KINGDOM
CROSS and
COMMUNITY

Guy F. Hershberger

KINGDOM
CROSS and
COMMUNITY

Essays on Mennonite Themes in
Honor of Guy F. Hershberger

Edited by
John Richard Burkholder and
Calvin Redekop

HERALD PRESS
Scottdale, Pennsylvania
Kitchener, Ontario
1976

Library of Congress Cataloging in Publication Data
Main entry under title:

Kingdom, cross, and community.

"A bibliography of the writings of Guy F. Hershberger, 1922-1976,
Elizabeth H. Bauman": p.
  Bibliography: p.
  Includes index.
  CONTENTS: Schlabach, T. F. To focus a Mennonite vision.–
Gross, L. History and community in the thought of Guy F.
Hershberger.–Kreider, R. S. Discerning the times. [etc.]
  1. Mennonite Church–Doctrinal and controversial works–Addresses, essays, lectures. 2. Christianity and culture–Addresses,
essays, lectures.
3. Hershberger, Guy Franklin, 1896-
I. Hershberger, Guy Franklin, 1896-
II. Burkholder, John Richard, 1928-
III. Redekop, Calvin Wall, 1925-
BX8109.K56   289.7   76-29663
ISBN 0-8361-1139-7

KINGDOM, CROSS, AND COMMUNITY

Copyright © 1976 by Herald Press, Scottdale, Pa. 15683
  Published simultaneously in Canada by Herald Press,
  Kitchener, Ont. N2G 4M5
Library of Congress Catalog Card Number: 76-29663
International Standard Book Number: 0-8361-1139-7
Printed in the United States of America
Design by Alice B. Shetler

CONTENTS

PREFACE

This book in one sense began in 1925 when a young man from Iowa arrived as a new teacher at Goshen College in Indiana. More precisely, the book was launched fifty years later, when friends of that scholar (now an active professor emeritus) proposed a *Festschrift* as an appropriate way of honoring the long and distinguished career of Guy Franklin Hershberger. With the active support of the Goshen College administration, the project advanced through the steps of forming an editorial committee, securing financial support, choosing editors, and selecting contributors to the volume.

Guy Hershberger's lifelong interests and work, centering at Goshen College but extending in influence through and beyond his beloved Mennonite Church, provide the focus for the book. The editorial committee, recognizing the wide range of Hershberger's contributions to church life and scholarship, sought to select topics and writers that would reflect the varied facets of his activity. This collection of essays is an effort to assess achievements, identify problems, and project directions for the community of faith with which Hershberger has been identified, namely, the Christian traditions that lay claim to the sixteenth-century Anabaptist heritage.

These writings suggest where Anabaptist-Mennonite scholarship now stands on major questions of ethics, social concerns, and the form and mission of the church. It is our hope that these chapters will foment a new level of interest in the contemporary relevance of the Believers' Church viewpoint, and that they will speak prophetically both to the Mennonite brotherhood and to a wider Christian audience. We believe that the book is a step toward fulfillment of the vision of the kingdom that inspired and motivated Guy F. Hershberger.

The book is offered as a tribute on the occasion of Hershberger's eightieth birthday, December 3, 1976. It is a modest but genuine expression of esteem, love, and gratitude from students, colleagues, and friends.

Acknowledgments
The editors herewith express their appreciation for:
—The overarching vision, sense of direction, and helpful counsel provided by the editorial committee: John A. Lapp, chairman; Leonard Gross, Leland Harder, Robert S. Kreider, Theron F. Schlabach, and the late Melvin Gingerich.

—The grant from the Schowalter Foundation that enabled released time for editorial work and secretarial assistance.

—Cooperation from administration and staff at Goshen College, and especially for the typing skills of Carol Wengerd.

—The conscientious labor of Elizabeth Hershberger Bauman in the preparation of the bibliography of Guy Hershberger's writings.

—The professional attention and personal patience of Paul M. Schrock of Herald Press in supervising the production of the book.

September, 1976   *J. R. Burkholder* and *Calvin Redekop*

Citizen of the Kingdom

Citizen of the Kingdom

Guy Franklin Hershberger is a pivotal member of that creative group of American Mennonite churchmen who, by rediscovering the potential contemporary power of the four-century-old vision that had inspired their European forefathers, carried forward the "quickening" of church life initiated a few decades earlier and brought the Mennonites into full engagement with the twentieth century.

The essays in this first section provide varying perspectives on the life and times of Guy Hershberger. Three historians offer their respective tributes to the man, along with their distinctive analyses of his work and influence.

"Hershberger's personal contribution was above all to bring into focus a Mennonite position on questions of peace and social justice," declares Theron Schlabach in his comprehensive study of the meaning and inpact of one man on several generations of thought and activity in the Mennonite world. He examines the several phases and multiple roles that gave expression to Hershberger's central commitment to spell out the meaning of the way of the cross as an ethic for the faithful church. Schlabach attempts to describe and evaluate the overall significance of Hershberger's labors in classroom, committees, conferences, and numerous publications.

Leonard Gross underlines the abiding continuities in the tradition of faith and the commitment to community that inspired and directed Hershberger's activity. He calls attention to the consequences for the life of the church that flowed from the self-conscious choice, by Hershberger and his colleagues, of *history* as a key to identity. An authentic conservatism motivated the recoverers of the Anabaptist Vision to chart a course for the Mennonite brotherhood that would minimize the eroding influences of competing movements that lacked this historical perspective and sense of corporate belonging.

As a fitting conclusion to this section of the book, Robert S. Kreider gives us a vivid picture of several crucial decades in the formation of both Hershberger himself and the brotherhood in which he lived and moved. Kreider's work illuminates the distinctive character of the selected epochs and reminds the reader of unfinished historical agenda. He asks provocative questions and suggests research topics for other scholars who may be challenged to further the self-understanding of American Mennonites.

1

To Focus a Mennonite Vision

Theron F. Schlabach

I

Guy Franklin Hershberger was born in 1896, in rural Iowa, to Amish Mennonite parents.[1] In the late nineteenth century the Mennonite Church,[2] including Amish Mennonites soon to merge with it, was undergoing change so profound that historians have called it the "Great Awakening." Whether or not it was that, certainly it brought a "quickening"—an increase in tempo. There evolved a host of bustling new activities, from Sunday schools and revival meetings through church publishing and a new college to missions and Boards and old people's homes and orphanages. The new tempo was more than simply religious, for a separated, previously unassimilated group was getting more and more absorbed into North American life. In private life and in church meetings, there were massive shifts from German to English. Some Mennonite and Amish Mennonite Church members left farms for business and professions. A sprinkling of bright youth pursued higher education.

Even religiously, the people of the Mennonite and Amish Mennonite churches were flirting with assimilation. They were taking more and more of their signals not from their own tradition but from North American Protestantism, especially from more or less revivalistic groups such as Methodists, certain Presbyterians, some Baptists, and the United Brethren. It was a matter of taking on cultural traits in a very special way: *by plugging into North American cultures at the particular point of revivalistic Protestantism.* That way gave the acculturation process an aura of religious vitality and sanction.

Without question the quickening was more than mere acculturation. It did bring genuine, new religious life to many Mennonite people and to stagnating congregations. But the cost was some loss of focus of Mennonite vision. People in the Mennonite and Amish Mennonite churches before the 1860s had shared a more or less common religious view. That view included a perception that Jesus' message had been

---

Theron Schlabach is a member of College Mennonite Church, Goshen, Indiana, and professor of history at Goshen College. His research interests and publications are in social welfare and the social history of Mennonites.

centrally a "gospel of peace"; a memory of persecution and rejection by the world, much reinforced by wide reading of an ancient Anabaptist-Mennonite book entitled *Martyrs Mirror;* a sense of peoplehood, dating back to sixteenth-century Anabaptist origins and reinforced by migrations and growing ethnicity thereafter; a commitment, at least in theory, to an uncomplicated and literal obedience to the New Testament; and a conviction that key sins were pride and desire for worldly station.

But the quickening brought other concepts. Religious life became more the product of a sharply defined, individualistic, public conversion. Response to God became less a matter of self-effacement and more a giving of oneself to aggressive "Christian service" in mission and uplift. Perception of church became more one of organization and program, somewhat less one of peoplehood. All this led to a loss of focus, especially since across the North American continent, Mennonite ideas and practices—both religious ones and those of language, education, and occupation—changed at different rates.[3]

The forces distorting the vision were so strong that during the first half of the twentieth century Mennonite Church leaders would devote much of their energy to refocusing—to redefining and restating what Mennonite Church people believed, who they were, what they stood for, what they understood to be the gospel.

To do so, Mennonite Church leaders tried to establish stronger authority, mainly in two ways. One was more centralized church structures, such as a denominational general conference begun in 1898, and three major church boards—education, missions and charities, and publication—established from 1905 to 1908. The other was more and more emphasis on correct formulas of belief and doctrine. The quickening had opened Mennonites to general Protestant currents, and of course the major battle within American Protestantism in the early twentieth century was that between "Fundamentalists" and "liberals," or "modernists." That battle coincided with Mennonites' own need for stricter definitions. More Mennonites took the Fundamentalist side than the other. There emerged a Mennonite version of Fundamentalism.

It was a "Mennonite Fundamentalism," not exactly a more standard Protestant variety. For instance, while many twentieth-century Mennonites have been premillennialist, and some of them dispensationalist, those positions never became required doctrine. Historian John Horsch, for instance, could vigorously denounce modernism and in many ways sound like a Protestant Fundamentalist—and yet remain an amillennialist. So too with Daniel Kauffman, editor of the official Mennonite Church paper, the *Gospel Herald*, from its beginning in 1908 until 1943, and a leader so powerful and so omnipresent in church councils that he could veto virtually any denominational decision. In many ways Kauffman thought and spoke like a Protestant Fundamentalist, yet he too drew back from premillennialism. On the other hand, Fundamentalist-leaning Mennonites added certain points to the more standard Protestant version; Mennonite doctrines such as nonresistance and nonconformity they treated in effect like additional "fundamentals." Theirs was a distinctly Mennonite version, but it was a kind of Fundamentalism.

High point in the authoritarian trend was a statement of fundamentals that the Mennonite Church's general conference adopted in 1921. In 1921 Guy F. Hershberger finished his first year at Hesston College, a Mennonite Church school in Kansas.

II

The structural centralization that developed in the early twentieth century would be important to Hershberger's career, for he would work primarily through his church's superstructure. And the Mennonite version of Fundamentalism would set outer limits on what he could accomplish within his denomination, produce some resistance to his ideas, and affect the style and idiom he would use. Nevertheless, Hershberger never got caught up in most issues that Fundamentalists found tantalizing, such as the mechanics of scriptural inspiration or the exact manner of Jesus' future coming. Instead, his interests lay with two other movements, tending to redefine Mennonitism in other ways: a growing emphasis on relief, service, and social concern; and the "Anabaptist Vision" school of historical theology.

In his youth Hershberger had been quite oblivious to Mennonitism's upheavals. Born in Johnson County, Iowa, on December 3, 1896, he grew up as a farm boy, attended four full years of public high school, and soon thereafter began to teach rural school. The Amish Mennonites of Johnson County had been slow to move with the late-nineteenth-century quickening. Any tensions among them still largely concerned internal Amish Mennonite issues, not debates imported from the outside. Hershberger's own family was somewhat acculturated and progressive. His maternal grandfather, for example, had been a schoolteacher, had taken a normal school course at the

University of Iowa, and in the 1860s had refused formally to join the Amish Mennonite Church until there was formed a new congregation with relatively tolerant leadership. Such were the roots of the East Union congregation, of which Hershberger at age twelve became a member.

In 1920 Hershberger and a neighboring schoolteacher, Clara Hooley, were married. By that time they had caught enough of the quickening's mood to dream of going to India as missionaries, so they enrolled at Hesston College. Hesston in 1920 had a fairly strong Mennonite-Fundamentalist, even premillennialist tone, which Hershberger for a time adopted rather uncritically. But never militantly. In fact, by his later recollection, he scarcely ever heard of premillennialism until shortly before going to Hesston, when his bishop and pastor Sanford C. Yoder mentioned the issue to him.

Sanford C. Yoder was mentor and patron for the younger Hershberger. Yoder too had grown up in a Johnson County Amish Mennonite family. Hershberger has since argued vigorously that those Iowa origins allowed Yoder to keep from lining up either with Fundamentalist-leaning Mennonites or with their opponents (1974d: 7-40); the inference for Hershberger's own career is clear. Since Yoder avoided both poles, and since he by talent was a conciliator, the Mennonite Board of Education called on him in 1924 to become president of the oldest Mennonite Church college, Goshen College. It was a fateful call—for Hershberger also. By 1924 Hershberger was teaching at Hesston. Now Yoder suggested that he join the Goshen faculty. Good college teachers, Yoder argued, were even scarcer than good missionaries (Hess, 1966: 22). In 1924-1925 Hershberger took time to earn a Master's degree in history at the University of Iowa, from which eventually, in 1935, he would also receive a doctorate. Summer, 1925, he attended the University of Chicago. In the autumn he began a long career of teaching history, sociology, and ethics at Goshen.

Goshen College in 1925 was scene and symbol of a Mennonite search for a way between full-blown Mennonite Fundamentalism on the one hand and what in the Mennonite Church was considered liberalism or modernism on the other (actually, very few within the Mennonite Church were really very liberal or modernist in the larger Protestant sense). In thirty years of existence the school had been victim as well as beneficiary of the late-nineteenth-century quickening's loss of focus and diversification. Some presidents and faculty had grown increasingly out of touch with their church. For instance, early in 1903 Noah Byers was a former principal of the college's predecessor institution, Elkhart Institute, and soon would become the college's president. From Harvard University, where he was studying, he wrote in an idiom more secular than Mennonite and declared privately that the college should be run by professionals on the basis of academic excellence, not by ministers. John E. Hartzler, who followed as president from 1913 to 1918, lashed out in a letter against "broadcloth religionists" and " 'regulation coat' divines" who were sure that the college suffered "liberalistic and atheistic educational appendicitis." Such people reminded him of "a hungry lamb; when they got a hold of the proper piece and the cream really begins to come, they don't know when to stop shaking their tails." Wiser folks, thought Hartzler, would have to "lift some of them up to the right tit [*sic*] . . . [*and*] hold them a little while till they get stronger."[4]

As for who was strong, in the end it was not the Mennonite Church but Byers and Hartzler who bent, for by the early 1920s both of them cast their fortunes with the General Conference Mennonites. Meantime, from about 1918 to 1923 Goshen College lived in a perpetual state of financial and other crises, until finally its Board closed it for the year 1923-1924. Thereupon, the Board invited S. C. Yoder to come, build a new faculty, and begin again. Yoder did so, but without ever moving Goshen as far to the side of Mennonite Fundamentalism as were the denomination's other two colleges, Hesston and Eastern Mennonite. It was the reorganized Goshen College, picking a precarious way between Mennonite Fundamentalists and Mennonite "liberals," that Hershberger joined in 1925.

To set forth what separated the two camps would require a major study. Their theological differences hardly seem to have been ultimate ones, but of course Mennonites have always largely understood belief in terms of real-life practice. Fundamentalist-leaning conservatives felt themselves to be the more orthodox and faithful. "Liberals" thought themselves more enlightened and up-to-date. Educated "liberals" thought that they were broad intellectually, and uneducated ones also thought themselves broadminded on matters of dress and behavior. But was it breadth or merely assimilation into North American culture?

The answer is that neither side had a monopoly on acculturation. Both sides had been influenced from the outside during the quickening. The conservatives, for instance, had changed Mennonite theology subtly but much more profoundly than they knew. Before and in the

early days of the quickening, Mennonites had spoken constantly of
"our gospel of peace" or "our nonresistant gospel." They had seemed
to keep their understandings of salvation, obedience, discipleship, and
lifestyle healthily integrated and whole (a wholeness Hershberger
would work hard to restore). But increasingly the conservatives
developed a formula that divided basic salvation from nonresistance,
lifestyle, and ethics. More and more they spoke of a "Plan of Salvation" as if it were something apart from what Christians receive from
God for their practical lives. In doctrinal formulations, for instance, in
several influential books by Kauffman (1898; 1914; 1928), they invariably put the plan of salvation idea high on the list of doctrines.
Ethical considerations such as nonresistance and the nonconforming
lifestyle appeared further down, usually after topics such as ordinances. And then ethics virtually always fell within a category that the
conservatives labeled unattractively as "restrictions." Salvation had
become primarily a matter of removing past guilt, not something vital
and inherent in the regenerated lifestyle itself. In that, the conservatives
harked back to Protestant Reformers rather than to their Anabaptist
forebears, and so gave evidence of one kind of acculturation.

The so-called liberals could also at times sound more early-
twentieth-century North American than Anabaptist or Mennonite. In
1919, for instance, a group of generally liberal young people from
various Mennonite branches who were working with the American
Friends Service Committee at post-World War I reconstruction held
what they called a "General Conference" of Mennonite reconstruction
workers at Clermont, France. Some speakers took potshots at church
authorities in terms that seemed to make American-style democracy
and individualism, rather than biblical or Anabaptist understandings
of church, the criteria. Or they fell into the optimistic language of
human progress so prevalent in certain liberal Protestant and other
circles in that day. They expressed deep social concern, but sometimes
they seemed to echo North American social gospel activism, without
questioning seriously how it all fit with Anabaptists' and Mennonites'
traditional distinction between church and world.

If neither the Mennonite Fundamentalists nor their liberal coun-
terparts had a monopoly on acculturation, so also did neither camp
have a corner on trying to be faithful, according to Anabaptist and
Mennonite understandings. The conservatives might separate
nonresistance and nonconformity from salvation, but they retained
those emphases among their fundamentals. And they probably

preserved a sense of obedience, discipline and discipleship, and close-knit peoplehood church life, albeit in distorted forms, somewhat better than did the liberals.

On their side the liberals deeply appreciated tradition. They called for more inter-Mennonite contacts between Europe and America, and more study of Anabaptist and Mennonite history. They strongly emphasized the pacifism of their tradition, and wanted to make it more positive in permanent programs of relief and service. Better than did the conservatives, they retained the earlier sense that peace is at the very heart of Jesus' gospel and therefore of salvation. Indeed, in significant respects the liberals anticipated the later "Anabaptist Vision" school of Mennonite thought which Hershberger would embrace and foster. But in 1919 and the early 1920s Mennonite Church leaders (unlike, for instance, post-World War II leaders, including Hershberger, who defended an analogous "Concerns" group) as a whole failed to see beyond the somewhat rebellious and sometimes alien language of the liberals. The leadership failed to appreciate their deep strain of loyalty to Anabaptist and Mennonite understandings.

Young Mennonite liberals followed their 1919 conference with three "Young People's Conferences" in the United States—in 1920, 1922, and 1923. But their movement soon fizzled, partly because Harold S. Bender, soon to be leader of the Anabaptist Vision persuasion, moved into leadership and then in 1922 delivered a manifesto saying that for himself he would work within established church authority. Liberals within the Mennonite Church and other Mennonite branches continued a weak voice from 1924 to 1928 by publishing a small paper, the *Christian Exponent*, edited by Vernon Smucker (who according to Bender's wife, Elizabeth Horsch Bender, was only minutely to Bender's left). But the *Christian Exponent* also died. Had its existence been a merely Mennonite episode, or had it demonstrated again that Mennonites were caught up with the larger society, wherein a "lost generation" of youth was challenging fixed values and the majority's dogmas? Whatever the answer, as the liberal movement languished, that of the Mennonite Fundamentalists went vigorously on. The conservatives made it their business, for instance, to see that Mennonite Church missionaries in India preached salvation rather than reform through education, or that people such as Hershberger who were concerned with peace did not consort too much with pacifists who were not orthodox on the "fundamentals" (Hershberger, 1967f).

Hershberger walked aloof from both camps. He read the *Christian*

Exponent appreciatively, was probably influenced by those emphases that anticipated the Anabaptist Vision school, and increasingly rejected the vehement premillennialism and dispensationalism of some Mennonite Fundamentalists. On the other hand, even late in life, he could write that what he understood to be the five classic fundamentals—scriptural inspiration, Christ's deity, the virgin birth, substitutionary atonement, the second coming—caused him no difficulty. Any difficulties with Fundamentalism, he would write, lay in accretions such as dispensationalism and eternal security and in failure to emphasize the church, discipleship, and ethics (1958d: 129-131).

Hershberger's style was noncombative. When he achieved he did it by solid hard work more than by angling for place. He emphasized the peace and ethical concerns that liberals wanted emphasized, but throughout much of his life—so long as necessary to avoid offense to Mennonite conservatives—he wore the "plain coat" (although usually with a necktie only half-hidden beneath it). And in a day (unlike 1976!) when slickness in dress and manner went more with Mennonite liberalism than with Mennonite Fundamentalism he kept a few hayseeds about him. "If you want to stay here," a Goshen colleague told him in 1925, "you'll have to quit walking like an Iowa plowman" (Hess, 1966: 20). Not only did Hershberger retain his farmer's walk, he carried other idiosyncrasies: pausing with mouth open in search for the right word, much erasing and rewriting on classroom blackboards, and the like. One friend has suggested that such mannerisms are marks of a mind always in process, never dogmatically fixed. No doubt true. In any case, Hershberger's 1925 colleague was wrong, for Hershberger continued his plowman's stride and yet stayed at Goshen. And even critics of Goshen College "liberalism" found his idiosyncrasies endearing.

At Goshen, aligned with neither camp, Hershberger helped gradually to develop new thought-categories for Mennonites—including the so-called "Anabaptist Vision." His Master's thesis was on the origins of the Anabaptist movement (1925b). In 1926 he and colleagues Harold Bender and John Umble launched what soon became the *Mennonite Quarterly Review;* throughout his career he was a productive associate editor, and briefly in the 1960s, after Bender's death, editor. While at first the *Review* seemed geared to the scholarly kind of Fundamentalism offered by J. Greschem Machen of Princeton, where Bender had studied, it was much more a vehicle of Anabaptist studies. The latter, of course, won it an international reputation.

Hershberger himself did not go on to pursue sixteenth-century Anabaptist studies; he wrote his doctoral dissertation instead on the Quaker experiment in governing colonial Pennsylvania (1935d). Thus his own articulations of the Anabaptist Vision were largely derivative. Yet they could be eloquent. Anabaptists, he summarized in 1958, had

> emphasized inward perfection, the way of brotherhood, and close personal relations within the group. They did not build their church coterminously with the general social order and then modify its ethic to fit this lower level. They built their church on the New Testament pattern and invited men and women to leave the world; to take up their cross and follow Christ into the life of the holy community, the colony of heaven, which was planted within the pagan world. The strenuous ethic of Jesus was accepted without question. They were not aggressors before the courts of law; they did not use the oath; they did not engage in war; they were indifferent toward the state; and they kept themselves largely separate from the economic struggles of the time. Their emphasis on brotherhood made for equality and simplicity of life, for the sharing of material possessions, and in some cases for actual community of goods. . . . [They] obtained a wide following in spite of opposition and persecution, and their influence was destined to be a great and far-reaching one. (1958d: 155-156)

Scholars may debate whether that view of Anabaptists is accurate, or idealized and mythical. But they can easily overlook an essential point: for Hershberger and his colleagues, the vision was normative, not merely a matter of history. For them it became more and more a vehicle for developing a third way of understanding the gospel, a way not locked into Fundamentalist-versus-liberal categories.

The third-way vision included social ethics. A peace-inspired social ethics was, of course, the main thrust of Hershberger's career and contribution.

III

Hershberger's personal contribution was above all to bring into focus a Mennonite position on questions of peace and social justice. Behind him stood two committees of the Mennonite Church's general conference: a "Peace Problems Committee" and a group that began as a "Committee on Industrial Relations" and became the "Committee on Economic and Social Relations."

The Peace Problems Committee grew out of World War I, just as

Hershberger's career was beginning. Hershberger had almost joined the reconstruction unit in France, and missed doing so only because while waiting for proper papers he finally signed a schoolteaching contract. World War I created for North American Mennonites a crisis of their own. Many of them felt forced to disobey government to one degree or another. Some one hundred of the brightest youths from the various Mennonite branches were dispersed to France, the Near East, and Russia for relief and reconstruction work. And the war thrust upon Mennonites a renewed consciousness of their own doctrines, history, and identity. Many Mennonites perceived that no matter how much they emulated North American Protestants in this respect or that, they could never fully identify with other denominations, because few Protestants had proven in the crunch to be pacifist.

Yet Mennonites did not want to be outcasts. They chafed under wartime taunts of "slacker" and "traitor," and really wanted fellow North Americans to see them as good citizens. So with complex motives they set out to prove that they were after all loyal and productive people, who simply worked constructively instead of killing. Out of all this came a new emphasis, close to what Mennonite liberals were calling for, on continuing programs of peace and social service. Hence the creation of an inter-Mennonite Mennonite Central Committee in 1920. Hence the evolution from 1917 to 1926 of a permanent Mennonite Relief Committee under the Mission Board of the Mennonite Church. Hence also the Peace Problems Committee, created by the Mennonite Church's general conference in 1917, and in 1925 reorganized with new, young leaders such as Christian L. Graber and especially Orie O. Miller in charge.

Not until 1959, near the end of its formal existence, was Hershberger ever a member of the Peace Problems Committee. But immediately in 1925 Miller and his group encouraged the young professor to take up research and writing on peace issues, which he did. Setting the tone of his career, in 1927 he published a substantial piece on "False Patriotism" in *Mennonite Quarterly Review* (1927a). It warned against nationalism in words as up-to-date as the U.S. Bicentennial. Later that year he traveled to St. Louis for a broadly based peace convocation sponsored by the World Alliance for International Friendship Through the Churches. Some Fundamentalist-leaning Mennonites, most notably Horsch, thought that to mix openly with such a crowd was to open the door to liberalism. Throughout his life Hershberger would make clear again and again that he considered

Mennonites' biblically based pacifism to be quite different from optimistic hopes for general human betterment that marked the pacifism of certain Protestant liberals. Yet in 1927 Hershberger returned from St. Louis arguing eloquently for keeping in touch with pacifists of various sorts (1928b).

He also came with a program for the Peace Problems Committee, or really an elaboration of one that the committee itself had set out in 1925. Among its points was to have church schools become study centers for peace and other of the church's principles. Soon Hershberger was pouring energy into that—starting what eventually became a Peace Society at Goshen College, building up a peace library, developing his pace-setting course on "War, Peace, and Nonresistance," and the like. Another point was to spread understanding of peace among Mennonites through Young People's Meetings, the Sunday school, and literature. To do that the committee sponsored some writings throughout the 1930s. Hershberger's most notable contribution was a long series of articles to his church's youth paper, the *Youth's Christian Companion,* published in the latter years of the decade, after his doctoral work was completed. Still another point was to keep in touch with pending legislation and poised to appeal to government on behalf of conscientious objectors. In February of 1935 Hershberger helped articulate what for the cause of conscientious objection on a national scale became perhaps the decade's most significant proposal.

Prodding Hershberger in 1935 were three stimuli: his just-completed PhD dissertation on Quaker politics in colonial Pennsylvania; a Mennonite peace conference at Goshen College, where he read a paper; and what had long been a subject in pacifist circles, the question of some more formalized and systematic plan, should another war come, for alternative service in relief units and similar projects, such as had begun to develop in World War I. For his paper at Goshen Hershberger developed that last idea. In a new war, he argued, a Mennonite or another peace-church young man could expect to go one of four ways: full participation, noncombatant service, noncooperation, or some sort of peaceable alternative service. He much favored the last, and sketched out how government might arrange it (1935b).

Later in the year his colleague Bender took the subject up with representatives of other Mennonite branches, the Friends, and the Church of the Brethren. The occasion was a meeting hosted by General Conference Mennonites at Bethel College in Kansas; the meeting, called to renew an earlier attempt at inter-peace-church cooperation, grew into a continuing Conference of Historic Peace Churches. In its main outlines Hershberger's was the plan that, after much negotiation, peace churches convinced the United States and Canadian governments to adopt as their World War II systems of Civilian Public Service and alternative service. Thus Hershberger, by making more firm an emerging idea, contributed to a broad development—not only to national policies for conscientious objectors, but in fact to historic traditions of freedom for individual conscience, and of separation of church and state.

Bender, dean of Goshen College, became chairman of the Peace Problems Committee in 1935, so that Hershberger was closer to it than ever. In 1937 the group gave Bender a mandate to draw up a position paper on what the Mennonite Church believed about church and state, and what its members would do in a new war. Hershberger was deeply involved with the community of thinkers who developed the statement. Later in the year the denomination's general conference made the paper its official pronouncement, and the statement still stands as a historic landmark. By then Hershberger was emerging, in effect, as first among Mennonite peace writers. In 1936 the Conference of Historic Peace Churches created a subsection on peace literature. While there was some question about whom to appoint as a second Mennonite representative (E. L. Harshberger, a General Conference Mennonite of Bethel College, was soon named), there was absolutely no hesitation about including Guy F. Hershberger.

Soon Hershberger was producing ever more thoughtful interpretations of Mennonites' nonresistance—not rapidly, propaganda-fashion, but characteristically only after much thorough research (and prodding from the Peace Problems Committee). In 1936 the committee published a booklet, *Nonresistance and the State,* in which Hershberger capsulized the argument of his 1935 University of Iowa PhD dissertation: that nonresistant Christians just could not, without hopeless compromise, run a civil government for a population that was largely nonpacifist (1936f).

In 1940, just in time for Mennonites and others to use as they faced the World War II draft, he and the committee collected some of his articles into a booklet entitled *Can Christians Fight?*—a title apparently borrowed from a Quaker pamphlet (1940a). Two years later he produced a 108-page study booklet for Civilian Public Service workers, *Christian Relationships to State and Community* (1942a). Although too brief to develop Hershberger's underlying rationale, the study guide stated concisely and clearly his basic position, especially on the proper functions of the state. Christians were to respect government. But there were some governmental functions, he asserted, which although legitimate for government were not suitable for Christians to participate in. There were others in which Christians could cooperate. Finally, there were areas where the church needed to provide alternate structures for welfare, social service, and the like so that Christians could do good without enmeshing themselves in the state's tangle of legitimate and illegitimate activities (1942a: 52-58).

Such points were vintage Hershberger—optimistic that there could be lines of accommodation without compromise, and favoring the alternative route rather than direct confrontation and challenge to the state.

Then, in 1944, came Hershberger's substantial *War, Peace, and Nonresistance* (1944c)—a full-fledged book that the committee had been prodding and advising him about since 1937, when he himself had suggested the need for a peace studies text. In it Hershberger combined three elements: biblical exegesis; a history of Christian pacifism from the early church onward, particularly as it developed through the Anabaptist-Mennonite line; and comment on up-to-date issues, especially the relation of Mennonite-style "nonresistance" to other forms of Christian pacifism. It was a broad-ranging and intelligent study, and the apotheosis of the Peace Problems Committee-related part of Hershberger's career.

It also openly challenged some of the more Fundamentalist Mennonites. That for Hershberger was hardly a new departure: he and the committee had to some degree gone against them throughout the late 1920s and the 1930s, as well as sometimes adjusted their words and actions to meet the conservatives' criticisms. Friction came mainly at two points. One was the committee's occasionally communicating to government its views encouraging disarmament and the like. This displeased the dispensationalists among the Mennonite Fundamentalists, especially a powerful Lancaster County, Pennsylvania, bishop, John Mosemann, Sr., for such persons held that in this age warmaking is a proper function of government and Christians ought not to question it. The other was the matter of consorting with theologically liberal pacifists. On that point leading critics were John L. Stauffer of Eastern Mennonite College and historian John Horsch. In *War, Peace, and Nonresistance* Hershberger stood up to the dispensationalists, especially where they argued that the Old Testament proved that at times war was God's will. Hershberger interpreted Old Testament passages otherwise. This brought him some rebuke from within his denomination.[5] Yet Mennonites as a whole were skeptical enough of dispensationalism and by 1944 esteemed Hershberger highly enough that they received his book quite well. Afterward their publishing house reissued it twice, in 1953 and in 1969.

On the matter of relations with theologically liberal pacifists, actually Hershberger and his colleagues made clear within the Conference of Historic Peace Churches that their nonresistance differed significantly from views they often found among Quaker and Church of the Brethren conferees. Throughout his career Hershberger generally preferred the term "nonresistance" over "pacifism." This it would seem was partly out of deference to Mennonite Fundamentalists, but partly also out of disagreement with many pacifists. Yet in *War, Peace, and Nonresistance* he explicitly accepted both terms, on grounds that both were biblical. Years later he would still say that the term "pacifism" was fine so long as it was "Christian pacifism," not merely some intellectual or humanistic variety. Indeed he would say that had he not been walking a narrow line between colleagues in the peace-church conference on the one side and Mennonite dispensationalists on the other, he would probably have written *War, Peace, and Nonresistance* somewhat differently. As for nonviolence of the Gandhian variety, Hershberger always considered it to be quite different from Christian nonresistance; it was still a strategy of coercion.

Yet throughout his career Hershberger insisted on keeping contacts with a good variety of pacifists. He did so against the wishes of Mennonite Fundamentalists.

The year 1944 marked a high point, but not the end, of Hershberger's Peace Problems Committee-related work. In 1951 he published, more or less at the committee's behest, *The Mennonite Church in the Second World War* (1951b). It was a history of the denomination's peace efforts since 1937, a yeoman's work rather than a grand or theoretical one, and evidence that Hershberger was still humble enough to take on such an assignment. In the late 1950s Hershberger initiated a new Mennonite Church statement on Christians' witness to the state, a statement that the church's general conference adopted in 1961. Actually the document was a product more of younger people, especially the upcoming theologian John Howard Yoder, than of Hershberger. But he promoted it enthusiastically, one of his graces being that he did not seem to fear or resent the younger generation. Finally, in 1959 the general conference belatedly made him the committee's executive secretary. He remained so until 1965, when the committee merged with another which he had led much longer, the Committee on Economic and Social Relations.

IV

Hershberger's Economic and Social Relations Committee (CESR) work began in 1939, and marked a second part of his career. The Mennonite Church had traditionally stood against labor unions. Unions smacked of oath-taking lodge organizations, put Christians into the unequal yoke with unbelievers, and used violence. (Like many North Americans, Mennonites were slower to see violence on the employers' part.) Besides, Mennonites were mainly ruddy, Germanic, agrarian, and small-business people, which probably helped to make the ethnicities and working-class philosophies of many unionists seem uncongenial. Once more, it was at least partly a matter of unconsciously selecting from among various North American signals. An official 1938 Mennonite Church statement used the language of the United States Declaration of Independence to assert that in the industrial world there were "certain inalienable rights." Then in the tones of North American business it asserted one such right to be that "of every employer of labor to conduct his own business, without interference by others, in submission to the laws of God and of his country." Elsewhere the statement professed not to be anti-union. Naively, it did not calculate that to protect business from all interference would make a sham of all effective unionism. It did not recognize that the policies of a business may well affect workers' lives much more directly than they affect owners' lives. Rather, it held that no Mennonite Church member should join a labor organization (or any farm or employer organization either, if joining involved an unequal yoke).[6]

In fact, however, church leaders were already searching for some kind of accommodation with unions. In 1935 some had persuaded a United Mine Workers local at Johnstown, Pennsylvania, to allow Mennonites to work without joining, if they would pay dues, and not work during strikes or lockouts. With this precedent and also some prodding from the Virginia Mennonite Conference, the denomination's general conference in 1937 formed a subcommittee to deal with industrial relations matters, which produced the 1938 statement.

Hershberger had nothing directly to do with all of this. But early in

1939 the Peace Problems Committee sponsored a second Conference on Applied Nonresistance and had him read a paper on industrial conflict. Upon invitation he read it also at the church's general conference in August. It was quite a *tour de force*. Not that it repudiated the traditional position; Hershberger was never the iconoclast or the revolutionary. He affirmed the stance against joining labor organizations and even strengthened it, with an argument that unions did not fit with nonresistance. For at heart the method even of nonviolent unions was coercion. "There is no difference in principle," he went so far as to say, "between so-called nonviolent coercion and actual violence" (1939c: 147).

But Hershberger's stance was no simple anti-union line. He insisted that employers were also "skillful in the use of peaceful coercion," and just as ready as unions "to resort to brutal violence." Hershberger shifted the chief burden to employers, emphasizing that Mennonite businessmen should create islands where ideal relations could exist between boss and worker without struggles for power. Such talk of course implied that employers held power, and should use it. Would that not involve coercion? He did not really face that anomaly. Instead he traced the historic changes that had created a large class or propertyless laborers and had drawn even Mennonites into the industrial work force. Explaining the industrial milieu of the late 1930s, he tried to communicate some understanding of how matters looked to the militant, rising Congress of Industrial Organizations (1939c: 137-150).

Admitting to influence from theologian Reinhold Niebuhr, Hershberger conceded that in a nation of large-scale, impersonal organizations, laboring people would never get justice without some use of power and coercion. But then he immediately departed from that Niebuhrian position: "Biblical nonresistance," he argued, "enjoins submission even to injustice rather than engage in conflict" (1939c: 147). Thus Hershberger concluded at a point again in keeping with established Mennonite Church understandings. But he had also added much that was fresh, and certainly more thoughtful than the 1938 statement.

Hershberger reached beyond Mennonitism for his ideas. He was enough Americanized that he began and ended his address not with Mennonite church fathers or Anabaptists, nor yet with the Sermon on the Mount, or Paul, or the prophets. Instead he cited Thomas Jefferson and Hector St. John de Crevecoeur, who had envisaged a pastoral

United States without large-scale industry and its evils. From there he went on to develop the main outlines of what in the next dozen years would be his and others' "Mennonite community" vision. In those years, moreover, he was regularly reading a New York publication called *The Christian Rural Fellowship Bulletin.* Among writers who especially influenced him was Oliver E. Baker, a U.S. Department of Agriculture economist whom a General Conference sociologist and life-long friend and collaborator with Hershberger, Winfield Fretz, had heard speak in a graduate school seminar and had drawn to Hershberger's attention. Baker had suggested, and continued to believe, that the traditional Mennonite community was a model other North Americans might well emulate. Some others of similar view who influenced Hershberger through writings and more direct contacts were Luigi Ligutti, a Catholic monsignor based at Des Moines, Iowa; Arthur Morgan of Antioch College in Ohio, at one time chairman of the Tennessee Valley Authority, and author of a book entitled *The Small Community*: and Walter Kollmorgen, another U.S.D.A. economist. Not all the input for the Mennonite community idea was particularly Mennonite.

In any case, from different angles Hershberger brought into focus a basic message for Mennonites: follow the Jeffersonian vision, and escape the capital-labor dilemma, by revitalizing Mennonite communities into ideal agrarian-and-small-business societies. But the professor was no romantic. He had grown up in a North America that had a penchant for organization, and he went on in his 1939 address to spell out in hardheaded terms what new programs and institutions he thought the Mennonite community would need. Prominent among them would be a well-organized system of mutual aid.

In 1939 the idea of organized systems of mutual aid was beginning to appeal to Mennonites. For a half-dozen years Social Security had been prominent in the public news. Since 1935 a committee of the Mennonite Church's general conference had been discussing the idea, as had some other Mennonites. Most importantly, Hershberger had just recently become acquainted with Winfield Fretz. Fretz had spoken at Goshen College on mutual aid, after completing a Master's thesis at the University of Chicago in 1938 on that subject. Even as Hershberger was preparing his 1939 address, *Mennonite Quarterly Review* was putting into print a two-part article by Fretz describing various mutual aid patterns throughout Anabaptist, Hutterite, and Mennonite history, and in a contemporary North American Mennonite community with exceptionally well-developed mutual aid arrangements, at Mountain Lake, Minnesota (Fretz, 1939). Mutual aid organization was the kind of idea that appealed to Hershberger, and he grasped it readily for his purposes.

"There should be," Hershberger explained, "a carefully managed financial organization to assist young people in getting a start farming for themselves." Instead of investing surplus capital in industrial stocks and bonds, wealthy Mennonites should channel it to help their own group. Mennonite communities should own some land for members who needed it; and if none were available near home, they should buy blocks of it in new areas, and help young families settle together (actually a time-tested idea among Mennonites and Amish). Mennonite missions, boards, and colleges could invest endowment funds in such ventures. Finally, Mennonite communities should do all in their power to attract their professional and other educated members to come back to settle and work. Teachers, for instance, should take jobs in rural schools. For medical doctors, "in some cases small Mennonite community hospitals might well be erected." Such a hospital could sponsor an "entire medical service" for the community, "managed and financed on a co-operative basis, giving equal medical services for all" (1939c: 153-154).

Soon Hershberger was given a new base for launching his message. The 1939 general conference decided to appoint him to a new, upgraded, five-member Committee on Industrial Relations. The other members quickly made him executive secretary. In 1951, its scope having expanded, the group became the Committee on Economic and Social Relations. Hershberger continued as its chief executive.

V

From that base Hershberger worked at two levels: practical solving of industrial relations problems for Mennonite Church members, and the development of his larger ethical and sociological vision. In the practical work, he and other committee members negotiated dozens of agreements with union officials, interceded when Mennonite workers had union problems, and the like. To Hershberger the 1935 accommodation with the United Mine Workers local was not satisfactory; Mennonite money still flowed into the union treasury, he pointed out in his 1939 paper, and therefore into the struggle for power. He agreed that the 1935 plan was the best to be gotten at the time—for to a point, Hershberger could always be something of a pragmatist. But his committee tried, with some success, to negotiate agreements that would channel dues payments to charity—a union sick-benefit fund, a local hospital, or the like. Also, where possible, he and his colleagues worked with unions' central officials rather than just with local ones. That made for fewer separate negotiations and broader agreements; and besides, the committee quickly learned that central officials often had the more flexible and more philosophical view. For a decade and more, Hershberger worked hard at such practical buffering. His feet remained on the ground, as they always did when he approached ethics and human relations issues.

Yet his eyes and mind ranged. From his committee position, Hershberger continued to ponder more farsighted strategies.

Throughout the 1940s and into the early 1950s, he continued to focus the Mennonite community idea. Although "alternative" was not especially his word, it is a key one for understanding what he had in mind. Indeed, the alternative service concept to which he helped give form in 1935 to deal with the military draft, and the CPS system in the 1940s, functioned as a paradigm of his larger effort. For his vision was to make of the Mennonite community an alternative way, so that Mennonites could opt out of many of the problems with industrialism, with the state, and with some of their nations' other patterns and institutions—but do so respectfully, without direct confrontation.

Hershberger's attitude toward his own nation was ambivalent. He continued consciously to draw on its traditions. As a Jeffersonian he even argued, as did the rural sociologists whom he was reading, that to strengthen the Mennonite community was to help "strengthen democracy in America." (This he wrote during World War II, when he might have felt some unconscious need to show again that Mennonites were good citizens and not slackers.) But in the same stroke he declared even more emphatically that "the Christian must always remember that his first obligation is to God and not to the state. . . . The better a society can meet its needs, without the aid of the state, the less the danger that the state will encroach upon those areas where it ought not to operate" (1944c: 196).

And so Hershberger's solution to church-state matters was twofold. One part was the scheme found in his *War, Peace, and Nonresistance* and other writings. In that scheme he called for general obedience to government, and suggested that there were cases where Christians and government could well cooperate. But there were also cases where although the state acted legitimately, Christians could not cooperate because to do so involved coercion. And there were other cases where the state illegitimately wanted to encroach on Christians' first loyalty, which was of course to God. That part of Hershberger's solution neatly combined accommodation and separation. The other part was of course the "Mennonite community" idea: create and strengthen sociological structures that would allow Christians, for ethical reasons, simply to bypass many of the goings-on in state and society. This was not exactly a call for withdrawal, certainly not one to an esoteric otherworldliness. Rather, it was a particular strategy for witness for *collective* and not merely individual witness. "We must remember," Hershberger wrote in 1944, "that the most effective testimony of the Mennonites in times past has been given through the group" (1944c:321).

The Mennonite community idea was by no means Hershberger's alone. It was itself a product of Mennonite community. General Conference Mennonite sociologist Fretz continued to contribute to it, especially to the idea of mutual aid. Mennonite Civilian Public Service (CPS) camps, operated by Mennonite Central Committee (MCC), also helped. In general the CPS experience surely made Mennonite young men much more aware of the problems of their people's relation to the social order. Specifically, MCC sponsored an ambitious system of courses and studies for CPS men that included along with Bible study various topics on Mennonite history, heritage, and life. For about a year in 1941 and 1942 Hershberger himself was educational director in a camp in Indiana, located first at Bluffton and then at Medaryville. Thereafter he often went to other camps to give addresses and courses on peace and Mennonite community life. At several camps there emerged "Farm and Community Schools." These began independently of his leadership, though he visited several of them and taught at one rather extensively.

Thus the CPS experience helped to spread and to develop the Mennonite community concept. It also brought forth young leaders to help promote the idea: for instance, Esko Loewen, Grant Stoltzfus, and Ralph Hernley. Loewen, a General Conference Mennonite, served as editor of *Mennonite Community Source Book* published in 1946, to make better known the sources CPS educational directors had found most useful. Stoltzfus and Hernley, of the Mennonite Church, both became active with Hershberger and others in a Mennonite Community Association organized in the same year.

Many helped, but no one articulated the Mennonite community

idea better than did Hershberger. During the 1940s he continually reiterated the vision. Mennonites should see in it more than the model for preserving American civilization that others saw, he emphasized in the Industrial Relations Committee's 1943 report to the general conference. Their primary motive for strengthening Mennonite community should be obedience to Christ. (In later years, in fact, Hershberger would feel that too many people had understood the vision too much in sociological terms, and missed the centrality of its ethics.) He amplified the vision in his books.

In 1942 at an inter-Mennonite scholars' conference on "cultural problems," fellow Iowan Melvin Gingerich, who was a member of the Bethel College faculty in Kansas and later a close colleague of Hershberger at Goshen, spoke on the topic, "Is There a Need for a Mennonite Rural Life Publication?" Of course his answer was "yes." But the Mennonite Church's publishing house decided that its constituency was not yet ready for an official magazine on social issues. So in 1946 a group of interested persons formed the Mennonite Community Association, which began in 1947 to publish the contemplated journal, using *The Mennonite Community* as its title (one year, incidentally, after General Conference Mennonites, out of somewhat similar interests, began publishing *Mennonite Life*). Hershberger was executive secretary of the community association, and associate editor of its magazine. Grant Stoltzfus served as editor.

Meantime Hershberger helped begin a formal system of Mennonite mutual aid. By the early 1940s the committee to which his church's general conference had assigned mutual aid questions, a stewardship study committee, had not yet produced concrete plans. Hershberger had of course taken up the mutual aid cause, and the general conference had encouraged his committee also to study the question. Finally in April 1943, somewhat impatient, Hershberger's committee sponsored a conference of church leaders on the subject. Hershberger himself was most interested in some health services plan. But he had also put forward the investment-loan idea in his 1939 address. And in the second version of that address he had expressed interest in the idea of Mennonite cooperatives, a suggestion that eastern Pennsylvania bishop John E. Lapp had advanced. At the 1943 conference Lapp spoke strongly for an investment-loan system. Still another idea afloat, a favorite of Orie O. Miller, was close to the investment-loan one: that CPS men would need much help to get established after the war. Reporting to the general conference later in 1943, then,

Hershberger's committee recommended strongly that the conference take action, especially for investment-loans and help to CPS men. Hershberger still wanted a health plan, but recognized that it could wait; he presented the CPS men's problems in the context of reestablishing the men in a way that would reinforce the Mennonite community.

The upshot was that in October of 1943 there occurred a meeting of Hershberger's committee along with Christian L. Graber of the stewardship committee. Hershberger took to that meeting the idea that the church should create a major new board to handle mutual aid. In December his committee took that and the October meeting's other ideas to officials of the general conference, who in turn authorized the creation of a formal, incorporated Mennonite Mutual Aid organization. By July of 1945 the organization was reality, and for years Hershberger served on the board he had proposed. Mennonite Mutual Aid, Inc., gave its early years to the investment-loan and aid-to-CPS-men tasks. But in 1949 it began to develop extensive quasi-insurance systems: a hospital-surgical and burial aid plan in that year, an automobile coverage system in 1955, and finally, after much wrestling with the Mennonite Church's traditional rejection of life insurance, a "survivors' aid" plan in 1961. These and other services that the system developed gradually overshadowed its original programs. Meantime the organization became more and more inter-Mennonite.

Implementing his ideas in still other ways, in 1947 Hershberger carried out an extensive survey of one Mennonite center, Fulton County, Ohio, to back his message with hard data. Beginning in 1945 his committee and/or the community association sponsored almost annually and sometimes oftener, until 1965, grass-roots Mennonite community conferences and workshops. These dealt with down-to-earth topics, especially employer-employee relations and other problems of small business, and thereby succeeded in involving not just "intellectuals" but "practical" people as well. Through the conferences, through church literature, and in various ways, Hershberger and others in the Mennonite Church and other branches built among Mennonites some insulation against American individualism and some new sense of social responsibility.

At its sharpest, in the late 1940s, the Mennonite community vision Hershberger projected was a remarkable and intriguing one. Sociologically it was intelligent, for it rested on a healthy understanding of North American (at least U.S.) history and social dynamics. And it was theologically astute, fusing as it did the sociological and the historical with the renewed Anabaptist Vision of the church as a peoplehood— God's people living and witnessing as loving communities. Quite certainly it was the clearest answer anyone ever gave to the problem of Mennonite diffusion. It was the most sharply focused alternative ever offered to the Mennonite Fundamentalist attempt to redefine Mennonitism through formulas of authority and orthodoxy. Yet by the early 1950s the Mennonite community idea started to lose focus. The community conferences continued until 1965. But the community magazine, always shaky financially, faltered. In 1949 the Mennonite Publishing House took it over; in 1954 the House merged it with *Christian Monitor* to create a new periodical, *Christian Living*. *Christian Living* continued more or less to cover community concerns, but gradually became a rather standard denominational family magazine. Even among Mennonites a family magazine sold better than one with a larger and more complete vision of community. The demise of *Mennonite Community* was but a symptom. More fundamentally, younger leaders were emerging who were not sure they wanted to return to the rural and small-town life that Hershberger seemed to envisage. Some of them began to suggest that the key was more in moving out as Christian cells into cities and elsewhere, overtly carrying the message of peace into society, its government, and its other structures. Hershberger and his colleagues had probably never meant to confine the vision to one sociological model. And to their credit, they wanted to meet the interests of younger people. Such new views had an impact, therefore, even on Hershberger himself. And besides that, urbanization, involvement in professions and large-scale organizations, increasing openness to national communications media, and a host of other sociological trends were all conspiring to blur any clear vision of Mennonite identity and community.

Indeed, a development of which Mennonites were quite proud probably contributed to the blurring. That was the growth of Mennonite voluntary service units—such as Hershberger himself had advocated in 1935, and strongly encouraged thereafter. The World War II alternative service programs had offered new vistas to young men dispersed from home communities. Following the war Mennonites spawned a host of new service ventures, in North America and throughout the world. To be sure, as Mennonites scattered explosively, they still went more or less corporately as people of a church, not as free-lancing individuals. So in one sense it all fit the Mennonite community idea. Yet there was a paradox. Hershberger's vision had been one of regrouping and consolidating. The new activities brought dispersion, and still another form of diffusion. They were exciting and almost sacrosanct, and so all the more effective. But in the long run they must have helped blur the vision.

Perhaps the change was less a blurring than a shift in focus. To a degree the Mennonite community idea has survived in certain Mennonite professional associations and in organizations such as Mennonite Economic Development Association, Church Industry Business Association, Mennonite Business Associates, Mennonite Disaster Service, and of course Mennonite Mutual Aid. In 1972 the Mennonite Community Association was reactivated, and it is now working for common understanding of the role of such interest-group and special-service organizations within the Mennonite concept of church. It is also a link to the recent intentional community movement, and under its auspices Hershberger plans (as this is written) to produce an article on "Mennonite Community in the 1970s." And if in the 1950s the Mennonite community vision lost some of its focus, the concept of the Anabaptist Vision flourished.

For Hershberger there was perhaps only a subtle shift in mix, from the sociological to the more theological. Harold Bender, who had never identified closely with the sociological part of the community vision, may have helped that shift along. In 1953 he wrote, "We should disabuse ourselves . . . of the notion that cultural Mennonitism has anything to do with the essence of real Anabaptist-Mennonitism. Agricultural contributions, economic achievements, strong family and community life, in which we sometimes glory, are all worthy and fine, but they . . . are not of the essence" (Bender, 1953: 36). Timed as Bender's statement was, it could almost seem the *coup de grace* of the sociological Mennonite community vision. Small wonder than that by the 1960s Hershberger's emphasis seemed more than ever to be on church, on being God's people, whatever the sociological or ethnic parameters. A subtle shift had seemingly taken place that may have been proper, but that blurred the Mennonite community idea.

VI

As is his style, Hershberger took the change gracefully and walked in stride with his church. From about 1941 onward, under its broader name of "Committee on Economic and Social Relations," his committee seemed more to address particular social questions and issues, and less to work for one overall community vision.

Contemporaries scarcely noticed the change. Hershberger and his colleagues continued many of their former activities—still negotiating with unions, carrying on workshops, publishing this or that, and the like. But they also tried new approaches: students-in-industry units in large cities, for instance, as a young Mennonite woman, Elaine Sommers, suggested after experience in such a unit sponsored by Mennonite Central Committee; or in 1958 and 1959 helping employees in a Mennonite-owned firm, the Hesston Manufacturing Company of Hesston, Kansas, set up a worker organization that Hershberger considered a model for fostering Christian relations between boss and workers. Meantime Hershberger capped his scholarly career by editing a major book in 1957 and publishing one from his own pen in 1958 (1957b; 1958d). After 1958 the Committee on Economic and Social Relations burst forth with a broad agenda of issues which Hershberger helped to put before the church.

Perhaps the issues-explosion came because Hershberger and others in his church (Mennonite Fundamentalists being no longer able to foil them) had vastly broadened their contacts. Hershberger's contacts had always been broader than the Mennonite Church, as his reading of the *Christian Exponent* illustrates. Not only had he been active in the Conference of Historic Peace Churches from about 1936, but he had attended at least two meetings of its predecessor, the Conference of Pacifist Churches, in the 1920s; and those organizations of course included not only Mennonites from different branches, but also Brethren and Friends. Hershberger was also active in a "Conference on Mennonite Cultural Problems" which emerged in 1941 and 1942 and continued until the late 1960s as a vigorous inter-Mennonite group for the exchange of ideas. His work for *Mennonite Quarterly Review* and related Mennonite-studies publications was inter-Mennonite. In the 1950s and 1960s he constantly attended conferences, seminars, and the like put on by the peace committees of Mennonite branches other than his own, or by the inter-Mennonite Mennonite Central Committee. In 1939 he participated and served as one of the secretaries in a meeting that for the first time brought together from seven Mennonite branches the various Mennonite peace committees and other peace-minded leaders. Out of that evolved what was first called the Mennonite Central Peace Committee, and then the Mennonite Central Committee's Peace Section.

Hershberger never played a major formal role in guiding the MCC Peace Section. But he did serve it from time to time by contributing to conferences or helping to train peace teams, and he helped other parts of MCC in similar ways. During World War II he was involved, of course, with MCC-operated CPS camps. Another concentrated and direct involvement with inter-Mennonitism came after the war, in 1949 and 1950, when he spent a sabbatical year in Europe. Partially supported by MCC, he helped lead a student tour and work-camp group; researched the status of conscientious objection in Europe, and other topics; distributed American and gathered European peace literature; served as MCC's representative on a European wing of the Conference of Historic Peace Churches, and helped arrange a conference session; gave addresses and held interviews to explain the rationale of biblical pacifism; and worked at keeping discussion of the peace issue alive among not entirely willing European Mennonites. Like his wartime CPS work, the efforts in Europe surely served to broaden his contacts and perspective beyond his Mennonite Church base. Perhaps too it helped to blur or at least change the Mennonite community idea, by calling for a conceptualization in terms larger than the local community.

As Hershberger moved into the 1950s his contacts spilled more and more beyond Mennonite circles. He had of course long cherished extra-Mennonite contacts, in his acquaintance with various kinds of pacifists, in the Christian rural life movement, in his reading, and the like. As his books became known in the 1950s, such contacts increased. Hershberger took pleasure, for instance, in the fact that in 1959 the Fellowship of Reconciliation asked him to conduct a devotional meditation at a conference where black civil rights leader Martin Luther King, Jr., spoke, and that in the same conference the younger Mennonite spokesman John Howard Yoder gave what became a much-discussed keynote address on the theology of Christian pacifism. Upon invitation Hershberger also attended some of King's Southern Christian Leadership Conference sessions. By the early 1960s he participated extensively with the National Council of Churches, in its Department of Church and Economic Life. But even as he worked with the National Council and with the Fellowship of Reconciliation, he managed to retain good rapport with evangelical leader Carl F. H. Henry and to gain a hearing within the National Association of Evangelicals, in its small social action section.

Perhaps the issues-explosion had other causes. No doubt

Hershberger had new energy available after his 1958 book. Perhaps he worked doubly hard from a sense of having only a half-dozen years left before retirement. Perhaps it came because by 1960, due to Hershberger's efforts at least as much as any other one person's, many more Mennonites were aware of many more social issues than, say, in 1939. There occurred, in any case, a similar kind of issues-explosion in other Mennonite forums, such as the MCC Peace Section. Perhaps the cause was the sense of crisis of the North America of the early 1960s, a mood that had grown out of the U.S. civil rights movement and out of problems of world leadership. Perhaps still-acculturating Mennonites caught the activism in U.S. President John F. Kennedy's New Frontier rhetoric (Hershberger himself used "New Frontier" in a title for a 1963 report). Perhaps the issues-explosion grew out of all of these.

Whatever the causes, by the final years of Hershberger's formal career the range of issues to which he and those close to him were seeking to apply the gospel had become broad indeed. Included were old ones: the 1962 community conference, for instance, was on alcohol and tobacco; and in the early 1960s Hershberger was chairman of a group that updated and reaffirmed the traditional Mennonite stand against suing at law. Sometimes the issues were old but set more or less in fresh terms: teaching of peace in Mennonite missions and younger churches, for instance. In any case the list included proper pay for church workers (was the church itself a responsible employer?); women's roles in the church; food surpluses in North America, and a lengthy inquiry into what constitutes a Christian standard of living, in light of world hunger; capital punishment and constructive criminology; student exchanges, internationally and with Negro colleges; conditions of migratory labor, especially a case study in an Ohio Mennonite community; Christian responses to communism and anticommunism, and to right-wing radio broadcasting; and many more. Meantime Hershberger and those around him were probing in the broadest terms questions such as Christians' proper response to an ever-developing, automating technology.

The outstanding issue in Hershberger's final working years was that of race. This was not surprising, given the way the Mennonite Church had long been swept along more than it knew in large North American tides. It took black Mennonite voices to pose the issues most sharply: a call in 1952, for instance, from Mennonite pastor and CESR member James Lark of Chicago for more emphasis on community development, or a pointed statement from Vincent and Rosemarie

Harding of Atlanta in 1962 on how Mennonites were involved in one community's pattern of segregation—how, for instance, Mennonites coerced and boycotted merchants on the liquor issue but refused to do so for racial justice. Meantime, Hershberger may have been a bit too satisfied with his contacts with King, or with getting statements on the issue adopted in church conventions. Yet he and his colleagues worked at changing grass-roots Mennonite attitudes also.

Already in his 1944 book Hershberger had included a section applying nonresistance to race. And in 1944 and 1945, as editor of a new section, "Living Our Faith," in the official church paper, *Gospel Herald,* he had arranged for a younger contributor named Irvin Horst to write a pioneering article to arouse the Mennonite Church to the subject. About 1951 the CESR began seriously to take up the issue, and in the 1950s sponsored consciousness-raising conferences and writings on the subject. As one might expect, at first such activities were largely a matter of white Mennonites talking to each other, although not entirely; with time, however, younger black Mennonites gained more voice. In 1955 the CESR enabled the denomination's general conference to adopt an uncompromising statement for racial equality and justice. In 1960 and 1963 the committee, along with other Mennonite Church agencies and MCC, sponsored Hershberger (in 1960 in company with MCC officials Elmer Neufeld and Dwight Wiebe), on tours of Mennonite congregations in the Southern states. The purposes were to investigate and to give brotherly guidance (like other North Americans, Mennonite leaders were less conscious of Northern-style racism). Hershberger gave guidance where he could and in 1963, for limited circulation, wrote a pointed report. Partly out of his recommendations came various Mennonite Church and inter-Mennonite efforts on race matters, for example, an inter-Mennonite conference on the subject in Atlanta in February of 1964. Actually the Mennonite Church was not much ahead of North Americans generally in race matters, or for that matter in many other social issues. But at least it had intelligent leadership. And it had genuinely nonresistant leadership, concerned with being Jesus-like in its methods, as well as being prophetic in pursuit of just goals.

Hershberger's social concerns in his final working years were many and diffuse. Of course he still believed, quite explicitly, in visible Christian community. But instead of the strategy of regrouping and consolidating, he and those around him seemed now to accept the fact that Mennonites would scatter. So they operated as if their mandate was to help Mennonites develop testimonies on the great societal issues they would face as they went. The newer strategy was surely realistic, in light of what was happening sociologically and culturally to Mennonite Church members. But it was less focused than the older strategy of Mennonite community.

VII

Capping Hershberger's later career was his 1958 book *The Way of the Cross in Human Relations.* Although he surely wrote parts with a Mennonite audience in mind, Hershberger just as clearly addressed the book to all Christians, especially Protestants. It was his mature statement of the third way between the liberally oriented Social Gospel and the Fundamentalists' and evangelicals' too-reactionary rejection of it—or really of a fourth way, since the neoorthodoxy of Reinhold Niebuhr and others was now in the picture.

This time Hershberger did not ground his presentation so much on U.S. history as he had in 1939, or on proof-texts, as he had to some extent in *War, Peace, and Nonresistance.* Instead he based it on a perception of the basic, prophetic, biblical message for justice and love, and of Christ's life and teachings as emphatically a part of that message. To be sure, the author was no Hebrew-and-Greek-quoting theologian. And while his book reflected broad reading, and intelligent synthesizing, it was not an intensely argued, deductive kind of discussion. Rather, it was (like all Hershberger's writing) the work of a person with both a respectable grasp of the theoretical and broad practical experience in ethical issues. Much of the book's main message was more axiom derived from long study and experience than logical argument.

Although he did not state them formally as such, Hershberger's major axioms at the peak of his career were:

> 1. The church is, to use a phrase he often invoked, "a colony of heaven." It is not a merely human institution, not mainly a mystical body, not a temporary expedient for one dispensation, not anything else short of real people living as cells of God's kingdom on earth.
> 2. That colony is a new community, a social entity. The Bible's ethical standards are, therefore, always social and never merely individual. They are not, as Fundamentalists saw them, primarily expressions of individual salvation. Nor is the Sermon on the Mount, as the neoorthodox school held, impossible for guiding social behavior and thus relevant only for personal ethics.

3. Human nature, human beings, and human society are indeed fallen. Sin is real. As neoorthodox theologians were arguing so cogently, proponents of the early-twentieth-century Social Gospel had indeed been too convinced that humankind was on a road of progress.

4.Human social structures, including nation-states and governments, operate outside the realm of God's perfection. Christians are to respect such structures in the functions that God has given them, although by no means in all the functions they are likely to claim. But neither nations nor human society at large ever constitute the primary realm in which God is working out His kingdom. That realm is the colony of heaven. At the heart of Hershberger's quarrel with every Protestant school of ethics lay what he believed to be the misunderstandings of this point. In ethics all of them, whether Social Gospel, Fundamentalist or evangelical, or neoorthodox, had failed to break with the Constantinian church-state synthesis, or with medieval Christendom's identification of church with society.

5. The primary, the absolute ethical imperative for the Christian is to follow Jesus in discipleship and obedience. It is not, in the last analysis, the "good citizenship" on which theological conservatives have tended to base their assumptions, or the necessity to live responsibly, as neoorthodox ethicists have emphasized. And Hershberger did not conceive of obedience narrowly as had early-twentieth-century Mennonites. For them it had often been an almost blind submission to an ethically inscrutable and perhaps even capricious God, since they so much divorced obedience from Jesus' saving work. By 1958 the Anabaptist Vision school had long since freed discipleship and obedience from the category of "restrictions."

6. Jesus' disciples follow Him in means as well as ends. The Christian should never become agent of any human institution in a way that violates this axiom.

7. Christ's life and suffering death are to be seen as demonstrating His ethical teachings.

8. There is distinct difference between biblical nonresistance and mere nonviolence. For Hershberger the question of *coercion* was at least as crucial as that of violence *per se.*

9. North American evangelical Protestants in the nineteenth century, before the unfortunate dichotomy between the Social Gospel and Fundamentalism, had struck upon what was pretty nearly a proper synthesis of personal religion and social concern. Early-nineteenth-century evangelist Charles G. Finney had preached judgment on slavery and other social sins; his later counterpart Dwight L. Moody had refused to take up arms in the Civil War ("In this respect I am a Quaker"), and had originally established his Moody Bible Institute to help the poor.

Upon these axioms Hershberger answered other schools of Christian ethics. Never the bitterly partisan zealot, he used a friendly tone and found much to commend. Among Social Gospelers, Baptist theologian Walter Rauschenbusch in particular had come near the truth. The more or less liberal councils of churches, particularly the World Council, at least recognized biblical nonresistance as a fully legitimate Christian ethical position. The neoorthodox school was quite correct up to a point, with Protestantism (and, between the lines, Hershberger himself) much in its debt—correct, that it, until it put responsibility for the social order above the call to follow Jesus.

Of all the schools, Hershberger seemed still to try hardest to speak to the Fundamentalist or evangelical. He professed agreement with the original five points of Fundamentalism, so far as they went. To be sure (almost as if in a family argument), he had perhaps his sharpest words for evangelicals. Fundamentalists had overreacted against the Social Gospel instead of taking the good from it. They had distorted their own good points with the likes of dispensationalism. And to cap their errors, evangelicals too often simply ignored profoundly Christian social concerns. Worse yet, even as they denounced those who preached social concerns, they themselves made the broadest kinds of social pronouncements, and those too often on the side of militarism, racism, and similar sins. Yet Hershberger found examples of real, biblical nonresistance among evangelicals, for instance in Culbert Rutenber's *The Dagger and the Cross,* in a pamphlet entitled *Strangers and Pilgrims,* by James R. Graham, and scattered among members of evangelical seminary faculties. Beyond the aberrations of right-wing radio preacher Carl McIntire, and beyond what he saw as the ultimate inadequacies of Carl Henry or evangelist Billy Graham, Hershberger still professed to see hope for the evangelicals.

Whatever the good words for the various schools of thought, the ultimate message of *The Way of the Cross in Human Relations* was an Anabaptist-Mennonite one, offered as distinct from all the others. Where by one formula or another each of the others confused the kingdom of God with human structures, Hershberger insisted that the earthly form of the kingdom was in the church, the colony of heaven, and that the church was sharply distinct from human society at large. It was not a matter of the church withdrawn; Hershberger presented withdrawal as a fallacy and a temptation. But neither was involvement, and responsibility for society, the ultimate good. Rather, whether to be involved always depended on two tests: first, putting the discipleship imperative above the "responsibility" one, putting faithfulness above the logic of nation, of social cohesion, and of human calculations of justice; and second, not letting involvement entangle one in a way that is contrary to the noncoercive, loving ethic of Jesus and His cross.

Hershberger's formula of Christians' relation to government was still consistent with his earlier effort to define areas where accommodation was legitimate and others where separation was necessary. Christians could not, of course, participate with the state in war or even in police forces. Except for minor posts, they probably could not hold governmental office without compromise, since most governmental functions, even many so-called welfare functions, involved much coercion. On the other hand, Hershberger did not rule out voting, and he thought that in a welfare state there were certainly quite a few civil service jobs that were essentially positive in purpose and suitable for Christians to perform. He was still optimistic that on matters such as military service, Christians could work out mutually satisfactory arrangements with government and yet not compromise their ethics. Overall, Christians were still to respect government. Hershberger was no political radical, at least in any direct sense, no matter how radical the origins of his theology.

On church–state questions Hershberger's 1958 book mainly updated his *War, Peace, and Nonresistance.* A significant new contribution was his analyzing and replying to other schools of Christian ethics. Another major contribution, not exactly revising but going beyond his earlier book, was in economic matters. The economic problem, Hershberger held, was but analogous to the political: how to find, without either total involvement or total noninvolvement, the patterns that expressed love and self-giving rather than coercion and selfishness.

If the political formula of *The Way of The Cross in Human Relations* seemed less radical than its theology, even more did the economic conclusions. In his long work in industrial relations Hershberger had moved much more among Mennonite businessmen than among Mennonite labor leaders, because scarcely any structure existed for developing leaders of labor. Hershberger affirmed private property. He affirmed it not as a mere social convenience or an inescapable historical tradition but as a natural, positive, God-given human right—and this when a few avant-garde Mennonite intellectuals were already edging toward sharing of goods. As for labor unions, Hershberger discussed them along with trade associations, agricultural organizations, and professional groups. In all such groups, he advised, there were probably times when the Christian had to refuse participation in one activity or another, or even resign completely. But he was openly more dubious about labor organizations than about the others. It was not, he argued, that unions were essentially less moral. Indeed they had grown from a genuine quest for justice. It was merely that labor unions defined their goals coercively, and *inherently* depended on tactics that violated the means-as-well-as-ends test.

As his matured word on the industrial relations question, Hershberger cited the experiences of the Lincoln Electric and the Nunn-Bush Shoe Companies, whose managements, he insisted, worked in close harmony with associations of the firms' own workers. These were not the classic "company unions," he argued. Company unions implied a domination by management that he thought was not present in these firms. These firms emphasized genuine profit-sharing, participation of workers in management councils, guarantee of year-round employment, and the like. The examples were obviously models for the Hesston Manufacturing Company plan that Hershberger helped develop shortly after publishing the 1958 book.

But in saying that they did not represent company unionism, he overlooked some important tests. Implicitly his analysis was only micro-economic—a most fundamental weakness. From a larger view such plans of course assumed a separating of workers from mutual interest with fellow workers in competitors' firms, and thus continuing them in competition with such fellowworkers. And by assuming profit-sharing and a voice in management they built upon an ideal of the workers becoming co-entrepreneurs with management in a still-competitive (and really still-coercive) economic order. Hershberger was asking workers to renounce competition and coercion along class lines against their employers. But implicitly he was calling on them to work in harmony with employers—while in the large marketplace still competing with and probably coercing other workers.

The plans he favored did limit the so-called "rights of management," especially the right to solve economic problems by laying off workers, and the right unilaterally to decide the allocation of income among wages, profits, and other considerations. In any case, Hershberger was optimistic. With some blurring of managerial and labor roles with some structures to facilitate communication, and above all with good, unselfish intent and noncoercion, Christians could establish some semblance of kingdom-of-heaven relations within a capitalistic structure of ownership, investment, production, and marketing. Changed motives could override whatever selfishness and coercion were implicit in the system (and, one might add, probably in all human systems). His optimism was evidence of his essential faith. But insofar as it ignored the coercion in the larger system, was it perhaps also premised just a bit on some assumptions that he condemned in the neoorthodox school: that in the end one had to choose among imperfect options? that there was no real alternative to involvement in sub-Christian societal structures?

Whatever the answer, in some sense *The Way of the Cross in Human Relations* was a book by more than Hershberger. Hershberger freely borrowed and summarized ideas from other Mennonite thinkers, often younger ones, usually quite approvingly. And if the practical applications of his essentially radical theology would look a bit conservative to academic thinkers a decade and a half later, they probably nevertheless at the time represented a fair amount of agreement among thoughtful Mennonites. Hershberger was never an intellectual individualist. Consistently with his theology, he let the peoplehood church help shape his thinking. Yet in another sense *The Way of the Cross in Human Relations* was uniquely his. If much of the responsible opinion of his church approved it, as it did, it was because for some years he had been first among that church's ethical thinkers.

Hershberger's 1958 book showed much more inclination than had his earlier writing to accept the modern organizational revolution as accomplished fact. It showed distinctly less tendency to offer the overall, holistic alternative. There were still elements of the older Mennonite community model. In his labor-management proposals there was clear continuity; so also in proposals, which he put forward, for special Mennonite trade, professional, and agricultural associations. But the older Mennonite community idea in its holistic form was no longer there—or at least he did not choose to elaborate it. Ideally, at least in the Anabaptist Vision sense (whether or not in Mennonite practice), the church and not so much the sociological Mennonite community was now the unit for God's action. And in place of the ethical testimony of the grand sociological demonstration, the emphasis now was upon giving "prophetic witness" to government and society on particular issues and particular concerns. Having picked up the current "prophetic witness" phrase, Hershberger devoted an entire chapter to it. Of course he did not rule out prophetic witness by the large sociological demonstration. But the emphasis and the language had changed. And with the changes had gone some of the earlier focus.

VIII

Reflective study of twentieth-century Mennonite history and thought is still in its infancy. When scholars examine the Mennonite Church (MC) in the first two thirds of the century, scarcely anyone except Harold Bender and perhaps Daniel Kauffman and Orie O. Miller will deserve as close study as Guy F. Hershberger. Some questions needing deep investigation will be:

Did the ethical concepts of Hershberger and his generation grow as much out of Anabaptist understandings as the generation assumed? Why did Hershberger so much approve nineteenth-century U.S. evangelical Protestantism, which, according to historians such as Perry Miller and Robert T. Handy, was busy fusing its version of Christianity with U.S. nationalism to form a new version of *corpus christianum*?

In his own lifetime, what precisely did Hershberger accept from Fundamentalism, from the liberal Social Gospel, from neoorthodoxy, and so on?

How "Mennonite" were the roots of the Mennonite community idea? How much were they Jeffersonian and the product of a certain movement in rural sociology, and how much did they really spring from Mennonite tradition and Mennonite theology? Precisely how did the various roots intertwine?

If Hershberger's practical positions were indeed to a degree accommodationist and even conservative, did those positions really follow from his theological and ethical axioms?

Do Christian labor-management relations based upon his axioms have to be conceived so much within the limits of the firm? In order to be noncoercive and Christian in an immediate, day-to-day and on-the-job way, must such relations necessarily draw a firm's workers into such close step with management that they cannot join organizationally with workers in other firms to respond to the broader kinds of market and other macro-economic considerations?

Was Hershberger's apparent de-emphasis of the Mennonite community vision and relative acceptance of the organizational revolution a step backward or forward in Christian ethics (or neither)? Was it sheer acceptance of historical reality? or what? Did it lead to a more or to a less abstract and intellectualized ethics, to more or to less ability to translate vision into hard sociological patterns?

How much did the race issue and consciousness of ethnic variety and cultural pluralism among Mennonites have to do with blurring the holistic Mennonite community vision? *Must* appreciation of ethnic difference within the church work against some such sort of holistic vision?

At any given time, did the degree of accommodation with societal structures, as so clearly symbolized by alternative service under the draft, solve the problem of involvement as well as Hershberger thought? Were the positions he advocated the best ones for prophetic witness?

A basic question is: How shall we read Hershberger? His positions are vulnerable to charges that he was just a bit too optimistic, and his solutions a bit too easy and not very cognizant of ethical paradox. But shall we read him as a theoretician whose thinking should have resolved all abstract contradictions? To do so is fair, because he criticized contradictions in others. But is it not more appropriate to read him as a practical person who found the delicate lines that Mennonites at a certain time in history could walk to preserve a strong and real sense of being God's people, and do so without withdrawing into irrelevance? If he is judged as a theoretician, he is probably vulnerable. If he is read as finding practical ethical positions to serve the church's life and witness, he succeeded admirably.

Scholars, to exercise their gifts, must read him honestly and analytically. Yet Hershberger is a person to be not only studied, but appreciated. Without him or someone similar we in his tradition would scarcely know what questions to ask. That is a fact of Mennonite history. Hershberger helped capture the Mennonite ethic when some were trying to focus it by putting it alongside an alien theology and squeezing it into the narrow mold of "restrictions." He with others recaptured its positive tone and found relevant new applications in rapidly changing times. Whatever accommodations he and his contemporaries have made from time to time, they have not hesitated to offer their alternative ethics to elements of the larger society, whether to the Selective Service System in wartime, to an increasingly jaded and pragmatic set of once-idealistic labor union leaders, to the most weighty theologians of other religious traditions, or to whomever. Inside and outside Mennonite circles, innumerable seekers after a truly Jesus-like ethics are in Hershberger's debt.

As a still active Hershberger enters his ninth decade we do not have a Mennonite vision that is quite as nicely focused as either the Anabaptist Vision or the "Mennonite community" idea of two and three decades ago. Even for Hershberger the effort to capture and hold a focused Mennonite vision has become difficult. But the process of *trying* to focus and hold it has unquestionably been a boon in the Mennonite quest for faithfulness. And in the last quarter of the century?

2

History and Community
In the Thought of Guy F. Hershberger

Leonard Gross

I

In the Jewish-Christian-Muslim *Weltanschauung,* history is set
in a framework of theology. This traditional Western vista of history has been rejected by many Western historians—and by their
non-Western disciples too—during the last two centuries and a
half. Yet I believe that every student of human affairs does have a
theology, whether he acknowledges this or not; and I believe that
he is most at the mercy of his theology when he is most successful
in keeping it repressed below the threshold of his consciousness.
(Arnold Toynbee, 1969: 90)

Above all else, Guy F. Hershberger has been a "student of human
affairs," and like Arnold Toynbee, decided to probe life's meaning
through the discipline of history. History has provided the backbone
for the whole of his literary efforts, whether in the field of Christian
ethics, or peace, or social concerns, or economics, or theology. For
Hershberger probed history, conscious of his theology; he probed
theology and Christian ethics, conscious of the impact of history upon
the current social scene. During five decades and more, Hershberger
has been aware of the organic connection of the one to the other, af-
fording him a highly significant motif that has of necessity been reinforced by the needs of the times.

But faith and life, tied as they were for Hershberger to history,
were tied to a specific stream of history, the Mennonite experience going back four centuries when it was revolutionary to live in obedience
to the divine call that comes to individuals which at times counters the
proclamation of the state and its government—revolutionary, furthermore, in that a fellowship of believers should dare to question traditional methods of maintaining the social fabric, and dare to set

*Leonard Gross is executive secretary of the Historical Committee of the Men-
nonite Church and director of its Archives and historical research program,
located at Goshen, Indiana. A member of the College Mennonite Church, he has
written on Hutterite and Anabaptist themes.*

countering patterns of a community consciously based on the conviction that true peace may not attempt to maintain itself through violence. Such is the tradition with which Hershberger chose to identify
himself.

In a highly condensed form, the Anabaptist-Mennonite
expression of faith underlying this tradition takes on something of the
following argument: Peace can ultimately find its fulfillment only
within brotherhood. But brotherhood can be maintained only through
historical continuity, and through an identifying with the faith of
preceding Christian brotherhoods founded upon that peace which
Jesus embodied and shared with His disciples (John 14:27); here is
where the substance of peace is to be defined. But brotherhood can be
contained only in community—it *is* community. It is, however, that
particular Christian community founded upon divine love; for God is
love, who reveals Himself through His Spirit of love and peace in every
Christian community.

The Mennonite brotherhoods have borne witness to something of
this vision in each generation through a continuity of close community,
combined with a central affirmation that their peculiar history, going
back to the Anabaptists of Reformation times, is an important part of
the divine design of history. For God is here at work currently; but to
understand how God is now working we also need to maintain a strong
sense of heritage.

Because of historical continuity within community, the Mennonite identity is still more or less intact; there is no need to establish a
new ethic or a new theology or a new philosophy of life. There is no
identity crisis unless we bypass the whole of our common faith. The
wish, occasionally found, to begin again at zero (a "new" theology of
missions, or a "new" approach to ethics, for example) means in effect
to substitute a foreign import for the Mennonite idea (no man works
from a vacuum), and so also to betray the vital center of faith as interpreted within a strong four-hundred-year-old tradition. For indeed,
we possess an identity, a Christian ethic, a faith-theology, all of which
is well established and simply needs updating, reaffirmation, and reap-
propriation.

This sense of identity has surfaced in most generations of the Mennonite brotherhood's existence; it has come to the rescue when individuals or groups have attempted to chart new paths incompatible with
the Anabaptist way. Somehow, the incompatible elements tend to be
cast aside; in other words, the church, whether of Swiss Brethren or

Dutch Mennonite origin, has always been recallable.

The rationale behind stressing Anabaptism to this degree is the brotherhood conviction that in Anabaptism there is something worth maintaining because it is essentially at one with the witness of Jesus, although this interpretation needs perennial reexamination and reassessment.

II

Guy F. Hershberger is an important link in this historical process of maintaining community for Mennonitism of the twentieth century. As a "student of human affairs," Hershberger has balanced his literary activities with an existential and localized concrete witness to people. The setting was Goshen College, and Hershberger ventured into this fragile mid-1920s setting at a time when a number of Mennonite educators were pessimistic about the future of Mennonitism. The genuine center of a faithful, creative brotherhood, as earlier defined in terms of brotherly reconciliation, mutual aid, and a strong community based upon Christian ethics and love, was in danger of losing ground to cultural and doctrinal imports. The great American Mennonite crisis surfaced in all its severity and is symbolized in the closing of Goshen College in 1923-24. A variety of approaches to solving the dilemma were being suggested to breach the rift, represented by the factions within Mennonitism: (1) nineteenth-century liberalism, (2) twentieth-century Fundamentalism, (3) the rigorous cultural fixation enthusiasts, and (4) the search for the essence of Anabaptism.

When Goshen College reopened, the option chosen by the Mennonite Board of Education is obvious in their choice of the new president, S. C. Yoder, whose key strength lay in gentle diplomacy and in the quiet affirmation that the heart is more important than reason (2 Corinthians 10:5). His approach was one of quiet determination to maintain the Anabaptist-Mennonite faith and way of life, based most fundamentally upon the idea of community and its existential expression. To this degree it was the option to maintain an authentic conservatism, rather than to attempt to begin with newer ideologies pretending to be the whole of Christian truth. Furthermore, it was hoped that another method of maintaining nonconformity to the world might be found than simply to fix, culturally, outward forms and structures.

The brotherhood spirit which won the day was a courageous venture, given the strong factions crying for another stance, whether this be Fundamentalism, or the recently-set culturalism, or a lingering of elements of classical nineteenth-century liberalism which were to a certain degree present in pre-1923 Goshen College. But the new force at work in Goshen was developing its own forms and building a power and strength which can be compared to a new rope created from individual strands. The clue to the gathering strength lay in the idea of teamwork, effected through the low profile but untiring efforts of the new president, S. C. Yoder, who was able to gather a strong new faculty, including the initiators of the *Mennonite Quarterly Review:* Harold S. Bender, Guy F. Hershberger, Ernst Correll, John Umble, and Edward Yoder.[1]

The question which lay central throughout the 1920s and 1930s was posed something like this: Wherein lay the answers to the deep-seated problems which were in large part fomented by the ideological imports from the then current American scene? The team members were well aware that a key threat, Fundamentalism, was in its (lack of a) historical approach at odds with the Mennonite faith. They also understood that this same Fundamentalism had permeated many a Mennonite congregation. However, the team was also of one mind that there was indeed a way through the maze; it would simply need to be found. And furthermore, they were convinced that this approach demanded an open and common search, if progress were to follow.

The platform chosen upon which to launch the next step in the program lay in a reaffirmation of history as a fundamental source for answers. What makes this answer all the more significant is that this was during a radically ahistorical era, when the forces of Fundamentalism, neoorthodoxy, and existentialism—all three ahistorical in nature—were gaining rapid strength throughout the countries of the Western world.

To have made this choice was not only being true to the Christian faith, which is by definition historical (see Hershberger, 1958d: 374), but it was also remaining true to the Anabaptist-Mennonite interpretation of biblical faith, which sees God's designs in history tied integrally to the whole of the history of His people, of whom the Mennonites claimed to be a part.

The choice of history allowed Hershberger, Bender, and the other team members to work gently but surely in helping the larger Mennonite brotherhood through current problems. History served the cause mightily; it was also the genuine Anabaptist approach—indeed, it lay at the center of Anabaptism. The decision seems not to have been politically motivated but was simply seen as the correct approach; it came from the heart, and turned into a lifelong quest in the search for a vision and a fulfillment of this vision. But there was also the feeling that the Anabaptist-Mennonite way of life lay deeply ingrained in the souls of many of the brethren, and simply needed reawakening and sharpening.

Church history in general, and Anabaptist-Mennonite history in particular, became the new platform. The method lay in a brotherhood approach whereby truth developed and emerged from the group, and not solely—or even primarily—from any one individual. Hopeful that a new era lay just ahead, the young Goshen team optimistically announced the new program to fellow youth of the Mennonite Church:

> The Golden Age of the Mennonite Church is not past; it is just ahead. The problems of the present are many; they are difficult. But problems are challenges. They are opportunities for consecrated talent. The time never was and never will be when problems are not present. Let vision and faith see problems as challenges.
>
> The present generation of Mennonite youth have unusual talent to consecrate to the present task. The number of young men and women trained and in training, whose heart is set on the work of the kingdom, whose loyalty is sincere, whose faith is deep, has never been exceeded. The church is ready to use this talent, this faith, this loyalty.
>
> The coming generation in the Mennonite Church is being given a carefully built, well-knit, efficient organization of activities. This organization is the equal of that in any Mennonite group and is quite compact, has rich resources and experience behind it. It covers the field of publication, education, missions, Sunday school, church music, and church history.
>
> The heritage of the coming generation in faith and practice is sound. The faith has been kept. The historic ideals of the Mennonite Church are still functioning. Whatever obscuring of New Testament faith and practice has been found at places can be remedied. The Mennonite Church still wishes to be a pure New Testament church.
>
> Youth of the Mennonite Church, the church of tomorrow! The heritage is yours, the organization is yours, the talent is yours, the problems are yours, the future is yours. Get the vision, follow the gleam, bend your back to the burden, consecrate yourselves to the task. You are needed, you are wanted, you are able. May God grant the will. (Bender, 1927:ii)

Here is a progressive vision, at once set apart from both modernism and a propositional truth approach which lay at the basis of Fundamentalism; for here was an open common search for the essence of our heritage, and the desire to review critically this heritage. This willingness to carry forward the search for answers is what has set the *Mennonite Quarterly Review* apart from Fundamentalism. To have taken history in the troubled ahistorical 1920s to solve the Mennonite problem may seem from the vantage point of the 1970s to have been a political expedient; it was also far more than this. History according to the Anabaptist-Mennonite view is central to the essence of the gathered community in that it is in community where God is at work; here, history—salvation history—is in the making. And the belief became clearer as the years went by that within community lay the foundation of faith, hope, and love, and the witness to truth.

III

It was the search for an authentic conservatism to which Guy F. Hershberger opened himself when he came to Goshen College in 1925, a search which marks all of his writings during more than half a century. But what was there to conserve? History provided the clue to finding answers. Where did the Mennonites in fact come from, and what were the consequences of their historical development? The idea of brotherhood was assumed; it did not seem to need articulation during the first fifteen or so years of Hershberger's search. But to save the brotherhood reality and idea posed quite a different question. And the method could not be disassociated from the answer; in fact it suggested the answer. For the answer lay in affirming how God had been—and had not been—working in the midst of (for our purposes) the Mennonites.

Hence, the lessons of history were a major clue to finding the meaning of salvation for the brotherhood. History could consequently not be separated from community, nor community from history. Indeed, the truth could not ultimately be captured in a codified system of thought (basic to Fundamentalism), nor in a hope in the saving powers of well-intentioned international spokesmen (one aspect of nineteenth-century liberalism), nor in fixing culture once and for all wherein salvation could be set in a static way of life (legalistic nonconformity). To be sure, truth could not be confined in any man-made box, but could only be experienced by the current generation of those gathered believers who were open to present revelation.

Even here, however, history substantiates and helps to check and balance current experience; for God's hand in the course of mankind can be traced historically, and although the greatest of precedents for seeing God's hand can be found in the history of God's people through ca. AD 100—namely in the Bible—this process of tracing the history of God's people indeed continued further into the Christian era. The Anabaptists and later Mennonites, among many other groups, found God at work in history. There were certain givens, just as had been the case throughout the scriptural eras: affirming the reality of God's people, and coping with the issues of cause and effect, substance and form, vision and hope, and the realization of faith and love.

It is significant that Hershberger started here in his open search for answers; it is also significant that Hershberger was not alone in this search, but worked closely with others in the same quest. It was an authentic team effort which in itself suggested something of the method used in finding answers: the brotherhood approach where truth emerges from the group. For this was the Anabaptist method from the beginning years of Zurich and Schleitheim.[2] Herein lay a clue for Bender, Hershberger, Correll, Umble, Yoder, and later on, many others.

In fact this clue is as significant as the idea of the quest itself—that Hershberger was willing to share in this common quest, and not attempt to develop it solely through his own efforts and out of his own mind and reason. His writings always found their way into the hands of fellow scholars for a sharp review before they were published. Indeed the volumes were generally initiated through the commission of the Mennonite brotherhood. Often Hershberger would run a "trial balloon" in the form of a shorter article in the *Mennonite Quarterly Review* or elsewhere before finalizing the text of a manuscript (for example, *War, Peace, and Nonresistance*), or he would find such critique directly from audiences, where he would lecture on human affairs and then finalize a manuscript (*The Way of the Cross in Human Relations*).

Hershberger began with Anabaptism in his life's search;[3] but significantly, he constantly balanced the historical with current issues, and in this manner was able to analyze the present (church and world) against the backdrop of the past, but also to align the past (cause and effect) with the present. His civil religion article (1927a) is an early and masterly example of this.

The idea of peace also lay at the center of this vision. Peace was an issue with which Hershberger grappled throughout the decades of his research and interpretation; it continues strong in his current writings and ideas. But again, peace cannot be separated from heritage (where peace is defined) or community (where peace reigns), so that for Hershberger the clue to the peace question also lies centrally in the message that history (and not only Anabaptist history) alone can provide. The maintaining of peace is always to be seen within the context of the brotherhood, although Hershberger at the same time extends the message of peace beyond this focal point as a witness for any and all to comprehend and accept. Peace was both a quality of life for God's people to embody in community as well as a way of life for them to proclaim and demonstrate to the world. Hershberger reached his great synthesis on the theme of peace and conflict in his *War, Peace, and Nonresistance* (1944c).

Meanwhile, during the 1940s, the Mennonite idea of (rural) community was itself being threatened by the new trend toward urbanization. The idea of peace consequently needed a broader defining than simply being a strong witness against war and overt violence. Brand-new social issues needed to be thought through, discussed, and dealt with, whether in the realm of labor unions and employer/employee relations, or in redefining how community can exist within the urban context. The efforts in this area resulted in a second great volume, *The Way of the Cross in Human Relations* (1958d).

Hershberger's *The Way of the Cross* is a high point in twentieth-century Mennonite scholarly literature. For here, Hershberger dares to analyze, for the first time in such depth and comprehensiveness, the whole spectrum of ideological imports into Mennonitism, including aspects of nineteenth-century liberalism and twentieth-century Fundamentalism and neoorthodoxy; he also takes on much of church history, including Luther and Calvin and their impact upon Western thought. All of this is set in the framework of a careful development of the theme of creation, with the Christ of history as the personification of God's new creation.

Certain of these recent Western ideologies merit further analysis, in light of their relationship to the theme at hand, namely, history and community:

Liberalism. Although Hershberger plays down the terms "modernism" and "liberalism" in *The Way of the Cross*, largely because the warm debate on this theme was already waning after the Second World War, the movements that were firmly based upon the nineteenth-century optimistic view of progress are set forth, along with their successors. Hershberger sums them up in his chapters "The Social Gospel" and "Christian Action." Within the social gospel movement, for example, there was a strong sentiment for pacifism. However, generally

> it did not produce conscientious objectors who took their stand for the law of Christ and the way of the cross in the face of a society given to militarism. When the war came in 1914 many of the social gospel pacifists were caught off guard since they were not expecting a major war to occur. They recovered their composure, however, when they were assured that this was the war which would end all wars. Since it was merely one of those obstacles which the pilgrim on the progress road inevitably encounters, the best must be made of it (1958d: 97-98).

If we understand liberalism within this larger nineteenth- and early twentieth-century context, then we may summarize the Hershberger argument something as follows:[4]   Liberalism is not the carrier of Christian truth not primarily because it is liberal, but because it is not tied to the reality of the gathered Christian brotherhood; it rides the back of nationalism and is hence ultimately divisive, vis-a-vis the church universal. The international Kellogg-Briand Pact (1928), which outlawed all war and violence, is one example of (political) liberalism at its best, but also an example of the limitations to the approach and substance of this idealistic movement. It overestimated man's goodness and what he can accomplish, and thus seems to be at odds with the realities of a mixed-up Machiavellian world and its realpolitik.

Another perspective of (religious) liberalism which tends to limit its usefulness in carrying Christianity is its essential marriage to current philosophies of society. Recent examples of such philosophies—although admittedly during an era which is no longer liberal, indeed, an era which also stands in reaction to neoorthodoxy—are the secular and God-is-dead movements of the 1960s, ideologies speaking to their time, yet which were not solidly founded upon lasting rock. Any new movement is to be reckoned with as a force in its day, but at the same time it must be interpreted in the light of history and community.

Fundamentalism. A still more current ideology which continued to strike close to home throughout Hershberger's era is Fundamentalism. His argument goes something as follows:

Fundamentalism, another import into the Mennonite stream, also is highly limited in its usefulness to those who affirm the brotherhood way of life, centering in the close Christian community, as the means of maintaining divine love and peace. For Fundamentalism tends to be both individualistic in its orientation, when compared to the close brotherhood approach, and is just as nationalistic as liberalism. It is largely devoid of (God in) history, and because God is pushed into the inner recesses of the individual, with the ultimate health of the nation at hand becoming a major responsibility of the church, the natural recourse is to identify rather directly with *one* nation and its society, and to mirror something of that nation's ethics, social concerns, and foreign policy. Hence, the Fundamentalist must by definition compromise in the area of war and violence, much as he would otherwise like to affirm the idea of peace. Consequently for Mennonites, Fundamentalism is a serious challenge to the brotherhood approach to Christ's universal kingdom already established here on earth.

Furthermore, the individualistic approach to the communication of the prophetic word within Fundamentalism is at odds with the gathered community approach of the Swiss Brethren and the Dutch Anabaptists, where truth emerges from the group wherein God's Spirit is at work, guiding and revealing truth. Although there is a need for the teacher and missioner in the group context, truth is no longer (if it ever had been) that of words forthcoming from the mouth of a person who in his own individual right tells others what truth is. An individual may, of course, represent the group, as did the Old Testament prophets in writing or witnessing by word of mouth. But it is the witness which grows out of the group that the individual prophet passes on, based on a historical consciousness of the gathered people of God, who are continuing His truth and way of life here on earth. Hence the prophet is an honest and genuine prophet only where he draws his truth from the community, and in this way embodies in his own being the carrying force of a historical continuity which resides squarely in the spirit of the gathered people; for his is a historical faith which is defined by the whole of the Christian heritage. The prophet who stands at all independent of community is to that degree by definition a false prophet.[5]

*Neoorthodoxy.*Although Hershberger does not dwell upon the twentieth-century crisis theology of neoorthodoxy at length, he does critique the movement at times:

> Its weakness, as this writer sees it, is an insufficient emphasis on redemption, on the power of the Holy Spirit, and on the lord-

ship of Christ. As in the case of the social gospel, the neo-orthodox theologians have identified themselves with the general social order, and their thinking is with that orientation. The difference is that whereas the social gospel would transform the nearly sinless kingdoms of this world into the kingdom of God with such ease that the help of God was barely needed in the process, their successors are so involved in the ambiguities of the hopelessly sinful social order that even God Himself is not powerful enough to enable a penitent soul to do more than to confess his sin and then keep on sinning. (1958d: 102)

At another place, Hershberger talks of neoorthodoxy's "underrating . . . heaven's power to change the human heart and to direct the ways of man into the path of Christian discipleship." (1958d: 4-5).

It is significant to note that Karl Barth never did write a comprehensive volume on eschatology in his great *Kirchliche Dogmatik*. This not only suggests something of Barth's theological priorities but also suggests indirectly an underlying problem within the neoorthodox approach to history and community. For to believe as strongly in the transcendence of God as Barth did minimizes to the same degree God's immanent working in history, where God is the proper establisher and foundation of His people.

Christianity as Faith and History. That Hershberger based his thought squarely upon the historical approach can be seen throughout the volume *The Way of the Cross in Human Relations*. A crowning passage on this theme merits quotation:

> In order to bring the way of the cross and the kingdom into proper perspective it is necessary to grasp the essential nature of Christianity as faith and history. Christianity is not primarily a system of thought or even a set of ethical principles, although these are included. Christianity is faith in a Person who acts in history. Divine revelation is a history of the mighty works of God which were manifest first in the creation, then in the redemptive work of Christ, and which the New Testament tells us will continue until their consummation in the age which is to come. (1958d: 374)

The above passage also suggests another clue to Hershberger's view, that the Christian way of life transcends mere ethics, an idea brought out in yet another passage on Christian discipleship which also suggests that the great faith and substance undergirding the Christian way has a spiritual dimension lifting it beyond a cogent system of ethics or even the greatest philosophical concepts of morality:

Girded by this confident assurance [of victory in life and in death] the Christian disciple enters into the redemptive experience with Christ, following His steps, conscious of the fact that as an ambassador of Christ, God now makes His appeal through him (2 Corinthians 5:20). Being a member of the colony of heaven, the Christian recognizes that his manner of life in this the end time must bear the image of his heavenly citizenship. The way of love and the cross must control both his personal and his social ethic. How else can men know that he is a disciple? How else can God make His appeal through him? "By this all men will know that you are my disciples, if you have love for one another" (John 13:35, RSV). (1958d: 382)

We note in passing that the Anabaptist scholar Robert Friedmann (d. 1970), during the last years of his life, mentioned in conversation that Christianity is "more than ethics." The Christian follows after the Jesus of history; his actions are not only or primarily the result of decisions based on ideas having their source in the mind and reason of an individual, but rather originate in a higher and broader voice, namely, that of Jesus and His church of gathered disciples, where His Spirit is operative. Such an approach to handling life contrasts sharply with the individual's attempt to do so out of his own sense of right and wrong. It is instead the community approach, which does not minimize the reality of the individual but provides him with the appropriate structure to develop and channel his human resources and potential. Here is true Christian community; here is continuity as long as community continues, which has been the case for the Mennonites through history to the present time; but here is also the source of action and of existential living.

IV

It is the historical approach which Guy Hershberger, H. S. Bender, and the other members of the team accepted as the foundation for understanding truth, whether in the questions of church and state, or community and world. Today, we either accept this same historical approach, or we begin at zero and find we need to formulate a brand-new—"Mennonite," or whatever—theology and ethic. But where there is continuity of community this is not only unnecessary, it is self-destructive for that community. Where there is no community it is still an option with high risk, for the brand-new idea may just as easily collapse as fulfill its promise of actually working.

For where there is continuity of community, we already have our faith and Christian ethics. We know where to begin to solve problems, and that is halfway to solution,

The historical question is hence at once both the community question and that of the historical substantiation of a movement, given the fact that one needs to choose, confessionally, to be a member of a voluntary group, but also to accept the consequences of that choice. But the Mennonite community goes back to the Zurich community of 1525 and the Schleitheim Confession of 1527, where truth was discerned as emerging from the group.[6] We also reap the consequences of this choice (for example, assuming less than a total allegiance to and responsibility for a nation's government), but find thereby as Christian disciples something of divine peace within community as we dwell within God's new covenant in Christ—albeit imperfectly, for we are human and fallible. But history has suggested the worth of this community movement and its historical reality; the best way of continuing the positive side of this tradition is to learn from history both what has led closer to the ideal and what has tended to lead away from the ideal.[7]

V

Anabaptism transcends an individualized Christianity; it is more than ethics; it views *Heilsgeschichte* as going beyond AD 99 and into the present time. Because its identity is still so strongly imbedded in the mind-set and life of the Mennonite community it therefore is a very present reality, and the foundation of a continuing "neo-Anabaptist" community (see Miller, 1975). We look to our long heritage and find an approach and a way of life which helps to bring balance currently, during yet another precarious time when so many "truth-bearers" are telling us so many answers, some of which seem to be only the product of their own fantasy and inner creative urges. The community approach also stands apart from the experiences of the world, which looks to its own heritage of wars and conflict, and can only hope that the next step beyond its present state of being will lead to better horizons—yet even here, history is the great leveler, bringing realism into focus, and exposing illusion for what it is.

The community where Christ's Spirit reigns, however, is grounded in God's kingdom, and as a nucleus of this kingdom, such community is already in its essence something far more substantial than a mere utopian dream; it *is* reality, imperfect to be sure, but a manifestation of the perfect. It is an imperfect casting of the ideal, but as such, embodies something of the substance of the ideal and vision—indeed, the vision has in a very real sense found fulfillment. For a true vision, in contrast to illusion, is a positive part of the human experience itself, in that all human beings live with a view to vision; this is what grants hope to the human soul, what impels man into a new day. Vision colors essentially the human experience.

But the gathered Christian community also selects from other traditions and experiences. Hershberger did so, selecting historical precedents from a consciously chosen grouping of traditions, all the way across the board, including other church groups and the wisdom of the world. But the clue here, in order not to become overwhelmed by the contrasts and contradictions, is again to be found in the historical approach, where the Anabaptist Vision and its reality—or lack of reality—has been kept carefully in mind.

For to test the Mennonite scene during the twentieth century is to test at the same time sixteenth-century Anabaptism—but also the whole of church history—within the context of the history of Jesus and how He turned the old covenant into a new one. His process of selection and rejection is an important clue to understanding this radical shift.

We also want to view Jesus and His church universal within the context of all of history; yet in a real sense Jesus is the central point of reference for both faith and history, in that here is the foundation and substance—to use Hershberger's phrase—for the "Christ-inspired concern for a new order here and now" (1975a: 4).

3

Discerning the Times

Robert S. Kreider

The children of Issachar . . . were men that had understanding of the times, to know what Israel ought to do. 1 Chronicles 12:32. 12:32.
To every thing there is a season, and a time to every purpose under the heaven. Ecclesiastes 3:1.
But can ye not discern the signs of the times? Matthew 16: 3.

To live eighty years is a major achievement and a gift. The years from 1896 to 1976 embrace an awesome expanse of history. It is a special gift not only to live through these eighty years but to be able to discern the times and seasons—to travel the road of change and to know the mountains and the valleys and to sense where one's people ought to be going. Guy F. Hershberger has been such a person.[1]

Melvin Gingerich was to have written this article but death intervened on June 24, 1975. Melvin and Guy both grew up as Amish Mennonite farm boys in Iowa, both attended Hesston College in the early twenties, both were historians, both went to Goshen College where they were faculty colleagues, both served together on committees and publications. The sixty-two pages of typed transcript of Melvin Gingerich's March 1975 interviews with Guy Hershberger (Gingerich, 1975) reflect an intricately intertwined web of shared experiences, convictions, and perceptions—and above all, shared joys in pilgrimage. In due course this series of interviews should be edited and published as a significant source of insights on this era just past and on the art of perceiving the times and seasons.

Theron Schlabach and others contributing to this volume write of Guy Hershberger and the infinitely varied links which bind the story of a man to the story of a particular people. Our task here is to savor these eighty years, identifying epochs and forces, reflecting on issues and motifs. We begin with a search for motifs or themes in the life of Guy

Robert Kreider is director of the Mennonite Library and Archives, and professor of peace studies at Bethel College, North Newton, Kansas. An active leader in the General Conference Mennonite Church, he was formerly president of Bluffton College.

Hershberger, which are at once motifs in the life of a people. We shall then proceed to the critical periods in this history. We shall comment on the issues worthy of continuing study. All this has a tentative quality—a prologue or an agenda. Most emphasis will be given to the earliest years and much less to the more recent periods. The focus of this essay is primarily on one branch of the Mennonites—the Mennonite Church (Old Mennonites). However, the experiences of this group are analogous to and intertwined with the experiences of other Mennonite groups.

During the past generation many scholars have been engaged in sixteenth-century Anabaptist studies. The needs of Mennonite people call now for a comparably intensified study of these past eighty years— a time of fantastic, frightening change for Mennonites and all groups. It cannot be proved, but it may reasonably be said that more than half of all the Anabaptists and Mennonites who have ever lived in the world since 1525 have lived since the birth of Guy Hershberger in 1896. Inescapably, then, it is imperative that a people know themselves in these latter days.

Motifs in the Life of Guy Hershberger

In Guy Hershberger—the scholar, the churchman, and the person—one finds a variety of motifs which seem appropriate to the role of prophetic leadership among a people cautiously seeking to maintain their identity in a time of rapid change.

1. He has been a scholar of the people. Much of his writing has been commissioned by his people through editors and conference committees: the Peace Problems Committee, the Committee on Industrial Relations, the Mennonite Central Committee, the editor of the *Youth's Christian Companion,* and others. Here is a prophet who has had an assured power base. His method has been to write and share a draft with colleagues, give the article a test run in a periodical, listen to advice and counsel, and then revise it for publication. No book of his is etched in stone as a definitive statement. Each suggests an invitation to further study and possible revision. And then, most important, he has listened to his people at scores of workshops and meetings in congregations, his radar picking up the language and concerns of the people.

2. All of his writing reflects a high seriousness toward the biblical record. In the Scripture he lives and moves and has his being. He reads with comparable seriousness contemporary history and church history—the Bible in one hand, the newspaper in the other. With his

constant attentiveness to biblical resources, Guy Hershberger's writing cannot be shaken off by the Christian right, center, or left. Biblical thoroughness and ethical seriousness have given him credibility and entree to the conservative and liberal sectors of the church. He is a bridge.

3. One senses that along with the biblical "thus-sayeth-the-Lord" theme is a pragmatic streak—the politics of peoplehood. He has been sensitive to words which offend—using "survivors' aid" instead of "life insurance," "nonresistance" instead of "pacifism," "progressive" instead of "liberal," and others. He continued to wear the plain coat long after others had laid it aside. He could accept a rigid doctrinal statement with an affirmative attitude—if even a bit less than enthusiastic: "It gave me no trouble." He has not allowed differences to break fellowship. He has been charitable to his opponents. Unlike many persons, he has seemed to enjoy opposition. Reprimanded by those in authority, he quietly went on with his studies. Perhaps this might be called the practicing of "revolutionary obedience" in the structures of the church.

4. He has had the courage to cross disciplinary lines. Not a systematic ethicist or theologian, he nonetheless ventures into the complexities of the world of Karl Barth and Reinhold Niebuhr. Not a biblical scholar by training, he dares in his studies of the Old Testament to take issue, for example, with the neatly contained systems of dispensationalism. This blend of biblical, historical, theological, and sociological materials is holistic. Today this might be called a systems or ecological approach—that is, recognizing that everything is related to everything else. He has seen peace relating to the gospel, education relating to evangelism, publications relating to Christian nurture, community relating to peace, and so on and on. He saw nonresistance as warp and woof of the gospel—not just an add-on, or a restriction peculiar to Mennonites.

5. He has continued to be a man of hope when the data gives scant basis for such optimism. This politics of hope runs through all his writing. Read the concluding paragraphs of his major books and each strikes a chord of hope. All disciples of Christ have the opportunity to live meaningful and faithful lives—at least in the world of the Christian community. Intertwined with the theme of hope is a desire to be identified with the forces of progress—an authentic, biblical progressivism. When one listens to his conversation with Melvin Gingerich about boyhood days in Iowa and student days at Hesston,

scores of times Guy and Melvin use the words "progress,"
"progressive," and "change," and always with appreciation: "a
progressive congregation," "in sympathy with the whole concept of
progress and change," "a lot of progressive ideas." He also speaks
words of approval for the conservative persons in his acquaintance—
often commenting something like this: "He was very, very rigid but he
was an intellectual." He respected a good mind—conservative or
liberal.

6. He has been a highly productive scholar. Certainly there are a
variety of factors which lead one to be productive: energy levels, attention span, singleness of purpose, a supportive community, affection for
one's work. In retrospect it seems good that Guy Hershberger was
spared extensive involvements in the institutional machinery. A
thoughtful but not a brilliant speaker, he was not made captive to a
busy lecture schedule. He chose carefully his areas of concentration:
peace, Christian community, brotherhood economics, race—all closely
interconnected.

7. Guy Hershberger's life is an intriguing study in the role of the
providential. It is interesting to speculate on meta-historical questions
("what-if" history). What if Guy Hershberger had gone to France with
the American Friends Service Committee team in 1918 and had been
present at the Clermont conference of the restless young Mennonites?
What if he had attended the more suspect Goshen College of 1920, as
he almost did, instead of the safer Hesston College? What if he and his
wife had gone to India as missionaries instead of preparing to teach at
Goshen? What if he and Harold Bender had entered the hazardous
field of biblical studies in the 1920s instead of the more acceptable field
of historical studies? What if he had chosen a field of study other than
peace and state relations for his doctoral study? Suppose S. C. Yoder
had not been his pastor and then later his patron? Of all the significant
questions which he could have chosen to study, why in the 1920s was he
led to study peace, a topic of shame to many Mennonites? Surely the
providential is in this record.

8. Guy Hershberger's life is associated with the genesis of many
ideas and programs. His story reflects how difficult it is to verify a
single parent for any particular achievement, suggesting rather that
most significant programs and ideas have multiple lines of paternity.
He acknowledges indebtedness to Baker, Ligutti, Kollmorgen, Eby,
Fretz, Nunn, Bender, and many others.

9. In the bitter, polarized climate in the Mennonite Church in the

1920s Guy Hershberger chose deliberately a middle way. He came to Goshen in 1925, young, clean, and unstained. He correctly assessed the forces of Fundamentalism and an older authoritarian polity to be in the ascendancy. Although a progressive and an emerging Anabaptist at heart, he sensed instinctively that Fundamentalism and authoritarianism could not be contained with a liberal counterrhetoric. He must have sensed that Fundamentalism called for an intensively biblical and a deeply historical Anabaptist response. The strength of Fundamentalism has been its serious biblicism, but its weakness has been its selective biblicism and inattentiveness to the story of the church. Guy Hershberger's inclinations led him into biblical-historical studies which helped to tame and shape powerful diversionary forces in the Mennonite Church. Here was an agent of change set in the image of continuity, caution, and conservatism. The conservative component was authentic and the progressive part was authentic. This is not unlike the latter-day reflective wisdom of a Robert Maynard Hutchins who was supposed to have said: "I would have made more rapid progress if I had proceeded more slowly."

Guy Hershberger's principal legacy may not be his books or the church programs he spawned. It may not be in the definitive, systematic statement of theological position and moral application. His legacy may instead be that of discerner of the times, a navigator-guide to the critical moral issues. He has been an ethicist for his people, keeping close to them, yet preserving dimensions of detachment—probing, exploring new territory, coming back and inviting others to join in the pilgrimage, always being a bit hesitant, groping, searching. In this process one feels assurance of authenticity. One sees him always moving forward with his people in pilgrimage, sometimes dragging his feet, sometimes running ahead, always in friendly conversation, never breaking relationships. In him have been the images of peoplehood, pilgrimage, peacemaking . . . discipleship, faithfulness, wholeness . . . the Bible, the Anabaptists, the blessed community . . . the process: "I press toward the mark for the prize of the high calling of God in Christ Jesus" (Philippians 3:14).

The Recovery of a Decade Past

To recover a feel for the decade eighty years ago when Guy Hershberger was born strains all our imaginative powers. Henry Seidel Canby described lovingly his boyhood world of the small town and called the decade "The Age of Confidence." At the beginning of the

decade the last of the Indian wars had been fought at Wounded Knee in
the state just west of Iowa. Dwight L. Moody was still alive and had
just established a Bible institute in Chicago. The United States was
growing, but in 1896, had only one-third the population of today. The
nation was not yet identified as a great power. Two years would pass
before the war with Spain. The United States still appeared to have
clean hands—no colonies, no Panama Canal, no great military establishment, no Pentagon, no CIA. But in two years this country would
give release to pent-up longings for overseas empire and to carry "the
White House's burden."

The Hershberger home in Johnson County, Iowa, in 1896, did not
yet have electric lights or a telephone. The family paid no income taxes.
Probably no one in Kalona, Iowa, had yet seen an automobile, certainly not an airplane. The year 1896 was the year when rural free de-
livery began, bringing to the home the Sears-Roebuck catalog and the
temptations of a dazzling new range of consumer goods. Gold had just
been discovered on the Klondike. Far away in Washington, D. C.,
Grover Cleveland was in the last months of his presidency. A month
before in the presidential elections William McKinley, friend of big
business, had triumphed with ease over the eloquent populist
Democrat, William Jennings Bryan. The populist protest against the
power of the railroads, Eastern banks, big business, and "The Cross of
Gold" had been turned back. This was the age of Morgan and
Rockefeller and Carnegie and expansive American industries un-
checked by regulatory bodies or unions.

In 1896 the Hershberger farmstead near Kalona, Iowa, reflected a
simpler agrarian life. Everyone in the family knew how to hitch a horse,
milk a cow, talk Pennsylvania Dutch, fire a cookstove, and play a role
at butchering time. In 1896 there was no *Gospel Herald,* no Goshen
College, no Hesston College, no inter-Mennonite bodies of any sort, no
general history book on the Mennonites, no overseas Mennonite
missions, and only recently the first city mission in Chicago. This
Amish Mennonite community had its problems, but it was a good and
understandable world. This was an age of confidence.

The writing of Mennonite histories in English is a post-1896
phenomenon. Written in tidy, parochial ways, many of these have been
chronicles of congregations, conference resolutions and institutions,
and biographies of the men who have been leaders. They tend to be
insulated from the accounts of other Mennonite groups, the broader
stream of national church developments, and the trends in a larger so-

ciety. They have skirted our conflicts, the explanation being that it is not good to have dirty linen washed in public or to open closets containing skeletons.

Guy Hershberger has been one of those writers who has seen history whole. When he writes peoplehood history he delineates those shaping forces of the marketplace and technology, of religious and national movements, of city, factory and university. When one paints history on that broader canvas he sees particularities and gifts not observed before; he is also made aware that a people's uniqueness is not quite so unique.

To illustrate the broad canvas approach, the influence of technology on Mennonite life and thought could be profitably explored. Perhaps Henry Ford has had as profound an effect on our people as Conrad Grebel, and Sears-Roebuck as Menno Simons. Henry Ford's Model T wiped out the one-room schools around Kalona, imposed on Mennonites uncomfortable problems about insurance, brought the city closer to the farm, changed patterns of entertainment and social life and weekday church programming, and displaced the age of the horse. One cannot conceive of Scottdale, Elkhart, and Akron without crowded appointment books, the long-distance telephone call, dictation equipment, the photocopier, offset printing, computerized bookkeeping and mailings, credit cards, rental cars for traveling executives, instant reservations by air to Kinshasa, and the presence of Imperial 400 Motels near international airports for conference boards and committees—none of these available in 1896. More importantly, add to this the emergence of young Mennonite managerial people with technical training and the vocabulary of the worldly professions adapted to the churchly programs: "feasibility studies," "management consultants," "corporate image," "inputs and outputs," "goals and strategies," and even "the bottom line." And then add to this tax deductions for charitable gifts. The corporate business model is as much a part of the Mennonite way of life as the Schleitheim Articles.

Then go back to Kalona and think of the Hershberger farm in 1896—a relatively self-sufficient farmstead with an annual cash income of only a few hundred dollars. This Amish community had been wrestling with the worldliness of Cyrus McCormick's attractive new farm equipment. The restraints of the church on the new farm technology steadily gave way to what was felt best for the economic man. Visit a Mennonite farm in Kalona eighty years later. The Green Revolution has arrived: $25,000 tractors, bulk milk storage equipment, hybrid seed, chemical fertilizers, self-propelled combines, conveyor belts to the feed bins. Large-scale capitalist agriculture has come to Kalona. For the Mennonite farmer, his accountant, banker, and lawyer may be as big in his life as his pastor. The art of paying only the minimum required income tax is one of his more recently acquired skills.

What did it take to start farming in 1896? $500? What is needed today? $50,000? Perhaps more. Every congregation now has those who are wise in the ways of corporate finance. In 1896 no one traveled very far—a few trips in one's lifetime to visit distant relatives and sometimes a trip west to spy out virgin land. But now eighty years later Mennonites spend more on overseas travel and other vacations than on all the conference budgets for overseas and home missions and Christian education. Today they pay more in taxes for the support of the military than they give voluntarily for the support of the local church program.

Nonconformity to the world came naturally to the Amish Mennonites of the Kalona community in 1896. In 1976 nonconformity has retreated before the frontal advance of central heating, electric power, indoor hot- and cold-running water, color television with movies in everyone's family room, wash-and-wear clothing, installment buying, and electric hair dryers. The old arts of subsistence farming, of canning, drying, and butchering are close to death. And women and children have left the farms to find jobs in the towns, each driving in his or her car on paved highways.

In the fall following his graduation from high school in 1915, Guy Hershberger began teaching in a rural school. When he entered college in 1920 at the age of twenty-four he could count only a few from his whole acquaintanceship who had ever gone to college. Now many Iowa Mennonite youth go, or are expected to go, either to college or into voluntary service—the latter not an option in 1915.

New machines and a new technology have slipped into our lives and have taken control. Technology, the servant, becomes technology, the master. The world of 1976 contrasts with the 1896 of Guy Hershberger's birth in many ways: (1) The enormous scale and massing of all human operations. The world's population has tripled in these eighty years. Massive quantitative changes bring qualitative changes. (2) The enormous complexity of all human operations. (3) The complex interdependency of all human operations. (4) The intensifying tempo. Less and less time is available between the introduction of a new idea or a new technology and the moment for the response.

Dividing the Waters —A Grasp of the Themes

If we have stretched our comprehension of the distance between 1896 and 1976, then how shall we allow the eighty years that have transpired to take form? Inescapably when one imposes static periods on the flowing river of history one is doing the impossible: freezing the waters and sawing the stream into blocks of ice. One is creating stereotypes, caricatures. One is simplifying, exaggerating, manipulating events. And yet despite its perils, periodization helps us to talk about our past in orderly ways.

In seeking a sense of period in history one looks for the clustering of events in a critical mass. One looks for crises which halt the flow of events and which release the flow of events. One looks for contrasts and similarities. One looks for symbols and personalities and critical events—not always because they are crucially significant—but because they illuminate the period. Hovering over this exercise in the identification of periods should be an awareness that later generations of scholars will come along with new sets of questions which will lead to the labeling of new historical periods.

The Eighteen-Nineties

The decade in which Guy Hershberger was born was a time of beginnings. For Amish Mennonite people it was a springtime in the church. In the 1890s came four-part singing, singing schools, a new hymnal—*Hymns and Tunes,* Sunday schools, Sunday school conferences, Sunday school lesson helps, "protracted" or evangelistic meetings, young people's meetings, a new publication—*The Young People's Paper,* weeklong Bible conferences with leaders from distant congregations. A few began to slip away to college. They were switching from hooks and eyes to buttons. The Amish Mennonites in Iowa had begun to use some English in their worship services. Meetinghouses were being built. A quiet revolution was in process.

Just before Guy Hershberger was born, the forerunner of Goshen College, the Elkhart Institute, was founded in 1894. A bit earlier the Russian immigrant Mennonites had started a similar school in Kansas, Bethel College. At first these colleges were little more than secondary schools. Some had a vision of a four-year Christian college. One was the widely respected evangelist and churchman, John S. Coffman, who as president of the board struck the keynote for the decade in his eloquent dedicatory address for the Institute—"The Spirit of Progress":

The Spirit of Progress was planted into man when Jehovah breathed into him the breath of life and man became a living soul. . . . The Elkhart Institute . . . is after all an evidence of the spirit of progress among us in the line of education. This is but the welling up of a pent-up stream that could no longer be suppressed. Disadvantages, opposition, fears of failure, all had to give way before the force that was driven into action by the deep consciousness of duty to God, to the church, to our young people, and to the cause of Christ in general. Here we are at an epoch that marks a transition period in our beloved brotherhood. It is really a final crossing over. . . .(Coffman, 1924:6-7, 24)

This was liberation theology for that small group of faculty and students at Elkhart who were to become the leaders in missions, education, and conference for the next generation. These were heady words for these first-generation college students: I. W. Royer, I. R. Detweiler, J. E. Hartzler, John Umble, Paul Whitmer, and the others. Four years later John S. Coffman was dead at the age of fifty-one.

In the eighteen-nineties Mennonite leaders like M. S. Steiner and John S. Coffman were busy in many areas of church program. They started publications, founded schools, opened orphanages, wrote Sunday school lessons, launched mission programs, led Bible conferences in the congregations, formed church conferences, and even wrote books and edited hymnals. This renewal was liberating and it was binding. Scattered congregations and their leaders were finding meaning, resources of help, and outlets for service through this intricately interrelated web of new programs. Young people—who now had new role-models in persons like the evangelist-churchmen John S. Coffman and M. S. Steiner and teachers Dan Gerig and N. E. Byers—saw opening to them a variety of options for church-related service if they would only stay with their people.

Other new institutions were springing to life. Missionary concern was breaking forth in a series of new agencies: the Mennonite Benevolent Board, then the Mennonite Evangelizing and Benevolent Board, followed by the Home and Foreign Relief Commission, and then the Mennonite Board of Charitable Homes. A Mennonite pastor in Elkhart, George Lambert, took off in 1894 for a trip around the world. He returned to write a book, *Around the Globe and Through Bible Lands,* in which he spoke enthusiastically of mission opportunities abroad. He followed in 1896 with another book, *India, the Horror Stricken Empire,* a plea for famine relief to India. Within months the several Mennonite groups were launching programs of relief and missions in India. The Mennonite Brethren in Christ were starting a mission in Armenian Turkey. The Mennonite world had suddenly opened up far beyond Johnson County, Iowa, and Elkhart County, Indiana. By 1900 there would be seventeen Mennonites from the various groups in overseas mission service. This would swell to 133 by 1920, and pass the 2,000 mark in the 1960s. In 1897 and 1898 the scattered programs and conferences were being brought together in the Mennonite Church in a General Conference for North America.

The seminal 1890s—plus or minus a few years—is an inescapably important period in the life of the Mennonite Church, not only for this particular group but for all Mennonite groups. This age of accelerating change, 1890 to 1917, needs to be studied as intensively as the Anabaptist period from 1525 to 1550. To comprehend this age of beginnings we need answers to many questions. How aware was any Mennonite group in the 1890s that other Mennonite groups existed in North America? What had happened to the inter-Mennonite camaraderie of John Funk, Jacob Y. Schantz, David Goerz, Christian Krehbiel, who had integrated the migration movements of the 1870s? What can we learn of the emergence of a missionary concern in this decade by a comparative study of the Mennonite Church, the General Conference, and others where similar interests were stirring?

The Elkhart Institute, Goshen College, Bethel College, Bluffton College, and the Mennonite Collegiate Institute all began within a span of ten years. The similarities are striking: those opening addresses of the founders, the exhilarating spirit of beginnings in the first student generation, the curricula, the apprehensive eyes of the constituency watching the new institutions. Too often we have assumed that the problems of Bluffton are unique to Bluffton or those of Elkhart to Elkhart. Again we need comparative studies of conference leadership among the several groups—studying a dozen leaders side by side: John S. Coffman and C. H. Wedel, N. C. Hirschy and M. S. Steiner, and many others. It would be helpful to study all the Mennonite publications of the 1890s to compare the issues being discussed and to discern whether there was in evidence an Anabaptist-Mennonite consciousness.

The Eve of World War I

Hesston College, where Guy Hershberger would later enroll, began in 1909—a response to a growing uneasiness with the progressive forces in the Mennonite Church that were not all properly under control. The Kansas-Nebraska Conference hoped that Hesston would be more safe and sound, less threatening than the recently established Elkhart-Goshen institution. The birth of Hesston is a significant date around which to cluster events.

This was a time of consolidation and centralizing in the Mennonite Church. The publishing program in 1908 was moved away from Elkhart County to Scottdale, Pennsylvania. Two periodicals were merged into the new *Gospel Herald.* The Mennonite Church began publishing a yearbook of statistics in 1906. It reported a total membership of 27,046 in 1906—one fifth the size of seventy years later. Mission agencies were combined into a new Mennonite Board of Missions and Charities. A hospital-sanitarium opened in La Junta, Colorado, in 1908, to which soon was added a school of nursing. A Mennonite Board of Education was established. Many of the leaders who had emerged in the 1890s served on several churchwide boards and committees, wrote for the publications, and traveled widely among the congregations speaking in local Bible conferences. They were farmer-preachers who had not attended Elkhart or Goshen and certainly not Oberlin or Northwestern. One who had attended Oberlin for a year, M. S. Steiner, died in 1911 at the age of 45. He would have been at retirement age of 65 had he lived until 1931. Would his presence have made a difference had he continued to give leadership through this next turbulent twenty years?

Among those who had welcomed changes in church life were many who were anxious now that change was too rapid, had been permitted to go too far. It was now time to slow down the speed of change, even to apply brakes, or to back up. It was time to recover respect and obedience for the authority of the elders and to assert sound doctrine. In 1909 the *Scofield Reference Bible,* the classic expression of the new movement of dispensationalism, was published. Premillennialist thought was making its inroads in the Mennonite Church in a variety of ways: periodicals, students who had studied at Moody Bible Institute, some speakers in the Bible conferences, the new Ontario Mennonite Bible School. *Gospel Herald* published warnings of the dangers of liberalism and higher criticism. A young evangelist, J. E. Hartzler, was writing a new book almost every year. In 1910 he wrote on the *Paths to Perdition,* warning of the perils of Satan, sin and hell, and detailing a series of such specific sins as the theater, dance, saloon, and secret lodge. Truth seemed to be truer when it could be numbered. Presbyterian Fundamentalists published their "five points": five "essential and necessary" doctrines. In 1914 Daniel Kauffman, together with a committee, edited a book for the Mennonite Church on *Bible Doctrine:* twenty-one doctrines, seven ordinances, nine Christian principles (duties and restrictions), four graces, and so on. This was a prescriptive age.

That first group of Mennonite leaders college-educated at Oberlin, Chicago, Northwestern, and Harvard found themselves increasingly estranged from conference-wide and district leadership. N. C. Hirschy left the presidency of Bluffton College in 1908 under a cloud. Five years later N. E. Byers and C. Henry Smith would leave Goshen. Others like J. E. Hartzler and Paul Whitmer succeeded them and also in a few years moved on. Such men were often identified—correctly or incorrectly—as modernists, higher critics, adherents of the Social Gospel.

Guy Hershberger's pastor and mentor, Sanford C. Yoder, was ordained bishop in 1913 of the East Union Church near Kalona, Iowa. Sanford Yoder describes appreciatively in his memoirs, *The Days of My Years* (1959), the more moderate tradition among the Amish Mennonite congregations of Iowa: more congregational in polity, less propositional in theology, more insulated from new movements such as premillennialism and liberalism, more charitable toward diversity, less prescriptive on practices such as dress restrictions. These Amish Mennonite congregations were cautiously considering the possibility of coming under the umbrella of the General Conference of the Mennonite Church.

Again many questions come to mind about this disturbing and intriguing period on the eve of the war. How were Mennonites responding to massive changes in their world: the automobile, the attractions of the marketplace, the invasion of aggressive new theological systems, and the thorny issues coming with higher education? Who was to decide the directions and the tempo of change for a people: the congregations or the bishops or the college leaders? Are the Fundamentalist and modernist categories helpful in understanding Mennonite thought patterns, or only stereotypes? Who were the true believers? Who were the faithful? How did those in communities like Kalona understand what it meant to be a Mennonite? What was the level of Anabaptist-consciousness? Were the books of the young Goshen historian, C. Henry Smith—the first Mennonite PhD—being read and having any influence? How shall one assess the influence of the Bible conferences—taking as a clue the following reflections from Sanford Yoder?

These meetings were important and on the whole edifying
and beneficial, but in the light of what has taken place since those
years and immediately following them one wonders whether they,
perhaps, did not accomplish more than they were expected to accomplish. As a result, there came a tightening up on dress regulations and a swing toward uniformity in this and other practices of
the church. Along with that there was in many places a trend
toward a much more rigid form of discipline . . . [which] later
resulted in unfortunate consequences and divisions in a number
of congregations. (Yoder, 1959: 108-109)

Finally, why were the Mennonites so ill prepared for the crisis of World
War I? Or were they?

The Crisis of World War I

Barbara Tuchman chronicles the two decades before World War I
in *The Proud Tower*. She speaks of the Great War of 1914-18 as lying

like a band of scorched earth dividing that time from ours. In
wiping out so many lives which would have been operative on the
years that followed, in destroying beliefs, changing ideas, and
leaving incurable wounds of disillusion, it created a physical as
well as psychological gulf between two epochs. (Tuchman, 1966:
XV)

At the end of her book she reflects:

When the effort was over, illusions and enthusiasms possible
up to 1914 slowly sank beneath a sea of massive disillusionment.
For the price it has paid, humanity's gain was a painful view of its
own limitations. (Tuchman, 1966: 544)

Guy Hershberger was twenty years old when the United States
entered the war. With the counsel of Sanford Yoder, Guy Hershberger
applied and was accepted for reconstruction work in France with the
American Friends Service Committee. The armistice came and he did
not go to France. Instead he finished his year of teaching and spent a
year selling books.

If Guy Hershberger had joined with the other young Mennonites
working with the AFSC team in France and had attended the
conference of Mennonites at Clermont en Argonne, Meuse, France,
June 20-22, 1919, he would have experienced the deep cleavage between
these young, idealistic, impatient, college-educated ascending leaders
in the church and the establishment of the Mennonite Church. Was this

polarization irreconcilable? Could there have been a reconciliation of those in their twenties and those in their sixties, of the college-educated and those who had not gone to college, of the progressives and the conservatives? Was it inevitable that a substantial portion of those educated at Elkhart and Goshen before 1919 would be wiped out of the Mennonite Church? We need a series of comparative biographical studies of this "lost generation," the men of Clermont. We need a biography of the talented and colorful J. E. Hartzler, who resigned from the presidency of Goshen College in 1918 and who in time came to be the symbol of dangerous modernism. Was the founding of Eastern Mennonite School in 1917, the year the United States declared war, an indicator of a war in the brotherhood? Finally, what were Mennonites writing and thinking and preaching during those years of the Great War? Were they aware of their mission in a world falling apart? Would they have recognized the world Barbara Tuchman was describing?

The Postwar Years —A Time of Tearing and a Time of Mending

In 1920 Guy Hershberger married Clara Hooley; he entered Hesston College that same year. Sanford Yoder, who was president of the Mennonite Board of Education and in four years would be president of Goshen College, advised him to go to Hesston rather than Goshen College. Goshen, which was running through a new president each year, must have seemed too risky a place to send a promising young member of his congregation.

The Hesston of the early twenties merits study because here were nurtured a number of students and faculty who survived the time of troubles and became leaders of the next generation. Here was the nucleus of a later Goshen faculty: Willard Smith, Noah Oyer, Harold Bender, Paul Bender, Glen Miller, Chris Graber, Melvin Gingerich, and Guy Hershberger. The *Hesston College Journal* for these years reflects a familial spirit not unlike the story of the early years at Elkhart, Bluffton, or Bethel. Chapel talks were practical and admonitional. Faculty instructed the students on etiquette and school spirit. Literary societies flourished. The campus with only two buildings was threadbare and poor. But it was a shared poverty. Outside stimulation was limited. Visiting evangelists and churchmen stopped by and occasional lecturers spoke, such as C. Henry Smith surveying Mennonite history and Orie Miller reporting on relief work in Russia. The faculty had not attended Oberlin, Wooster, or Harvard and so there were no pretensions of Hesston becoming an Oberlin of the West. For some like Guy Hershberger the Hesston experience was liberating, but for some óthers it was restrictive.

Theron Schlabach has recounted in another chapter in this volume the details of the tearing and the mending in the Mennonite Church in the 1920s. Our focus here is on the character of the period and the significant issues which emerged. One must read Mennonite history for this period against the backdrop of general social history: the Jazz Age and prohibition, heresy hunts and red scares, depression on the farms and a booming stock market, the golden age of sports and mediocrities in the White House. Mennonite leaders must have felt apprehensive about their youth entering this kind of world.

Mennonites carried into the 1920s a burden of guilt. They had been ill-prepared for the World War just past. The church had failed to provide adequate peace teaching in the congregations, or vigorous inter-Mennonite action in advocacy of conscientious objector rights, or solidarity against the hysteria of war bond drives. Adding to their secret shame was the knowledge that they had been enriched by war-time farm profits.

The issues of 1909 had not been resolved by 1920. Change was accelerating in the surrounding society. In the Mennonite Church some viewed things as falling apart. Various groups, each in their own way, were digging trenches to withstand the advancing waves of secularism and offensive change. Daniel Kauffman, editor of the *Gospel Herald,* had one of the more comprehensive strategies: adherence to sound and systematized doctrine, obedience to a more centralized locus of authority, and conformity to prescribed dress regulations. The Fundamentalist-influenced leaders seeking to establish control of the Bethel of 1919 saw their line of defense in the imposition of doctrinal tests. In some of the Russian immigrant congregations in the West the trenches were dug on the line of the German language in worship or the common communion cup. Many among the General Conference Mennonites saw the last line of defense in a rigid enforcement of the ban on secret societies. The Mennonite young men at Clermont in France saw the trench of no-retreat in a vigorous reaffirmation of the peace witness. All this is oversimplified, but common to all must have been an anxious concern for the retention of a people's integrity in a time of frighteningly rapid change. The Mennonites in the 1920s did not have an adequate Pauline doctrine of the diversity of gifts in the unity of the body of Christ.

When one reviews the multitude of changes—a veritable revolution—to which Mennonite pastors and elders accommodated themselves in the 1890s and the early years of the new century, one must ask: "Over how much change can one leader preside?" Few persons in history can lead more than one revolution. Most mortals must dig in their heels at some point, and on some issue let it be known that they are not captive to drift and permissiveness. Who was there in 1920 in the Mennonite Church who could bridge the polarities stretching from the young men of Clermont to the officers of the conference, the teachers at Goshen to the bishops of the Indiana-Michigan Conference, the Amish Mennonites of Iowa to the guardians of the faith in Virginia? M. S. Steiner, who had died ten years before, was not available. Most leaders were in their sixties and seventies. Sanford Yoder's time had not yet come.

We need comparative biographies of the church leaders of this era, particularly Daniel Kauffman and Sanford Yoder. Kauffman was president of Goshen College the year before it closed in 1923 and Sanford Yoder the year it reopened in 1924. Why was it that Sanford Yoder could put it together and Kauffman could not? Or were the issues more basic than style of leadership? The closing and the opening of Goshen is a highly significant story not only for the Mennonite Church, but also for every Mennonite group—each of which has had traumatic experiences with the task of fitting a college into a conference program. It is difficult to see how these long-brewing conflicts, with increasingly intransigent polarized forces, could have been resolved without some people winning and some losing, without some congregations being split, without some getting hurt, without a college closing so that it could reopen again with a new staff and new management.

Here the role of Sanford Yoder is crucial. He had only started college himself. He had not been corrupted by attendance at a prestigious eastern college. However, he had a power base. He was a farmer-bishop, secretary of the Mennonite Board of Missions and Charities, president of the Mennonite Board of Education, and a former moderator of General Conference. He had not been entangled in the bitter polity struggles of the Indiana-Michigan Conference in which Goshen College resided. He was known and respected at the grass roots as a teacher in many local Bible conferences. He knew his academic limitations and so brought with him from Hesston a well qualified dean, Noah Oyer. It was as though he and Oyer came riding out of the West, clean and credible, to rescue the maiden of higher education in distress. Retaining his mission board secretaryship, which gave him entree to otherwise closed congregations, he helped to legitimize in the Mennonite Church the place of higher education and the processes of deliberate, cautious change.

The Mennonite landscape was strewn with losers in the 1920s. Among the apparent losers were the young people—at the Clermont conference, in the Laymen's Movement, and in the Young People's Conferences—who felt that their voices were not heard. They were the faculty members at Goshen before the closing who felt that they could not make the adjustments required to be acceptable to the brethren of the establishment. They were the writers and readers of the *Christian Exponent,* the voice of the young loyal opposition. Guy Hershberger was one who read the *Exponent* with interest and profit but regretted that the writers were not at peace with the elders. The pages of the four years of the *Exponent* call for critical analysis. Again we need comparative biographies of these youthful dissenters of the twenties. Particularly helpful would be an analysis of any correspondence between these young churchmen and their elders.

Missing from the leadership group in the twenties were pastoral persons who could listen to the liberal, impatient, and sometimes arrogant youth and who could understand them. Needed always in times of transition are caring and respected patriarchs of the establishment who will run interference for the young, will sometimes caution them, and will say publicly in crisis situations: "These are our boys. We, of course, don't always agree with them. They are impatient like we once were, but their hearts are good. They love the Lord and they love the church. We must find ways in which we can work together with them." One cannot detect such pastor-churchmen voices in the twenties when they were so needed. Again the elders were cautious. Many were fearful of the critics in their own ranks. They had blessed an earlier revolution in the church. They did not have the strength to bless, as well as carefully correct, a second revolution associated with youth coming out of the colleges and World War I.

One of the major stories of the Mennonite Church in the twenties is how the study of Anabaptist history was used to spring a people out of the trap of polarization between liberal and Fundamentalist. Harold Bender, Guy Hershberger, those who started the *Mennonite Quarterly Review,* and many others saw the act of going to the Anabaptist sources in the sixteenth century as a way of recovering a sense of movement and vision in the twentieth century. It was a way of appealing to an authority prior to the recent hard-line orthodoxies of Fundamentalism and liberalism. The study and possible recovery of the Anabaptist vision was eminently a task for a college faculty. Thus, higher education would slowly recover its legitimacy in the life of the church. In the Goshen experience one notes that the reaffirmation of the peace witness was linked to Anabaptist studies, which was linked to the effort to recover a people's purpose. Guy Hershberger, who joined the Goshen faculty in 1925, was in the eye of this strong wind of change.

Here we digress to urge that by 1976 we should have reached a level of maturity as a people so that we can examine critically and openly the conflicts of our past. If we are to be ministers of reconciliation, peacemakers, conflict regulators, then we should be able to look at the conflict beams in our own eyes and learn the art of removing beams, learn the discipline of living by Matthew 18, and receive the gift of peacemaking. To that end we should be able to study the many conflicts strewn through the records of our past eighty years.

One senses that the agenda—including both the tensions and the healing processes—of the twenties continued on into the thirties, making the two decades one period for study. In both decades Mennonites lived through another crisis experience, which has been little described in our literature, but of profound significance. This is the Great Depression, which continued, though with declining intensity, up to World War II. The Depression, followed by the prosperity of World War II and after, may have been a potent agent of Americanization for the Mennonites. At last they had a war—be it an economic war—where they could shoulder arms with their American neighbors, where they could display their battlefield scars, where in the best *Poor Richard's Almanac* tradition they could show their valor in thrift and hard work. They, too, had earned the honor of being Great American Go-Getters. With the Great Depression they, thus, became Americanized and then vulnerable to a new set of American temptations in the subsequent age of affluence.

The Exhilaration of World War II

During World War II, Mennonites in America gained a new sense of identity. Guy Hershberger was one of many who came into his own in this period. He contributed ideas which helped shape the alternative service program, Civilian Public Service (CPS), which became the largest and most sustained inter-Mennonite and interchurch program in Mennonite history. In midwar appeared both his first major work, *War, Peace, and Nonresistance,* and Harold Bender's presidential address to the American Society of Church History "The Anabaptist Vision." Mennonites of all groups were better prepared for this crisis than the one of 1917. Mennonites appear to have been pleased with themselves in their demonstrated ability to mobilize resources to administer a program of Civilian Public Service for 5,000 young men, Mennonites and others.

In this CPS program they found themselves almost unexpectedly conducting an extensive nonformal educational program for an emerging new group of church leaders. The rapid expansion of domestic and overseas service programs immediately after the war added what in effect were quasi-professional internships. Here was a large, sprawling educational enterprise, most of it on an inter-Mennonite basis. Increasingly the freshly articulated rhetoric of Anabaptism was used to give reason for programs and policies. The Anabaptist perspective was gradually displacing earlier perspectives.

Not all were of one mind. Substantial numbers of young Mennonites entered military service without hesitation. In many Mennonite groups in World War II the historic peace position appeared to have been reduced to a fragile minority position. In 1943 leaders from six Mennonite groups founded Grace Bible Institute, evidence of deep dissatisfaction with the established conferences and their schools. The concerned Mennonites who published the *Sword and Trumpet* also reflected a disquietude with what was now becoming the main stream of doctrine and practice in the Mennonite conferences.

The Mennonite experiences of World War II were radically different from those of World War I. Mennonites were inconvenienced but rarely suffered. In fact they were often praised for their wartime services. Mennonites were demonstrating what they could do in church programming by adopting the ways of the American managerial revolution. It was a time of planning, a time of hope. In many ways for Mennonites the war had been an exhilarating experience. They had met the challenge—or what they thought was the challenge. They were gaining self-confidence and sureness of purpose so that the 1950s would become their Age of Confidence.

The Mennonite Age of Confidence

Daniel J. Boorstin in *The Americans: The Democratic Experience* speaks of the emergence in the nineteenth century of the American Go-

Getters—the builders, the organizers, the producers, the answer people. They were the ones who had confidence that problems could be solved if they but concentrated their minds and resources on the issues. They had a practical, daring-do spirit, an assurance that if something was wrong it could be fixed. Mennonites after World War II evidenced more than ever before in their history this spirit of confidence that they could meet issues with statements and problems with programs. The day of the Americanization of the American Mennonites had come. Among all the Mennonite groups one witnessed an explosion of institution-building and a proliferation of programs. Mennonites were learning to project their image with the once-forbidden arts of drama, film, radio, and television. More and more they began to tell themselves that they had a message not only for themselves but for the wider society. Others told them this as well. For the Mennonites this was their delayed Age of Confidence.

We are still so near the years following the end of World War II that it is difficult and dubious to divide this time into periods. It would help immensely if we better understood those pivotal periods in an earlier history: the time of new beginnings in the 1890s, the years of anxiety preceding and during the first Great War, and particularly the times of tearing and the times of mending in the twenties and the thirties. If we could discern more accurately the record of our people in those periods, we might be better able to understand where we have just been and where we now may be going.

Only those are free who have a sense of pattern in history, who discern the times and seasons, the great themes—the rhythms, the tempo, the fragility of life and the durability of life, the capacity of God's people to walk again after they have stumbled, and the mystery of it all. I yearn for a series of cameo histories of the Mennonite people in America during these past eighty years, each focused on one of the periods, each done with an inter-Mennonite perspective and each seeking linkages of understanding with that wider community which presses in upon them.

Guy Hershberger has helped us to understand better the great issues of Mennonite people in his lifetime. We pray that the gifts of discernment and faithfulness he possessed may live on in the scholars and prophets of his people in these latter days.

Foundations of
Kingdom Community

Foundations of Kingdom Community

The central importance of the community of faith in the process of understanding what God desires of His children has been demonstrated in history and is evident in many ways today. The koinonia groups of the early church, the monastic orders, some of the pre-Reformation movements, the Radical Reformation, and later Christian communal movements all serve as models of faith because a community of believers had allowed the Holy Spirit to reveal the Lord of history in a corporate setting.

It can be said that the Anabaptist movement owes its character to the emphasis on community. That is, when a prophetic voice or stance was proclaimed, it came out of the cradle of the covenanted community. The early Anabaptist martyrs; the Mennonite leaders espousing religious freedom and integrity in the face of the Revolution and slavery in America, or against military conscription in Russia; the conscientious objectors in recent wars—all these and many more emerged out of the community of faith which created and sustained them.

In this section we examine elements of faith and practice that are essential to the creation of genuine Christian community. Millard Lind suggests an approach to hermeneutical method that attempts to be faithful both to the received faith of the fathers and to the demands of the contemporary historical setting. He finds the model for authentic interpretation in the actual unfolding of the meaning of revelation in a hermeneutical community—the people of God in the Old and New Testaments.

The following essay by Norman Kraus shows how a specific period of recent Mennonite history has both distorted and clarified the theological self-understanding of the church. Kraus emphasizes the need for an alternative to both liberalism and Fundamentalism that would give new theological coherence and direction to the disciple community and projects an agenda for further development.

Harold Bauman, after sketching the contemporary quest for new forms of congregational life, looks for clues from the Radical Reformation experience, and then spells out the functional implications of insights derived from the Believers' Church concept of community. Illustrations from actual church situations, along with more extended analysis of such themes as salvation and decision-making, enhance the discussion.

The chapters by Lawrence Burkholder and Calvin Redekop engage some particularly vexing issues for the ethical self-understanding of the nonresistant church. Burkholder presses the inadequacy of nonresistance as a foundational ethical principle, and inquires about its negative psychological implications. Finding support in the example of Jesus, he urges a more comprehensive approach that would deal realistically with matters of power and ambiguity in actual life situations.

Burkholder's suggestion that Mennonites have accepted in practice what they have rejected in theology is echoed in Redekop's treatment of the perennial problems of power and institutionalization. Utilizing insights from biblical theology, church history, and sociological analysis, Redekop proposes helpful new understandings for coping with these questions.

In the final chapter in this section, J. R. Burkholder surveys three decades of Mennonite ethical writing in order to locate the theoretical problems in the articulation of a Believers' Church ethic. The analysis moves from criticism to exposition to the call for congregational involvement in ethical decision-making—a theme that brings together the theological hermeneutical community from Lind and Kraus, the specific problems focused by Lawrence Burkholder and Redekop, and a functional church life as proposed by Bauman.

4

Reflections on Biblical Hermeneutics

Millard C. Lind

Guy F. Hershberger demonstrated his interest in hermeneutics as he sought to establish biblical bases for guiding the life and work of the church in the world. He gave careful attention to matters of biblical interpretation, particularly the question of the relation of the Old and New Testaments, in his two major books on Anabaptist-Mennonite ethics.[1] Through his use of sociology, ethics, and history to elaborate the theological message of the Bible, he has contributed significantly to the development of my own thought.

My intention in this essay is to set forth a few reflections on a valid biblical hermeneutic, from a perspective informed by the Anabaptist tradition. These are the reflections of one who seeks to stand within that tradition, and who is in conversation with modern biblical studies within the ecumenical church and synagogue.[2]

By "hermeneutics" I mean the twofold effort to understanding the original language of the Bible within its ancient settings, and then to translate those understandings into modern language in its social context. This view of hermeneutics thus includes both biblical exegesis and biblical homiletics, which have often been considered as separate aspects. Such an approach demands a knowledge of the ancient languages and worlds, a knowledge of contemporary languages and worlds, and a method for moving from one to the other.

By "Anabaptist" I mean that movement which began in Europe in the sixteenth century as the result of the rise of humanistic biblical studies within a certain social-economic-political milieu. These studies led to the formation of a body of believers who saw themselves set apart from the world in which they lived, by virtue of their faith. They dared to act in freedom from that world, in response to the sovereignty of the resurrected Christ whose living presence they confessed.

A revolution has occurred in biblical studies since the sixteenth

---

Millard Lind is professor of Old Testament at the Associated Mennonite Biblical Seminaries, Elkhart, Indiana; his research interests include worship, warfare, and political theology in the Old Testament. He has served as pastor and in teaching ministries in the Mennonite Church.

century. Textual criticism, literary criticism, form criticism, arch-aeology, the recovery of whole libraries of ancient literatures—these have all contributed to a knowledge of the Bible which is greater now than at any time since the first century. Followers of the Anabaptist tradition, with its genuine interest in biblical authority, should wel-come these advances. Within the context of ecumenical debate (a characteristic of sixteenth-century Anabaptism), we need to approach the Bible anew in every generation. Our new knowledge confirms some of the central insights of the sixteenth century, though it may set those insights within new perspectives, and may serve to correct others.

Despite, or perhaps because of, the hermeneutical revolution of the past century, there are some Anabaptist understandings that I find helpful in the interpretation of the Bible.[3] They are:

1. The congregation as a hermeneutical community.

2. An understanding of the authority of both Old and New Testa-ments in a relationship that is not "flat" but historical, that is, a pattern of promise and fulfillment. (I am not sure that the early Anabaptists were as negative to the Old Testament as have been some Mennonites of the past generation.)

3. The emphasis on discipleship, with the consequent demand for discerning between true and false hermeneutics.

4. The challenge to prevailing concepts of political power, grounded in an analogy to the experience of the biblical people of God in their Near Eastern and Mediterranean context.[4]

For me, these points have an abiding relevance for the herme-neutical task of the faithful church.

Hermeneutics as Exegesis and Homiletics

Hermeneutics as we have defined it is divided into two parts, exegesis and homiletics. Exegesis is the attempt to discover what the original language meant. This original meaning is not easy to fix; it may refer to the oral tradition behind the text, or to the meaning of the text as a unit of written tradition, or to the meaning of the unit within a larger edited whole. In any case, we must realize that when we read the Bible we are crossing cultural barriers of both time and space. Bible translations which obliterate these barriers in order to make the Bible read like a modern book may have their uses, but they also have their debit side. They may remove the reader even further from the culture and milieu of which the Bible was a part. The very nature of the biblical faith, centered about certain prophetic-historical events, excludes methods such as allegorizing that deny the Bible's historical character. All readers of the text should make their journey back into the strange world of the Bible, to the extent that their ability and calling permit them.

Biblical hermeneutics also demands a knowledge of today's languages. Along with moving back into history, the reader must move forward into the modern age. One must be able to say, in terms that modern man can begin to understand, what the mystery of the gospel means today. This problem is compounded when we remember that ours is a missionary task, and that we must communicate the gospel not only to ourselves, but to those who have no commitment to it, those to whom the Bible is utterly foreign. Here we can learn much from a prophet like Hosea, who seized the central myth of Baalism, broke it off from its mythological moorings, and used that language to proclaim the Yahwistic faith, or from Paul, who translated the Hebraically oriented gospel of Jesus into the milieu of the Greek world.

The Home of Biblical Hermeneutics

Viewing the congregation as a hermeneutical community is an important contribution of Anabaptism to biblical hermeneutics. This perspective enables the specialist to see himself as part of a team concerned with the larger hermeneutical question. It may deliver him from trivial and unprofitable questions in research, although there may be a difference of opinion as to what the important questions are. It should also help one to realize that we cannot stop everything to deal with the problem of hermeneutics but that we must deal with it "on the run." The results must constantly be tested in the midst of the community in its relation to the world. For the community itself to enter into the exegetical and homiletical process, the specialist must exercise his skill as a genuine leader rather than as a dogmatician.

The concept of the hermeneutical community includes also an epistemological dimension. The hermeneutical question is shifted from "What does the text mean to me?" to the more basic question, "What does the text mean to us?" Slight as this shift may seem, it emphasizes that the Bible is a *public* book. It is to be used and interpreted within its own public life situation. Therefore its historical and sociopolitical dimensions, as well as its psychological implications, are a part of its relevant theological message. Otherwise, if the Bible is seen only as a book for private devotions, an adequate hermeneutics becomes impossible.

I do not want to minimize the difficulties of the movement back-

ward to the Bible and forward to the twentieth century. But by accepting the congregation as the context for the Bible's life situation, the
process is quite a different one from that in which it is assumed that
there is no twentieth-century life situation in which the Bible is truly at
home. If the latter is true, the hermeneutical process is indeed questionable and largely meaningless. It is only within the life situation of
the hermeneutical community that the fundamental analogies are
experienced which make the Bible historically credible.

A Biblical Unity

There is a tendency on the part of some modern Mennonites to
disregard the Old Testament. The Old Testament is essential, however,
to an understanding of the New. This is true not only because the Old
Testament community provides the cultural womb for the New Testament, but even more because of the nature of the biblical faith itself.
We cannot understand a reality outside our own previous experience,
except by a process of analogy in which similarities and differences
stand out. The biblical faith, however, witnesses to certain once-for-all
prophetic-historic events that never happened elsewhere and which,
therefore, have no analogies outside the biblical stream of history. The
history of biblical scholarship is replete with perversions of the biblical
faith caused by interpreting the unique, unrepeatable event in the light
of the repeatable events (mythologies or philosophies) of surrounding
cultures. The "sacral kingship school" of Old Testament science has attempted to reinterpret Israel's origins in terms of the state structures
which surrounded Israel (Hooke, 1958). The "mystery religions
school" of New Testament science has tried to reinterpret the meaning
of Christ's death and resurrection in terms of death and resurrection as
celebrated by the mystery religions of the Graeco-Roman Empire
(Angus, 1925). Anselm in his theory of the atonement used pagan
analogies that have distorted the biblical view of atonement in orthodoxy and Fundamentalism to this day. Bultmann, captivated by
Heidegger's existentialism, follows a similar method (Neill, 1964: 228
ff.). But one cannot capture the biblical reality in the mythologies or
philosophies of this world without paganizing the biblical faith. If this
is true, and if we can understand something new to us only by analogy,
where are the analogies by which we may understand the biblical faith?

Our answer is that the biblical stream of history provides its own
analogies; this is the importance of the biblical understanding of
promise and fulfillment and of typology.[5] When the New Testament

church looked for analogies by which to understand the Christ event, they went to the Old Testament: "This is that which was spoken. . . ." No doubt Jesus' own self-understanding was largely shaped by Old Testament analogy. The Old Testament was indispensable for the early Christians not only because it was the matrix for the New Testament community's culture, but because through the Scripture they experienced that newness of the Word of God, which provided analogies for the understanding of the unique event that had happened among them. It is only by use of these analogies within the stream of biblical history that we can escape from a paganization of the Jesus event.

The Old Testament is necessary, however, not only to provide analogies for the faith event, but also because the great themes of the faith, such as the understanding of God, the understanding of the world (creation), sin and salvation, mankind and peoplehood, are presented as continuities in the two Testaments (Brunner, 1963). The New Testament event may alter the character of some of these emphases, but the continuities are dominant, and without the Old Testament we cannot fully understand these themes.

It is also true that the Old Testament is to be understood in the light of the New. But this presupposition is not a dogma to be enforced by an allegorical method. If we merely read the thought of the New Testament back upon the Old, we deny the value of the Old Testament. When, however, we view the Old Testament narrative within the context of the Near East, with its historic struggle between assimilation to and rejection of that culture, it becomes evident that the New Testament as fulfillment is no longer an arbitrary dogma. As a result of biblical research, one can now say that while the Old Testament developed in the ancient Near Eastern environment and the New Testament within the Graeco-Roman environment, neither was really at home in its environment. Both were closer to each other than they were to their environments. Both are to be interpreted in the light of each other, rather than in the light of their environments, though these environments are important to their understanding.

The Bible in the Context of the Ancient Near East and Mediterranean World

Since the time of the church fathers it has become traditional to contrast Jerusalem with Athens. Such a contrast of the Bible with its environment is much more ancient than the Hebrew-Greek clash, however, for in fact it goes back to pre-kingship Israel. This ancient contrast is not so well known, however, because until recently, ancient Near Eastern history was unknown. The Old Testament jutted into the modern world like a rocky promontory from the past; readers of the Bible knew next to nothing of the environment with which it interacted. Thanks to archaeology and the discovery of ancient libraries, this isolation no longer exists. Today the volume of the ancient Accadian literature is at least as great as that of the Greek and Latin literature which has come down to us. This means that we are able not only to compare the Bible with Athens, but to compare the entire story from Abraham through Jesus and Paul with the Near East and Graeco-Roman world. With this larger perspective, we can observe not only the Bible's rejection of outside cultural items, but also its assimilation of many of them.

In contrasting the Bible with its environment, scholars have usually emphasized formal differences. For example, William Klassen has called attention to Auerbach's judgment of the literature of Greek antiquity: "We are forced to conclude that there could be no serious literary treatment of everyday occupations and social classes . . . of everyday customs and institutions . . . in short, of the people and its life. Linked with this is the fact that the realists of antiquity do not make clear the social forces underlying the facts and conditions which they present" (Auerbach, 1957:27). Over against this the literature of the Bible "portrays something which neither the poets nor the historians of antiquity ever set out to portray: the birth of a spiritual movement in the depths of the common people, from within the everyday occurrences of contemporary life, which thus assumes an importance it could never have assumed in antique literature. (Auerbach, 1957:37). This difference of form is obviously connected with the content, however, and it is questionable whether emphasis on merely formal categories can adequately portray the real contrasts.

Scholars have also emphasized the formal category of history in attempting to distinguish the Bible from the Near East. Mowinckel makes a typical statement: "While the other peoples experienced the deity in the eternal cyclic process of nature, the Israelites experienced God in history."[6] Certainly there is some truth in this statement, but it is misleading as a generalization. Clearly the gods of the Near Eastern states participated in their people's history also, since they were always considered decisive in the fighting of wars. For example, Assyrian art provides us with an example of the divinity fighting alongside the king. In a relief of Ashurnasirpal there is a complete conformity between the

warlike movements of the god and the king. Before the battle, king and
god advance with bow drawn toward the enemy. After the battle, both
have their bows slung in celebration of victory (Mendenhall, 1973:
Figs. 10-13). Thus, we cannot say that Yahweh acts in history and that
gods do not act in history. The point is rather to observe *how* Yahweh
acts in history as compared to the gods.

The Bible's Self-Consciousness

We are on safer ground for comparative work when we let Israel
speak for herself. What was Israel's own self-consciousness of her difference from the nations?

The ancient poetry of the Pentateuch reveals that Israel was
strongly aware of such a difference: "Lo, a people dwelling alone, and
not reckoning itself among the nations!" (Numbers 23:9, RSV). This
self-consciousness is delineated again and again, in the oldest as well as
the more recent sources. For example one of the oldest sources of the
Pentateuch contrasts Yahweh's call of Abraham with the self-willed
character of the primitive democracy of a Babylonian city state
(Genesis 11 and 12, tenth century BC). The Book of Hosea, a polemic
of Yahwism against Baalism, concludes with an attack on kingship as
rebellion against Yahweh, although it is fitting to Baal.

This polemic against kings is found throughout the Bible: Yahweh
against Pharaoh in the escape from Egypt (Exodus 1-15); Yahweh
against Sennacherib (Isaiah 37:23-29, eighth century BC); Yahweh
against the king of Babylon (Isaiah 14:4-21, seventh or sixth century,
BC); Yahweh against the prince and king of Tyre (Ezekiel 28:1-19,
sixth century BC). Outside of Israel, kingship was considered as "let
down from heaven," a blessing of the gods (Pritchard, 1969: 265).
Within Israel, kingship was regarded as human rebellion, a rejection of
the rule of Yahweh (whose will was communicated not through the
king, but through His prophets) to become "like all the nations"
(1 Samuel 8; 12;cf. Judges 8:22,23;9:7-15; Deuteronomy 17:14-20).

William McKane has shown how the problem of political power
was at the heart of the prophetic conflict with the political wisdom of
the ancient Near East. The prophet's

> main concern is not that power should be stripped of the fearful
> crudity and grossness of which it partakes in the awful insecurity
> of our world—the world of the twentieth century. He does not
> principally work for the refinement or ratification of power, for
> this implies gradualism and is a political rather than a prophetic

solution. The prophet urges rather that the concept of a balance of power is unreal, because it leaves God out of the reckoning. The Israelite prophets and the contemporary prophets assert that power is not built in with historical existence in the way that the statesmen suppose. God reserves all power to himself and so the *locus* of power is outside historical existence. From this flowed the doctrine of instrumentality in the Israelite prophets. God moves the nations like pawns on a chess-board, but he is the only real policy-maker and reserves all power to himself.

In this case the statesman ought not to concern himself with power, for, if this is the situation, all that is left for him as for the rest of us is to know the will of God and do it. Beyond this everything rests with God. The statesman will say that the crudity of the balance of power in our world today is a true reflection of the tensions and perilous insecurity of the international community and that it is the unresolved, intractable problems, daunting in their magnitude and delicacy, which will have to be tackled and solved one by one before there is any betterment. But the prophet believes that faith has a creative potential and can transform a situation. If we had faith in God and loved our neighbour and were prepared to take the absolute risk for the sake of Christ, the world would cease to be an armed camp. (McKane, 1965: 129 f.)[7]

Yahweh's law and leadership were not experienced through an office of institutionalized violence, but in the reality of covenant relationship and worship, and in the office of the prophet who communicated the divine will to the people. This revolutionary kind of government reached its climax in the suffering servant of II Isaiah who went out to win the nations for Yahweh, armed only with Yahweh's word (North, 1956). That his enterprise ended with suffering and death and that it is this psalm of suffering and death which was decisive for the early church's understanding of Jesus shows that both Old and New Testaments are dealing primarily with the problem of political power.[8]

Jesus' own self-consciousness in relation to the nations had to do precisely with the question of leadership and the exercise of power. Jesus declared to His disciples, "Among pagans it is the kings who lord it over them, and those who have authority over them are given the title Benefactor. This must not happen with you. No; the greatest among you must behave as if he were the youngest, the leader as if he were the one who serves. For who is the greater: the one at table or the one who serves? The one at table, surely? Yet here am I among you as one who serves!" (Luke 22:24-27, *The Jerusalem Bible*; cf. Mark 10:41-45; Matthew 20:24-28) The unity of this saying with Jesus' words about the cross should be obvious. The self-consciousness which set off both Old and New Testaments from the nations had to do with the question of political power. The Bible's radical answer to this central question of power gave new structure to the biblical faith and new form to the literature.

This suggests that in our study of the Bible we must interest ourselves in more than the theology of the Bible. Biblical sociology, politics, and psychology are essential to the understanding of the biblical God. Israel had no concept of separation of church and state. Yahweh was Lord of her entire life. Her concept of separation was not between religious life and secular life, but between herself and the nations. Israel was different from the nations, though she was tempted to become like the nations. This difference of Israel from the nations is the Old Testament paradigm for the "separation" of church and state.

The Kingdom of God and History

Israel testified that this self-conscious difference from the nations was not due to her own acts, but to the action of God in her behalf: "Did any people ever hear the voice of a god speaking out of the midst of the fire, as you have heard, and still live? Or has any god ever attempted to go and take a nation for himself from the midst of another nation, by trials, by signs, by wonders, and by war, by a mighty hand and an outstretched arm, and by great terrors, according to all that the Lord your God did for you in Egypt before your eyes?" (Deuteronomy 4:33, 34, RSV)

In my opinion the possibility of independent structures for the faithful church stands or falls with the question of the relation of the biblical tradition to the historical event to which it points. If biblical tradition has no fundamental relationship to historical event, then faith today has no real relationship to history either, and we are doomed to a kind of spiritualism which the Bible abhors. Biblical faith claims that God acted in history for the salvation of mankind. If God did not so act in history, then biblical faith is a fraud.

This raises the question of historical method. The significant difference in Old Testament historical method does not lie between Martin Noth and John Bright,[9] but between Noth and Gerhard von Rad. Von Rad argues for the omnicompetence of the analogy of historical event as the fundamental basis of modern biblical criticism.[10] This means that to understand the rise of Israel the historian must get behind the unique claims of the Exodus and Sinai traditions to show that the real history of Israel's beginnings was more or less the same as the origin of nations elsewhere. In von Rad's view, any uniqueness in Israel's religion was not caused by the juncture of word and deed in an actual theo-historical event, but by theological reflection which re-constructed past history.

In contrast to von Rad, Martin Noth writes:

> Yet in spite of all these historical connections and possibilities for comparison, "Israel" still appears a stranger in the world of its own time, a stranger wearing the garments and behaving in the manner of its age, yet separate from the world it lived in, not merely in the sense that every historical reality has its own indi-vidual character, and therefore an element of uniqueness, but rather at the center of the history of Israel we encounter phenomena for which there is no parallel at all elsewhere, not be-cause material for comparison has not yet come to light but be-cause so far as we know, *such things have simply never happened elsewhere.* (Noth, 1958:2, 3; italics added)

Noth's treatment of the Reed Sea event illustrates his method. His examination of all the relevant sources of the Pentateuch uncovers much contradictory detail, but also one common agreement: the act was Yahweh's alone, and Israel did no fighting at all. This common agreement, Noth feels, is the more remarkable in the light of the contradiction in detail (Noth, 1962: 119 ff.) This evaluation and examination of the sources is as far as the historian can go, though it is evident that Noth accepts this common testimony. If one were to reject it, he would then need to explain the absurdity and tenacity of the bib-lical tradition, in face of overwhelming odds from ancient to modern times. A similar question about the assumptions of historical method is also involved in the quest for the historical Jesus.

The Hermeneutical Community and Miracle

The question of miracle is a crucial one, for it involves not merely peripheral events such as healings, but the fundamental events on which biblical faith rests—the Exodus and Sinai, the resurrection and present rule of God in Christ. It is my opinion that miracle is an essential element of biblical faith.

Miracle, however, is not to be understood in terms of the nineteenth-century argument between science and religion, but in terms of the biblical doctrine of creation. From this perspective, miracle is strange and offensive not only to modern man, but to ancient man as well. Had an Egyptian or Mesopotamian thinker encountered the biblical doctrine of creation he most likely would not have understood it; had he come to understand it, he would have been shaken to the foundations, largely because of the biblical assumption of freedom. As Christopher North points out:

> The concept of creation is not obvious, nor does it come naturally to mankind. Everywhere except in the Bible, interpretation of the universe is naturalistic, and worship is, in one form or another, worship of "the great god Pan." This is true of the religion of classical Greece, of "polymorphic" Hinduism, of humanism in its various forms, of the current concept of "one single branching metabolizing protoplasm," and of the popular idea of "the life force" as the creative agent in the universe. Outside biblical theism all interpretations of the universe are so many more or less refined forms of what the OT stigmatizes as the worship of Baal, Baal being conceived as the personification of the life process. (1964:14)

This concept of creation originated in Israel not as speculation on what had happened "back there," but through the present experience of the newness of Yahweh's creation of a people. This is evident from the relationship of the creation event to salvation history. In Nehemiah 9:6-37, for example, the thought of Yahweh as Creator is brought to bear upon what appears to be a frustrated salvation history, that is, Israel's slavery to the Persians. (Psalm 33; Isaiah 43:19; 65:17)

Remarkably, Israel projected the creative act of Yahweh in her own prophetic-historical experience onto Yahweh's relation to the entire universe, past, present, and future. While by His creative activity Yahweh gives order and regularity to the whole, at the same time He is making all things new in the creation of His people. There is no conflict between Yahweh's regular ordering of the seasons, and the new act of salvation history; both are based on His promise.(Genesis 8:21-22 and 12:1-3)

Yahweh's free creative act on behalf of His people was thus a promise of His creative presence both now and in the future. If we can believe in the possibility of miracle in this sense—that God is free to create something new in biblical times, in the present day, and in the future—this is of greatest consequence for a truly biblical hermeneutic, for it enables the break with the immanent cause-effect pattern of the secular historian.

The Hermeneutical Circle

We have now come full circle in our hermeneutic of the Bible. For it is only by the experience of the new creation that we can realistically affirm with the prophets "that power is not built in with historical existence in the way that statesmen suppose" and that "God reserves all power to himself and so the *locus* of power is outside historical existence" (McKane, 1965:129). The experience of creation alone will make us bold to believe—not that our faith has the creative potential to transform a situation, but that God has already acted creatively in the situation, and by our response to that act we can enter into the freedom of His suffering in making all things new.

It was faith of this character that enabled the Anabaptists of the sixteenth century to act in freedom from the power structures and political assumptions of their age. In a similar manner, Guy Hershberger challenges the "colony of heaven" to "the good fight of faith, overcoming evil with good—with love, nonresistance, and the way of the cross, even as Christ overcame the world by going to His cross" (1958d:55).

In the biblical pattern of promise and fulfillment, it is God's new act of covenant in Christ that provides a solid bridgehead which His people may occupy in the midst of the violent history of the twentieth century, in full confidence that His creative word is the determinative power leading to the future.

5

Toward a Theology for the Disciple Community

C. Norman Kraus

In his chapter "To Focus a Mennonite Vision," Theron Schlabach suggests that the "Anabaptist Vision" of H. S. Bender, Guy F. Hershberger, and others "became more and more a vehicle for developing a third way of understanding the gospel, a way not locked into Fundamentalist-versus-liberal categories." This is in part true; however, as Schlabach himself notes, the development of alternatives in theology and ethics was definitely limited by the mood of the time and by the current pressures to make the Mennonite Church conform to the Fundamentalist model. At the time Hershberger was seriously formulating and publishing his position, any form of liberalism as an option for Mennonite scholars had been decisively rejected by denominational leadership. Even though the theological climate at Goshen College (where he taught) was explicitly conservative, and the faculty considered men like J. Gresham Machen their theological mentors, suspicions of liberalism by the constituency continued to trouble them. Thus a Mennonite "third way" could not consider alternatives to liberalism and Fundamentalism because they were not free to face the issues that liberalism was raising.

Orthodoxy and Fundamentalism

The theological debate in the Mennonite circles during the period 1925-1950 actually reflected the differences between the conservative or orthodox theology of Calvinist and Arminian vintage and dispensationalistic Fundamentalism which was offering itself as the logical, biblical, anti-modernist position—the true heir of seventeenth-century Protestant Orthodoxy. During this period the theology of "Old Princeton"—of Purvis, Warfield, Machen, and Vos—played an influential role at Goshen College. Even as late as the decade of the fifties, Harold Bender knowingly took his clues for preserving a de-

---

Norman Kraus is professor of religion and director of the Center for Discipleship at Goshen College. A member of the Assembly in Goshen, he has written and lectured extensively on the history and nature of the Christian movement.

nominational tradition from the strategy of the Christian Reformed Church. At Eastern Mennonite School the same theological tension was evident. C. K. Lehman, who had studied at Princeton, was constantly countered by men like M. J. Brunk, who had studied at Dallas Theological Seminary, and J. B. Smith, who had drunk deeply at dispensationalist springs.

Until we understand some of the basic differences in methodology and assumptions between these two schools of thought, we cannot see the real shape of the alternatives proposed in the Mennonite debate. We should not be misled into thinking that the debate was between Fundamentalism and liberalism, simply because men like Hershberger were sometimes called "liberal." It was fairly common for Fundamentalists to claim that the more traditional conservatives were unwittingly subverting the orthodox cause.

In a real sense, Fundamentalism is a *modern ism, i.e.,* a system that attempted to adapt to the new methodologies as a part of its apologetic. Traditional conservative theology maintained its methodological base in Aristotelian logic, and its theological-biblical synthesis had been worked out already in the seventeenth and eighteenth centuries. Fundamentalism left this methodological base for a popular and sometimes pseudo-empirical approach. In Bible study, for example, it stressed a direct inductive approach, although it lacked the historical sensitivity and linguistic apparatus of the later inductive English Bible method developed at Biblical Seminary in New York and associated with men like Kuist, Sweet, and Traina. It developed its own "dispensational norm," ostensibly based on direct Bible study, and began the task of erecting a new synthesis. C. I. Scofield, who was its early synthetic genius, published his annotated edition of the Bible in 1909; not until years later did L. S. Chafer develop a full-blown dispensationalist theology based on Scofield's work (*Systematic Theology,* 8 vols., published in 1948).

A further example of its empirical or pseudo-empirical stance may be seen in Fundamentalism's appeal to empirical data to refute evolution. From Harry Rimmer's popular descriptions of natural facts in support of a supernatural creation to the Moody science film series (*e.g.,* "God of Creation"), Fundamentalism has claimed that evolution does not fit the *facts.* It has always argued that secular science has misconstrued the empirical evidence to support atheistic theories, and not that scientific evidence should be ignored. I am not, of course, suggesting that Fundamentalism's interpretation of the empirical data is correct, but only that it made a significant methodological break with rational orthodoxy.

By way of contrast, while Orthodoxy was also quite unwilling to accept evolutionary theories, its critique was based on different grounds, namely, opposition to a naturalistic system. Charles Hodge simply called evolution "atheism." On questions like the age of the earth and mankind, Orthodoxy more easily adjusted its views to fit the evidence. Its biblical hermeneutic did not call for literalism. B. B. Warfield, for example, concluded that the Bible does not speak definitively to the question of the antiquity of man and left that open for science to decide (Warfield, 1952:238 ff.).

Fundamentalism also modified the more rationalistic view of language as a vehicle for *ideas* into a view of words as technical vehicles to describe literal realities. Meaning came to be associated with the words themselves. Some of this, of course, had already happened in Orthodoxy, but Fundamentalism moved much further in this direction. I once heard Allan MacRae, then dean of Faith Seminary, say that there was no essential difference between the language of the Bible and that of a medical dictionary!

A second difference may be seen in the lack of historical tradition and perspective in Fundamentalism. Orthodoxy was significantly, if only relatively, more sensitive to historical dimensions of faith. Its claims of continuity with the historic creeds of the Reformation, its understanding of the covenant as a historical link between past and present, and its postmillennial eschatology all illustrate aspects of its more historical stance.

In Fundamentalism there was little or no appreciation for the slow, historical development of religious and social tradition, or for continuity with previous generations. It emerged at a time in American history when there had been rapid expansion, development, and change. Development was not viewed in terms of organic growth, but of mechanical invention and construction. So historical events were viewed as virtually unconnected constructions in time rather than space. This lack is clearly seen in the dispensational concept itself and in an eschatology which stressed an "any moment" rupture of the historical process.

Third, in contrast to Orthodoxy, Fundamentalism's concept of the church was spiritualized and individualized. They understood the church simply as a group of "born again" individuals meeting for spiritual fellowship and evangelism. It was only tangentially related to the sociopolitical order, and quite incidentally and unfortunately had become institutionalized into denominations. Orthodoxy had viewed the church as a social institution, based on the family, that related responsibly to the ongoing political order. As a social institution it defined membership in terms of profession and sacramental attachment rather than the revivalistic experience of spiritual new birth. It continued to expect the individual to find his self-identity in a denominational tradition, while Fundamentalism developed a nondenominational theology and praxis. For the Fundamentalists, church provided a spiritual identity, but their social identity was provincially or nationally defined.

Mennonite Alternatives

Now with this overview let us return to the proposed Mennonite alternatives of the period 1925-1950, particularly as they are reflected in Hershberger's writings. My thesis is that the Mennonite alternatives of this period represented a modification of the orthodox tradition in contrast to the new dispensationalism which was the heart of Fundamentalism. They do not as such represent a third alternative to the Fundamentalist-liberal controversy.

The overarching issue for Mennonites following the rude awakening of World War I was the preservation of a consistent community of religious and ethical practice that would give them a distinct identifiable reference in dealing with the sociopolitical world. On the one hand they faced a whole new set of social and technical adjustments. On the other, they had been reminded by the war that they must always be ready to give a defense of their nonresistant faith. In this situation the watchwords became *nonresistance* and *nonconformity,* while *consistency* became a primary ethical criterion. Thus the questions for Mennonites were not, strictly speaking, theological, but social and ethical. Theologically, the question was: What base could give the most consistent and adequate rationale and authority for the maintenance of the religious community? Liberalism had been ruled out. Pentecostalism was viewed as a proselytizing opponent, so holiness theology was given little consideration. Lutheranism was itself a minority theology in America. The broad and dominant Reformed tradition, influenced by revivalism, was the most obvious and amenable theological position at hand.

It did not occur to most Mennonites that from their own historical perspective significant modifications of such doctrines as God, man, creation, person and work of Christ, and the like, might be indicated. It was assumed that Mennonites held these in common with conservative theology. There was, to be sure, a definite rejection of predestinarianism. Indeed, George R. Brunk I used to say that while Calvinism was not so dangerous as modernism, it was nevertheless heresy; and inasmuch as Fundamentalism taught "eternal security" it was in that respect unbiblical. But in spite of the rejection of this specific tenet of Reformed theology, the Reformed system furnished the categories and definitions for theological discussion. The Mennonite distinctives were largely conceived as additions to a conservative or Fundamentalist base. It was sometimes said that the problem with Fundamentalism was that it was not fundamental enough—it did not include all the fundamentals!

Several examples of how the Mennonite discussion was influenced will suffice. Mennonites of both the conservative and dispensationalist orientations agreed on the ethical separation of the church from the sociopolitical order which they identified with the world. They agreed that the church is called to follow the ethic of *agape* revealed in Jesus Christ while the world ethic was based on law and the wrath of God. Differences developed, however, in their understanding of the nature of the church and its mission in the world. Those of a conservative bias reflected a clear denominational approach. This is in line with the older Mennonite multidimensional view of the church as a full-orbed social community encompassing all of life's activities and offering a distinct social as well as personal ethic for Christians. One might even call this a para-political view of the church. Those of a dispensationalistic bias on the other hand tended to think of the church as a spiritual reality, restricted to explicit religious disciplines and evangelistic activity. Following the lead of Fundamentalist mentors, they restricted the church's interest largely to personal ethics and dealt with social issues by negation, with a strong emphasis upon noninvolvement. Hershberger, who in this instance represents the conservative option, explored the social dimension of Christian ethics and eventually wrote *The Way of the Cross in Human Relations*—a subject well outside the realm of dispensational interest.

We see this same tension in intra-Mennonite debates about nonresistance and God's will for Israel in the Old Testament. Hershberger in chapter two of *War, Peace, and Nonresistance* used the categories of progressive revelation and God's "active" and "permissive" will to argue that God's highest will for mankind has always been the way of nonresistance. In this way he attempted to explain God's apparent change in covenant regulations. His more dispensationalistic opponents felt no need to explain such a change. God was free to change the terms of the covenant, and from their point of view had obviously done so. Nonresistance was for the church only. Furthermore, they suspected that Hershberger's argument from progressive revelation contained a covert contradiction of verbal inerrancy and the literal interpretation of Scripture.[1]

The Unfinished Theological Agenda

These examples suffice to show the tenor of the argument and the shape of the Anabaptist-Mennonite alternative that was being proposed. In the 1950s even J. C. Wenger, who knew neoorthodoxy firsthand and in some respects adopted its apologetic stance, saw the problem of Fundamentalism as only "a narrowness of spirit," a lack of social ethic, and a dispensationalist interpretation of eschatology (Wenger, 1954:13-14).

From the perspective of the latter part of the twentieth century, it seems evident that Mennonite church leaders in the first half of the century identified too quickly with Fundamentalist definitions of both the issues and answers. Thus, they failed to develop their own unique implicit insights. One must use the word "implicit" because American Mennonitism had not developed an explicit theology of its own. Indeed, one can quite properly speak of the Mennonite involvement with the Fundamentalist controversy as a loss of theological innocence! Basic questions and implications that were overlooked or brushed aside in the heat and anxiety of the moment were bound to reemerge and demand a more open reexamination.[2]

Let me suggest some of the unfinished agenda items. The first question, which was not even explicitly recognized as a question, was, "What kind of theology is indicated by the Mennonite experience and understanding of Scripture?" Since it was assumed that theology is simply the orderly, comprehensive explication of biblical teaching and nothing more, the question of a distinctly Mennonite contribution to the ongoing theological discussion, growing out of its own spiritual history, did not occur to them. Wenger's theology, coming at the end of this period, did deal with the question, but he resolved the issue by keeping his explanations nonspeculative and closely related to piety. His view of the method and role of theology conforms to that of Fundamentalism and Orthodoxy.

The theological models of Protestant Orthodoxy presented systems of rational explication of the various creeds which were in turn based on the Bible. Theology sought to be faithful to the Bible as understood in the confessional statements. Fundamentalism presented a popular nonscholarly version of this kind of theology. For the classical creeds it substituted abbreviated statements of "fundamentals," and instead of logical systematic explication, it claimed to present purely biblical explanations often published under titles like *Great Doctrines of the Bible.*

The Mennonite brotherhood, however, was not a creedal church, and since they did not make the practical equation of faith and orthodox belief as Protestant Orthodoxy had, one might have expected a different approach to theology and a different role for it in the church. This question remains largely unexplored to the present time.

A second question is that of the nature and locus of authority. How is God's authority recognized in the church? Some of the men who had been influenced by liberalism in the first decades of the century had incidentally raised this question, as well as the related question of the nature of theology, but the authority question was too existentially threatening, and the options offered by liberalism too open-ended and individualistic, for the question to get a hearing in Mennonite circles.

The question of authority is always a complex one, and to oversimplify the problem is to falsify issues. Authority in the traditional Mennonite community grew out of a long-standing community consensus about the thrust of the biblical message and its embodiment in a way of life. The power to convince, *i.e.,* its sanction, lay in the community which embodied that way of life, and it was related directly to the degree of one's involvement in that community. In other words, it was *church* authority, based, of course, on biblical understandings and always open to challenge from the biblical text itself. This pattern of authority is closely related in form to authority in churches with a creedal tradition, but differed in that the criterion was a style of obedient response rather than a system of belief.

The Fundamentalist alternative differed from both of these by placing the locus of authority for the individual directly in the words of Scripture. In Fundamentalism, no living, responding community, and only the most minimal doctrinal statements, are conceived as necessary to embody the authoritative Word. The words themselves, *i.e.,* verbal symbols, under the direct influence of the Holy Spirit bring rational convincement. (This process is rational in nature even though supernatural in source.)

Theologically, the Mennonite leaders of 1925-1950 accepted and verbalized Fundamentalism's concept of authority, although they tended to keep that authority in the hands of conference rather than relinquish it directly to the individual under Scripture. Attempts to reexamine the concepts of authority were strongly resisted as late as the decade of the fifties, and it is only as central church authority has eroded that the possibility for theological reconsideration has opened.

A third and related question was the nature of Scripture and its role in the church in relation to the authority of the Holy Spirit. Protestant Orthodoxy has usually discussed the nature of Scripture under the rubric of inspiration and revelation, but from the perspective of the Mennonite heritage the question of Spirit and Scripture in the life of the church is of equal if not more importance. On this subject the American Mennonite brotherhood was strongly influenced by the biblicism of Menno Simons, who himself reflects some of the bias of Reformed theology in contrast to some of his South German brothers. Consequently, it is quite understandable that Mennonites accepted Fundamentalism's statement of the biblical problem as a question of verbal inspiration and that they rested content with the answers which Reformed theologians like B. B. Warfield gave to the question of the Bible and the Holy Spirit in the life of the church.[3] Indeed, this definition of the issue was accepted by Mennonite scholars as the basis for classifying the various types of Anabaptists. Those Anabaptists who allowed for more freedom and authority of the Spirit to direct the life of the church were dubbed "spiritualist" and classified as peripheral to the movement.

The Brunk brothers revivals of the early nineteen-fifties reopened the issue of the Holy Spirit's work in the life of the believer, when the two brothers took the respective positions of Keswick and Pentecostalism on the question of the baptism of the Spirit. But this discussion did not deal with the larger theological issues of Spirit and Bible, freedom and authority. Again, the advocates of the recent charismatic movement have argued their position in terms of biblical literalism, but the broad implications of the issues raised have not yet received extensive theological reexamination.

The fourth doctrinal concept for which the traditional Reformed categories were adopted is the nature of salvation. In the traditional Mennonite understanding, salvation was experienced as a belonging to and relationship in the religious community. One was saved when by a free decision (repentance and commitment) he came under the rule of Christ who is "head of the body, the church." To be saved meant to be in church order. To be outside the church was to be outside of Christ, and thus to be unsaved. That was the implicit theological heart of the matter that underlay church practice. In its more pristine form it was stated by Hans Denk who wrote, "No one can know Christ unless he follows him in life." For Mennonites that life was in the church.[4]

In the post-Civil War Mennonite communities this concept had become too legalistic and inflexible to offer a satisfying rationale for a dynamic Christian experience. Furthermore, the validity and sanctions of the community were being challenged by the dominant, more free, individualistic, democratic, and self-consciously American community in its religious guise as revivalism. (McLoughlin, 1974.)

In this situation the doctrine of salvation rather obviously needed to be reexamined, and it was. But the reexamination took the form of adopting the revivalist definitions with their distinctly individualistic, noncommunity bias. This kind of salvation experience was promoted through the introduction of revival meetings, instead of working at the dynamics of Christian community experience and new understandings of the church as the community of salvation. Mennonite emphases, such as insistence upon marks of genuine repentance, the necessity of works to demonstrate faith (sanctification to follow justification), and the rejection of election and eternal security, were added to guarantee the validity of the new salvation experience. But these were attachments to an imported theological understanding. The categories of definition were clearly those of revivalistic Protestantism. The "salvation" item remained on the church's theological agenda for reexamination from more distinctly Anabaptist-Mennonite perspectives.

Perhaps the church as a separate doctrine need not be added to this list. All of the agenda items thus far are *church* issues. But in spite of the fact that no theological topic has received more attention by Mennonites over the past fifty years, I am still inclined to say that it remains an agenda item.

Mennonite discussions of the church have been largely in terms of the Free or Believers' Church versus the State or *Volks* Church. We have insisted that on the human side the church be gathered by the free commitment of individuals, *i.e.,* not coerced by political or social sanctions, and that it be free to respond to Christ as Lord without political hindrance. But in all this we have tended to consider the church under the model of a democratic institution rather than as the "body of Christ." Put crassly, but with more than a grain of truth, we have viewed it as a nonprofit corporation formed by freely contracting individuals (its actual legal status under the United States Constitution) for their mutual purposes of nurture, inspiration (worship), and evangelism. From this perspective the church, however solemnly we speak of it, belongs to the *bene esse* and not the *esse* of salvation.

That the church is not essential to the salvation of the individual was, of course, the position of the Reformers in reaction to the medieval Roman Catholic position. That was one reason why they did not need to take the visible church with the same seriousness as the Anabaptists did. Revivalistic Protestantism further attenuated the relation between salvation and life in the visible church. Salvation, even when received in mass meetings (hardly a model of serious community), was essentially a private matter which was to be taken care of independently of and prior to considerations of church membership. The individual who had already experienced salvation in the revival was then exhorted to find "the church of his choice." This stands in sharp contrast to the experience of having found salvation in and through relationships in a vital community under the lordship of Christ.

Thus the fundamental theological issue of the nature of the church as a manifestation of and witness to the new creation in Christ is still very much with us. How is it related to salvation in Christ? What does it mean to call it the "body" and "temple" of the Holy Spirit (1 Corinthians 12:13; 3:16) into which persons are baptized and in which they participate in the Spirit (Philippians 2:1)?

Some Preliminary Theological Considerations

If we are to consider a theological alternative to Fundamentalism, we must first recognize that liberalism raised many legitimate questions at many of the right places, even if we remain dissatisfied with all of its answers. Part of the problem in earlier Mennonite theologizing stemmed from its *out-of-hand* rejection of liberalism. Happily the situation has now changed in a number of ways so that issues can be discussed in a less reactionary manner.

In the first place, the shape of the whole discussion has greatly changed, resulting in reformulation of the questions as well as the answers. From within liberalism itself came the challenge of what William Hordern has called "The New Reformation Theology"—

sometimes referred to as neoorthodoxy or biblical realism. This movement challenged both Fundamentalism and modernism.

As a result the patterns of discussion between Fundamentalism and liberalism have also begun to change. A new conservative theological position has emerged which calls itself "evangelicalism." While it claims not to be compromising on the fundamental doctrines and has made biblical inerrancy—carefully defined so as not to mean dictation—its touchstone for intra-evangelical discussion, it has opened many other Fundamentalist positions for reexamination. George E. Ladd's *Crucial Questions About the Kingdom of God* (1952) was a harbinger of this new stance.

While evangelicals did not accept many of the ideas of neoorthodoxy, they opened themselves with a new attentiveness to dialogue with the theological and biblical scholars of that persuasion. The effect has been theological ferment of unanticipated proportions, especially among the younger scholars.

Some Mennonite scholars were among the early evangelicals who began to engage in this new dialogue. Already in the nineteen-fifties some teachers at Goshen College Biblical Seminary and Mennonite Biblical Seminary were reevaluating their position vis-a-vis Fundamentalism. A careful study of Anabaptist origins, along with biblical studies that stressed inductive and historical methodology, opened new understandings of the biblical message. Indeed, as John H. Yoder has observed in his *The Politics of Jesus,* much contemporary historical exegesis has raised the same kinds of theological and ethical issues that the reexamination of Anabaptism was also raising. Perhaps in this new climate of critical openness we can look anew at some of the agenda items.

Without going into the time-worn aspects of the liberal-Fundamentalist debate, let me in closing sketch a few preliminary considerations for the construction of a disciples' theology, following the agenda items raised in the last section.

Theology serves a number of purposes, and accordingly a variety of approaches are possible. The suggestion of one particular approach should not be taken to imply that all other approaches are invalid.

Without falling into the error of attempting to write *the* Mennonite theology in a dogmatic sense, we may nevertheless ask: What distinctive role for theology does Mennonite experience indicate? What might be the Mennonite contribution to the wider theological dialogue?[5]

A Mennonite theology *as a theology for the disciple community* could make a real contribution at this point in history to the ongoing discussion. Such a theology should grow out of and be related to the life of the grass-roots church—the *koinonia* or *Gemeinde*. Its data will be the ongoing experience of the disciple community under the guidance of the Holy Spirit in the light of the Scripture. It will begin with and bear witness to the reality of the Spirit of Jesus Christ alive and present in His body. Because the Spirit is precisely the Spirit of Jesus, the biblical materials remain its primary source material.

To refer to the data of theology in the above order does not make the Scripture secondary to present experience, but rather gives theology its proper setting and approach to Scripture. Theology should describe and point to a *present reality* and not *present theory, past experience,* or *eschatological prediction.* When it deals with past reality it is for the sake of the present life of the church. When it enunciates theory it is to provide a framework for understanding experience. When it explores eschatological dimensions of the faith it is in order to gain perspective on and provide a strategy for the present.

Theology should be a functional discipline in the life of the congregation. There is little value, for example, in rational speculation about the essential nature of the Godhead, which in any event must of necessity remain mystery (1 Timothy 3:16). What we need to know is how God is related to and deals with us—in Calvin's phrase, not God "as He is in Himself" but "as He is to us." Scripture itself presents God as "the God of Abraham, Isaac, and Jacob," *i.e.,* God in historical relation to mankind. Its purpose is for "discipline in right living" (2 Timothy 3:16-17, NEB). In these respects the Bible itself should be a model for a disciples' theology.

This suggests that in some real sense a disciples' theology must be situational, *i.e.,* have a specific location in time and space. Classically the ultimate goal of theology was the formulation of dogma—an official unchanging (timeless) doctrinal formula. While the idea of infallible dogma was challenged in the Reformation, post-Reformation theologians continued to operate with this model of theology. They attempted to set forth an "orthodox" system which would be the final criterion for Christian belief. I suggest that the goal of theology is not to establish dogma but to serve the church in understanding its message, mission, and strategy. These things have to do with time and place, and this means that theology should be done for a time and place. For example, we should not expect the categories and terms framed in Europe and America over the past centuries to serve with the same validity and usefulness in Africa and India. Neither should we expect our statements of truth to be timeless. This does not mean that ultimate reality changes, but only that our partial knowledge and experience of it changes. Theology is inevitably tied to our experience of reality.

When we turn to the question of authority in theology, we must begin with the recognition that it is the Holy Spirit who continues to have authority in the church. The Spirit is the fundamental requisite for the existence of the church. He is the creative source of its life and as such He is Lord of the church. He is not limited to or under the control of either an institutional hierarchy (Protestant or Roman Catholic) or Scripture in the exercise of His authority. As Author of Scripture He remains Lord also of Scripture. Spirit precedes Scripture. Spirit belongs to the *esse* of the church, Scripture to the *bene esse*.

Now the problem for theology is how to reckon with this acknowledged priority of the Spirit's dynamic and authority in the church. Protestant Orthodoxy, in opposition first to Roman Catholicism's concept of tradition and later to liberalism's emphasis on experience, maintained that the locus and instrument of the Spirit's authority lay in Scripture alone. It insisted that the Bible not only be given primary and prior authority to experience (and tradition) but that it be given sole authority, independently of experience! Accordingly it made Scripture the ground of authority for theological assertions and that which in turn gives them convincing power. This position is summed up in the popular phrase of Billy Graham, "The Bible says!"

Liberalism, particularly in its early formulations by Schleiermacher and the Ritschlian theologians, placed the locus of the Spirit's authority in the experience of Christians in the church. Perhaps in their reaction to orthodoxy the pendulum swung too far, but certainly we must find a way theologically to maintain a dynamic synthesis of the two—Scripture and experience—as the locus of the Spirit's authority.

The authority of a religious message must be based on a word which remains alive and functioning in the midst of a community of response. There is no way to capture and hold such authority either by a doctrine of inspiration or the legal prescriptions of an institution. Scripture has no realized authority apart from the continued living response of Christians to the authority of the Spirit as the Author of Scripture.

Thus it is the Bible providing its guidance and inspiration in the midst of a discerning, reconciling community that carries authority and has convincing power. It is not the Bible without the community, and certainly not the community without the Bible; but both together in dynamic involvement. A theology that springs from such a reality will derive its authority from its source.

This leads more specifically to the question of the nature and authority of Scripture itself. Scripture had its origin and point of departure in the everyday life of God's people. It is part of the ongoing work of the Holy Spirit leading the disciples into all truth (John 16:13). It is not only a historical report and explanation of past events; it is part and parcel of the continuing action—what the Spirit of Christ continued to do in the forming of the new community. If it is to have its proper use and authority, it must remain an instrument of the continuing action of that same Spirit. Fundamentalist theology is much too facile in its separation of the continuing work of the Holy Spirit in the church and the authority and use of Scripture.

If we put this same point in terms of the doctrine of inspiration, we would say that the authority of the Bible is derivative. It does not have an independent or autonomous validity or authority of its own, such as a logically argued essay or a technical scientific work describing empirical data. Its derivation from and dependence on the Holy Spirit is, I take it, the fundamental idea in the concept of inspiration. Fundamentalism, and Protestant Orthodoxy before it, treated the concept of inspiration as though it gave to the words of Scripture an independent informational authority, and then built a rational speculative theology on that information. But the inspiration of the Holy Spirit is not simply a past, finished action imparting an independent quality of perfection to Scripture. It is both a historically past and historically present inspiration. The Bible's authority derives from the continuing work of the Holy Spirit leading into all truth. Even the validity of what it reports about the earthly historical Jesus (past event) is not simply the validity of an accurate report about the past. When it bears witness to Jesus it is not simply a historical report about One who lived in the past and whose memory can continue to inspire us. It speaks of One whose present life and activity can only be comprehended in the light of what He "began to do and teach" in an earlier stage of His activity. This gives the Bible a distinctly present tense, confessional character and gives us a clue for its use in theological discussion.

Finally, a theology in the Anabaptist-Mennonite tradition should, it seems to me, be a salvation theology. Orthodoxy has generally begun its theology proper with God as Creator. But a theology that takes as its subject "God as He is to us" and that seriously aims to be a theology for discipleship in the new community might properly find its locus in God as Savior.

This does not mean that we would limit theology to soteriology or even necessarily begin with it. Rather, we would take salvation instead of creation as the primary theological category. In this way we would acknowledge theologically that in history, both history in general and our own personal histories, we know God as Savior-Preserver. He is the One who even now in Christ is creating "one new humanity" and thus is making peace.[6] The conception of God as Creator is implied in our experience of Him as the all-sufficient Savior, not vice versa.

In Scripture itself the concepts of salvation and creation often merge. Salvation is spoken of as a new creation; creation is described as salvation from chaos. It is the self-disclosing, saving Word who is also the life- and light-giving Creator (John 1:1-5). The "new nature" which is being renewed in knowledge, righteousness, and holiness is created after the image of its Creator (Ephesians 4:23; Colossians 3:10). Other examples could be given, but these will suffice to make the point.

To do theology as salvation theology grounds it in the present activity of God—the new creation which is in process. It gives it an immediate standing place in a visible community of salvation which is sign and witness to the new creation. It makes incarnational categories of *agape,* righteousness, and reconciliation primary for ethics. It directs us toward a hopeful future, as colabores with God.

The basic question for the church today is: What is the shape of the new thing that God is creating among us and how shall we respond to it in obedience? A disciples' theology should help us toward answers to this question for our time.

6

Forms of Covenant Community

Harold E. Bauman

The search for meaningful church life goes on. The revival of interest in the churches following World War II led to a focus upon liturgical renewal. Expressed in designing church buildings for liturgy and worship, the liturgical focus spilled over into the sixties.

The ferment of the sixties in the streets and campuses reached into many congregations. It caused unrest and dissatisfaction on the part of some persons. The focus for some continued to rest in the worship service as the place where the most important matters in church life were to happen. The decline in attendance at worship services and the unrest on the part of many persons indicated that all was not well with congregations. Reformations in worship are short-lived, perhaps because they are substitutes for deeper spiritual problems. (Jones, 1954:288-293).

Movements in the secular world indicated that many persons were seeking for experiences that would make them whole persons. The dominance of rational technological thought in American culture in the first half of the twentieth century had its impact upon congregations. The services focused primarily upon the spoken word, emphasizing the importance of preaching. The liturgical renewal in the fifties sought to give more place for emotional expression but continued to do this largely through what happened in the chancel of the church.

The search for security in an affluent society also had its impact upon congregational life. Affluence and the search for position and privilege led to the desire to keep the status quo. The law and order movement of the late sixties and early seventies was an expression of those who wanted to keep privileged status.

The counter movements gave evidence of the desires of people for something different. The rise of sensitivity training labs in order to express and find oneself as a person indicated the need for a more

---

Harold Bauman is executive secretary of Mennonite Board of Congregational Ministries, Elkhart, Indiana. A member of the Assembly in Goshen, he was formerly campus pastor at Goshen College.

holistic expression of personhood. The counterculture of youth as protest against the dominance of the military-industrial complex in the American scene and the war in Indochina was a statement of different values over against the dominant values of society. The formation of many communes by young people expressed a desire for experiential and communal relationships. Within the Christian scene, although not within the church, the rise of the Jesus People also expressed the desire for close community in expressing the Christian faith and meeting needs within the person.

It is evident that the signs from our society in the past several decades are pointing toward the crying needs on the part of some people for a deeper sense of community and personal wholeness. The attempts outside of the churches to meet these needs have come and gone. The ferment is reaching into congregations in an attempt to establish deeper community within them. Can the churches meet these needs?

The Quest for Community

The approaches to Christian community have varied. The historical Catholic approach has been that of a parish, a geographical area for which the church feels responsible. The focus of the church within the parish has been the scheduling of activities and seeking to solve the problems of the people (Clark, 1972: 12-14). Historically, the Protestants also used a geographical parish approach, although more recently the emphasis has been upon the calling of widely scattered people to a church building, focusing upon functions which take place within the building.

Those groups which emerged from what is called the radical wing of the Reformation have tended to focus more upon the quality of life among the believers as it is expressed in a community of relationships. One expression is found among the Hutterites who formed close communities with common possessions. Thus the geographical location, the holding of property in common, and sharing many common activities and life together were all bound into the concept of community. Other groups in the Radical Reformation, commonly called the Anabaptists, also focused upon the church as a community, emphasizing mutual relationships and common activities which expressed faith in Christ. Oftentimes these groups lived together in a close geographical area. Thus geography and common activities were bound up in the community.

In the migration to America, Anabaptist-Mennonite groups often located in geographical clusters for the sake of church life together. These communities covered a limited geographical area and developed cultural patterns which they held in common. Thus the common life of the community involved both the religious life and the cultural expressions in geographical proximity.

Most of these groups that came out of the Radical Reformation and kept their identity for centuries in geographical cultural communities have now been influenced greatly by the surrounding culture. Differences in dress and language for the most part no longer exist. The rapid means of communication brought new religious beliefs and ideas that infiltrated the religious thought of these communities and altered their religious faith. Some of these groups have borrowed extensively from other religious groups and are in the process of losing their identity.

One of the strong voices that sought to combat the disintegrating influences upon Mennonite communities and to project a vision of a vital functioning community of the future was that of Guy F. Hershberger. Hershberger's vision called for a community that was based upon a spiritual foundation drawn from the Scriptures and the life in Christ directed by the Holy Spirit. It was a community which had a large geographic dimension to it. The ideal of the family farm was to be maintained. For those in industry there was a focus upon wholesome employer and employee relationships. Small industries were to be established within the Mennonite community. The agricultural and business persons in Mennonite communities had the obligation to set Christian standards for others in these industries. Such communities should establish schools and include in the curriculum emphases upon preparation for life in the Mennonite community. There was to be an enlarged and wholesome vision of recreation and social activities to combat the commercialized amusements of the larger cities. The Mennonite community was to have also an evangelistic and service vision. Hershberger wanted to move beyond the back-to-the-farm movement. It was a call to Christian community in the fullest expression of Christian discipleship (1948b: 7).

The evolution in Hershberger's thought can be observed by his comments nearly two decades later to a conference on Christian mutual aid. He observed that the Mennonite community is a reality and documented this by the service and mission programs which originated in the two previous decades. He acknowledged that the Mennonites were decreasingly rural and increasingly urban. The basis of the community continued to be its roots within the gospel and the Scriptures (1964c: 21). The same shift is noted in one of Hershberger's major works, *The Way of the Cross in Human Relations* (1958d: 43 f.).

Is it necessary to drop the idea of a close geographical participation in order to have covenant community? The answers to this will vary from group to group. Lyle Schaller sees the benefits of a geographically defined community being offset by the present-day requirements of residential and vocational mobility. Therefore, a geographically defined community does not appear to be on the list of options for today (1975:26).

Schaller notes further that the basis of community today is seldom defined meaningfully in only geographical terms. The church cannot ignore economic, social, cultural, educational, racial, and ethnic considerations or it will only produce frustration. "The churches seeking to bring the gospel of Jesus Christ to persons outside their own membership tend to be more effective when they define community in terms of people and the characteristics of people rather than in geographical terms" (1975:25). He notes that for church leaders who ask how to serve this community, the answer may be simply: "Create a sense of community" (1975:31).

The many attempts today to build community within the church have given rise to various foci. There are those groups who attempt to build community around a new understanding of the teachings of Jesus and thus focus upon the question of ethics. Some of the house churches in the Kitchener-Waterloo area tend in this direction.

There are those groups seeking community who focus primarily upon the sharing of material possessions. There are other groups who see one of the primary purposes to be that of creating the extended family to provide strength for family relationships in the face of current cultural pressures which the nuclear family is seldom able to handle. The Church of the Redeemer in Houston, Texas (Harper, 1973), and the Reba Place Fellowship (Jackson, 1974: 180) are current examples. There are other communities which focus upon the functions within the congregation such as worship, teaching, mutual support, decision-making, and witness or service, expressed in a variety of forms.

Is there any guidance to be gained from the Believers' Church faith in seeking meaningful Christian communities? Does its theology have anything to say to the functions and forms of the Christian community? How are the forms determined?

Deep in the conviction of the Believers' Church faith is the understanding that forms of the church are determined by the functions which the Scriptures enjoin upon us. The forms must always be flexible to the growing understandings of what it means to be God's people. We shall look at how the guiding understandings of the Believers' Church faith point toward functions which are necessary in the life of God's people and some forms by which they may be met.

Voluntary Commitment to Covenant Community

Central to the Believers' Church faith is the conviction that the church is composed of those who freely accept the Word of God, turn away from the life of sin, and voluntarily are baptized into the body of Christ as expressed in a visible congregation. The church consists of persons from all races, social classes, and nations who voluntarily confess Jesus Christ as Lord and Savior. Such a faith that is uncoerced leads to voluntary baptism and involvement in a congregation. Membership on the basis of infant baptism or citizenship in a given geographical area cannot be the basis of constituting the people of God. In brief, the church is composed of those who voluntarily confess that Jesus is Lord and identify with a congregation of God's people.

The faith which characterizes the relationship between the believer and Christ is seen to include fundamental attitudes, feelings, perspectives, and the commitment of one's whole life. It is much more than just intellectual assent to some theological propositions. The commitment requires a degree of understanding that only a person who knows the tension between self-centeredness and allegiance to Christ can possess and come to a thorough repentance. The believer must be deeply aware that he has said "No" to self-centered living and "in whole heart and soul and body set out to live for God and his church" (Littell, 1964:xv).

Coming to new life in Christ occurs in the history of both the individual and the congregation. This basic truth is the ground for the uncompromising effort to work out with integrity a Christian witness. Thus, the baptism of the believer is not only the indispensable sign of incorporation into the visible fellowship, but it also marks a juncture of individual discipleship with corporate discipleship. By baptism the believer covenants with the congregation to become submissive to its discipline and to participate in its formulation and functioning. Thus, baptism is a public witness to faith in Christ, to the baptism of the Holy Spirit, to a covenant with the visible church, and to the ordination of the whole people in mission and witness (Groff, 1969:69).

Such is the voluntary decision on the part of the believer. It is a response freely made to the call of God in Christ with an awareness of turning from self to the kingdom-style enacted in Christ. The invitation is to all people and is not to be fenced in by national or tribal commitments. To respond is to become a member of the community of faith, the people of God, in a way which opens their resources to the believer who in turn shares responsibility for others.

Thus the form of the congregation is that of a voluntarily gathered group that covenants together in regard to their witness of the lordship of Christ and to the Holy Spirit binding them together. These covenanted believers constitute the essence of being the people of God in contrast to finding the essence in a clergy, a sacred building, a sacrament, or a preaching service.

The common commitment to the lordship of Christ is crucial. The commitment is the basis for motivation in joyful obedience to God's will and for responsible participation in the people of God. It is at the point of such a commitment that the realization of the biblical view of the church as a covenant community will ultimately rise or fall (O'Connor, 1963).

The Believers' Churches have been influenced by a view of salvation which is partial and individualistic: if one confesses the bad things one has done and loves Jesus one is ready for baptism, which unites one with the invisible body of Christ. (The child evangelism movement has promoted this view.) Membership in a congregation can be decided later and is not essential to living the Christian life. In some denominations the decision to say no to self is viewed as a "second work of grace," "the second blessing," or "entire sanctification," which is essential for those who want to go on and be disciples of Christ.

The Believers' Church faith follows Peter's invitation in Acts 2:38-40. The person must repent—confess Jesus is Lord; and be baptized—a public witness to allegiance to Christ, the cleansing from sin, and the receiving of the gift of the Holy Spirit. One is then to change crowds and be added to the believing community. Such a covenant of commitment is essential if the biblical view of the church as a believing community is to be realized.

Mutual Responsibility

The Spirit binding believers together leads to a second understanding of the Believers' Church: the church is a covenant community of mutual responsibility. Coming into the visible church, symbolized by believer's baptism, brings reciprocal responsibilities. The awareness and acceptance of these responsibilities forms the covenant in belonging to the community of faith (Williams, 1969:116). Such a covenant is based upon the priesthood of all believers: each person is a minister for every other person. There is an interdependence upon one another which grows out of an intimate caring, prompted by the love shed abroad by the Holy Spirit.

The covenant of belonging and mutual responsibility is expressed and symbolized in sharing in the Lord's Supper (Littell, 1957:xii). It is expressed in sharing in faithful admonition and teaching. There is participation in the "means of grace"—meeting together for Bible study, for common prayer and communion, for study of decisions in Christian life and witness, and for admonition and encouragement. The believer is healed in such a worship fellowship and is equipped for the alternate time of separation and service. Teaching, admonition, and exhortation are touchstones on which the believer can check his or her own sense of the leading of the Holy Spirit.

While special leaders and ministers are chosen to help equip the believers for their work, every believer is to be a minister. The true role of every believer begins at the point where the lordship of Christ and the governance of God the Holy Spirit in the church are asserted in practice. The integrity of the witness of the church requires that all those baptized in the faith, not just those with technical education, should pray, discuss, and determine the shape of the Christian witness in the world.

A further implication of being bound together by the Holy Spirit into a covenant community of mutual responsibility is that there is now a place where one is accountable to follow through on one's commitment to Christ. The integrity of one's commitment involves implementing it in daily life. The Believers' Church is aware of its own fallibility and tendency to self-deception. It does not accept the notions of Western individualism that personal and public morality are matters of private relationship to God. The Believers' Church seeks to find ways through which supportive confrontation can take place to aid members in fulfilling their commitments to God (Redekop, 1970:125).

Mutual responsibility involves caring about total needs of believers. Selfless sharing grows out of the motivation of love rooted in the relationship to Christ. There is responsibility for those who suffer illness and economic hardships. Material possessions need to be shared as there is need. Encouragement, admonition, and spiritual support are also needed in the mutual life together. Witness to this continuing stream in the life of believers is found in the Lord's Supper which is a testimony not only to the memorial work of Christ and a renewal of one's covenant with Him, but also a witness to the mutual fellowship of believers in the visible body of Christ.

The constraining force within the Believers' Church for mutual admonition and discipline is found in the believers under the guidance of the Holy Spirit searching the Scriptures until a consensus is reached. In the voluntarily gathered church, the only constraint that can be used to gather persons into the fellowship is the persuasive constraining power of the Holy Spirit. Once one is in the church, the ways of persuasion include teaching, loving entreaty, exhortation, admonition, rebuke, and finally, if necessary, the loss of privileges within the fellowship. The impact of decisions made by the congregation is a means of such persuasion.

The implications of the mutual responsibility and accountability functions within the covenant community in regard to form are great. Many groups have been attempting to search out forms adequate to facilitate such functions with covenanted believers. There are those groups who feel that the small house church which grows no larger than fifteen or twenty people is the best way to carry out such covenant responsibilities. The house churches in the Kitchener-Waterloo area are an example. Other groups believe that most of these functions need to be carried out in a primary group setting where intimate personal knowing is possible. Such groups may range in size from eight to fourteen persons. It is here that the inmost questions, hurts, and pressing decisions can be shared and dealt with under the guidance of the Holy Spirit and the Scriptures in the context of believers who love and care. Such groups need to be bound together in a congregation for the functions of worship, exposition of Scriptures, and broad policy decision-making (the intergroup functions). The tendency to follow one's prejudices and biases means that these groups need the counsel of other groups and cannot be autonomous and self-sufficient. Thus, the covenant life of mutual responsibility of the congregation demands both primary group settings as well as the larger setting for the functions appropriate to the size of the gathering.

The Fellowship of Hope (Elkhart, Indiana) is one example of a search for faithfulness which uses the extended household for the small-group functions and a gathering of the households in a congregation for the intergroup functions. Combined with this is community ownership of goods, Reba Place Fellowship in Evanston follows a similar pattern, though the gathering of all the households constitutes a congregation of several hundred persons.

A second example is the Assembly which functions in the context of Goshen College. While there is no common ownership of possessions, there is attention to sharing as each has need. Though there are a few extended households, to be a member of the Assembly one must be a member of a small group. These groups meet weekly to fulfill the needs of mutual support and accountability. They come together in three congregations on Sunday for the intergroup functions, with interested noncovenanted persons participating in both the small-group and Sunday gatherings (except members' meetings which are held frequently on Sunday evenings). Out of the conviction that for congregations to function in decision-making they should be no larger than from 80 to 100 persons, the Assembly functions in three congregations. These three congregations meet together every seventh Sunday for worship and a fellowship meal. Intercongregation coordination is effected by a group of six persons.

The search for adequate forms to express the mutual responsibility and accountability functions of the people of God in a mobile society will continue. Fundamental to the search is the conviction, expressed by Guy Hershberger in his day, that these functions are biblically enjoined upon us.

Decision-Making

A third understanding of the Believers' Church, out of which grows another function, is that the church lives by the spiritual governance of the Holy Spirit and the Scriptures through the believers gathered for decision-making. The church as it gathers asserts the sovereignty of the risen Lord and the Spirit of truth in the midst of believers gathered around the open Bible as the guide for faith and practice. Here is found the basis for the spiritual life and spiritual governance of the Believers' Church (Littell, 1964: 94).

Thus the congregation of believers is responsible to make any decisions which affect its life and work. Those persons who are chosen to give leadership to the teaching of the Scriptures and the shepherding of the flock facilitate such decisions but they do not make them. The Spirit working through the Bible is viewed as a force more powerful than any other human instrument of persuasion or authority. Christian practice must flow from inner commitment and experience. To remove

basic decisions in regard to Christian living from the bosom of the congregation and the shoulders of those who must ultimately practice
them is to weaken these believers. The exercise of self-determination
under Christ is viewed as essential to the vigor of every community of
faith.

The absence of power structures and authoritarian rule beyond
the congregation does not mean congregational anarchy or particu-
larism. Church unity is implicit in the very idea of the church. The need
for mutual counsel and correction of selfish interest is just as essential
between congregations as it is between individual believers and small
groups. Larger gatherings or conventions are needed to promote
consensus through discernment, sharing, and admonition, but in ways
which do not take from the congregation the responsibility for self-determination (Peachey, 1956: 217).

The Believers' Church finds the truth of Christ as the believers
gather around the Scriptures with the conviction that Christ is the
norm of truth and is most fully revealed in the New Testament writings
which are given by the Holy Spirit. The whole body of believers joins
together in discussion until a consensus is achieved. God's people live
in the confidence that God has yet new light to break forth in understanding the written Word. The capacity to be corrected and to discuss
and pray through decisions until a consensus is reached is fundamental.
The power of the Holy Spirit unlocks the Scriptures to make the revelation to believers in their present need. This avoids the normlessness of
the spiritualist who believes the Spirit gives individuals inner visions
without testing or the normlessness of individualism found in much of
the Western world today (Littell, 1961: 65).

Again, the implications of the form of the covenant community
are urgent. The agenda of the congregation needs to grow out of the
needs within the groups where the will of the Lord is sought. Such seeking for discernment means that each believer must share through bringing insight and conscience to the discussion, refusing to exist in isolation. The essential matter is the cultivation of a frame of mind and
readiness of action which makes for a quickened response to the will
and guidance of the Holy Spirit. As the small groups study the Scriptures and bring their insights to the larger gatherings, the congregation
is better equipped to find discernment and guidance. As questions and
alternatives are discussed in the congregation, these can be tested in the
small group meetings with reports coming back again to the congregation. Such a pattern is used by the Assembly in Goshen.

Discipleship

A fourth essential understanding of the Believers' Church is that participation in the community of faith leads to a life of discipleship, which inevitably results in tension with the world. Discipleship means that the life of the believer in all areas should be fashioned after the teachings and example of Christ. The life of discipleship is important, for the kingdom of God is both "a coming world, ardently expected, and a world already in the making here and now by practicing brotherly love and accepting suffering for the sake of the kingdom" (Friedmann, 1967: 10.) As a consequence there is a reshaping of man's outlook concerning a new hierarchy of values—now drawn from the teachings of Christ; a new social orientation—without one's brother there is no discipleship or following of Christ; and a new understanding of history—a powerful drama between the two kingdoms.

The fellowship of believers aims at nothing less than to follow Christ as He asked His disciples to do. Such a group discipleship leads believers to consider themselves as strangers and pilgrims on the earth with their determining citizenship in heaven, hence they are a mobile community.

It is out of such a community that the shape of discipleship is found. The Believers' Church is aware that people are self-centered, that they see things in their own interest, and that they can be totally and unintentionally unaware of their own motivations and desires. The mind can be darkened by the seductive powers of the world. Aware of its own sinfulness and dependency upon God, the Believers' Church structures itself to deal with subjective self-deceit and to confront the Scriptures under the Holy Spirit (Redekop, 1970: 123). The counsel and the consensus of the believers as a prophetic community are essential in discerning the path of obedience. The root of all true Christian ethics is fellowship ethics growing out of a community of faith (Littell, 1957: 124).

Thus the form of discipleship must be found as believers gather around the Word. The agenda of the meetings of believers, whether on Sunday morning or at other times, must focus upon the exposition of the Scriptures and the testing of the understandings in the light of the current context. The form of the church must allow believers to wrestle with the questions. As small groups make their discernments and report their findings to the congregation, each believer is involved. As the congregation formulates questions, the small groups can wrestle with them and report back. The counsel of other congregations can be found in larger gatherings and conferences as the path of discipleship is sought.

Involvement of members in decision-making around the Scriptures is integral to many new forms of the church as they seek faithful discipleship. The issue of the authority of the leadership group of the congregation is still present. In the Reba Place Fellowship the board of elders has considerable authority in contrast to the coordinators of the Assembly in Goshen. The internal convictions of the believers and the springs of Spirit-led motivation are essential to avoid a new legalism.

Witness

Finally, the Believers' Church holds that wherever God gathers a believing community, there witness and sharing of the message of Christ will take place, motivated by love in the face of any kind of opposition and conflict. The conviction is strong that the Spirit who gathers and governs is also a sending Spirit (Littell, 1964: 110).

As the Holy Spirit binds people together who have turned from self-centeredness to the shared life in the love of Christ there a witness is given in regard to God's act in the world. The congregation itself becomes a witness to the fact that God sent Christ to change people and bring into being a new order of community (Yoder, 1969: 273). The essential base for the witness which any group wishes to give must root in its own life as an evidence of the work and power of the Holy Spirit. Only when the Holy Spirit binds people together in a caring, shepherding, and discerning community is there an adequate base for witness that goes beyond. This means that the form of the congregation must make provision for mutual support and for discernment in primary and larger groups in reciprocal relationships.

It is out of such groups then that witness will emerge. Persons will be invited to observe in the small groups and see how Christian people can live in openness and acceptance one with another. Out of such groups love will flow in deeds of witness which are then explained as questions are asked. The deed and the word are held together under the work and witness of the Holy Spirit.

When God's people give their witness, conflict will arise from those who hold values of a different order. It is here that suffering love and nonresistance take on meaning. Such nonresistance is God's method of the cross as the word of witness goes out (Hershberger, 1958d) and a participation in the victory of Christ over the powers of the age (Yoder, 1969: 269).

In summary, the forms of the covenant community must grow out of biblical understandings on the functions of the people of God. New forms must provide channels to release these functions in a changing age. Each generation will need to rethink its forms so that they do not become the goal in themselves.

7

Nonresistance, Nonviolent Resistance, and Power

J. Lawrence Burkholder

It would be difficult to exaggerate the influence of Guy F. Hershberger upon Mennonite life and thought. His writings bring together ideas which were implicit within the Mennonite tradition but which were largely inchoate before his time. He helped the Mennonite Church to make explicit its ethical norms and its basic stance toward society. He was so clear and decisive that his social position has come to be regarded as an important alternative in contemporary Christian thought.

His book *War, Peace, and Nonresistance* set forth an approach to peace which has been regarded by many not simply as a volume on peace but by implication on ethics as well. It was written in the midst of World War II. It came at a time when only a discriminating position on peace and war would help the Mennonites to resist the national pressures and passions of the time.

Not only did Hershberger articulate a Mennonite position but he was most intent upon distinguishing it from other religious and humanistic approaches to peace. In so doing he reinforced the ideological consciousness of Mennonites and their sense of identity. He helped to provide an ideological framework not only for several generations of pastors and laymen but for young scholars as well.

The question must be raised, however, as to whether Hershberger's way of stating the peace position is adequate for our time. Much has happened since 1944. The Mennonites are no longer a rural people. They are now involved in business and the professions. Their scholarly endeavors have brought new understandings of the world. Today their conscience is informed by the findings of psychology, sociology, political science, metaphysics, and ethics. This means that Mennonites today view the world as a complex reality far

J. Lawrence Burkholder is president and professor of Bible and philosophy at Goshen College. He was formerly professor in the Department of the Church at Harvard Divinity School and has served the Mennonite Church in pastoral and educational leadership.

removed from the simplicity of rural life. It is incumbent, therefore, upon the present generation to rethink many aspects of the Mennonite position if it is to serve our times. This brief essay is intended to lift up just one of the major concepts which were elaborated in *War, Peace, and Nonresistance.*

The main problem has to do with Hershberger's understanding of nonresistance as the determinative if not exclusive principle of peace.

Hershberger attempts to delineate a view which he considers at once biblical and consistent. He insists that nonresistance is precisely what the word means. It means that one does not resist in any way an enemy or those in power, even for the sake of justice.

One can, of course, refuse to obey authorities when what is demanded violates a biblically based principle. However, he makes it abundantly clear that one does not resist for the sake of "getting justice" for oneself or others. Rather, one "does justice" for others. One does justice in personal relations and turns the other cheek when oppressed.

Nonresistance is really a way of life which is called "the way of the cross." Nonresistance eventually becomes a total approach to life that not only defines the response of Christians in actual cases of conflict, but results in a stance that is deliberately calculated to avoid conflict. Cross-bearing takes the form of nonparticipation in the struggles of society—particularly struggles in the political arena. Nonresistance and cross-bearing become the search for neutrality.

A perfect illustration of the implication of nonresistance for social action is found in Hershberger's proposal for nonparticipation in the labor struggles during an earlier period of American history. Hershberger proposed that Mennonites work in the union shop with the understanding that they would pay union dues but have nothing to do with the struggle for economic power either on the side of management or labor. Thus nonresistance becomes a kind of nonpolitical quietism and voluntary weakness.

Hershberger goes to great length to contrast "biblical nonresistance" with "nonviolent resistance." He quotes Reinhold Niebuhr in support of his claim that these conceptions are distinct and that the one is biblical and the other is not. He says in agreement with Niebuhr that "with clarity of analysis he [Niebuhr] shows that the doctrine of the New Testament is an absolute nonresistance which makes no compromise with the relativities of politics." (Hershberger, 1944c: 224.)

Hershberger goes on to show that there is no place in the life of the Christian for nonviolent resistance. In this connection he contrasts biblical nonresistance with Gandhi's concept of *satyagraha. Satyagraha,* however nonviolent, is a form of coercion. Gandhi, as is well known, used *satyagraha* as a method by which to force British compliance.

As Hershberger says, "Besides fasting and prayer, *satyagraha* uses such methods as negotiation, arbitration, agitation, demonstration, the ultimatum, the general strike, picketing, the sit-down strike, economic boycott, nonpayment of taxes, emigration, non-co-operation, ostracism, civil disobedience, and setting up a new government to take the place of the old" (1944c:221).

, Thus, by making such a hard and fast distinction between nonresistance and nonviolent resistance and turning them against each other, Hershberger cuts the theoretical ground out from under those who would participate directly in social action. The reason is simple enough—nonviolent resistance is resistance; resistance is a form of force; force is inadmissible in any form.

In reality the ramifications of nonresistance as an absolute, all-pervasive principle of life, of course, go further than withdrawal from the relativities of political life and revolutionary processes. It produces a psychological type. By exalting the absence of conflict rather than the peaceful resolution of conflict, it encourages passivity. By cutting across normal aggressive tendencies, nonresistance implies a kind of goodness which is measured more in terms of the number of people not offended than the number of people loved.

It should be pointed out, however, that it has been possible for Mennonites to make a significant nonrevolutionary, nonpolitical contribution to society even within what are ordinarily regarded as the limits of nonresistance. I refer to many good works of a personal nature under church auspices in relief work and various kinds of services.

Mennonites have found ways through which human suffering has been alleviated and local needs have been met in a sacrificial manner. Voluntary service has become a way of life. However, Mennonites have found it difficult to go beyond personal and institutional services. They have found it especially difficult to effect social change through political and social structures. The difficulty has a number of roots, but the main root is nonresistance interpreted as the absolutization of the freedom of others.

The question arises, however, whether the difference between nonresistance and nonviolent resistance, while analytically clear, can be and needs to be the sole theoretical principle operative in loving service and peacemaking. I would contend that we have driven ourselves into an unnecessary ideological trap. Without denying the essential difference between nonresistance and nonviolent resistance, I would claim that, rightly interpreted, there is a place for both in the life of the Christian. By making a place in principle for nonviolent resistance, it is possible to enlarge one's scope of activities in the world.

What is the basis for nonviolent resistance? It is the same as the basis for nonresistance: namely, the life and teachings of Christ. It can be shown, I believe, that Jesus in His life brought together attitudes and actions, some of which incorporated the principle of nonviolent resistance and others that demonstrated nonresistance. It is instructive to see how these are related to each other. Their relationship throws light not only on ethics but also on psychology.

That Christ died a nonresistant death is without dispute. When the authorities arrested Him in the Mount of Olives, He did not resist. Rather, He accepted the cross in the tradition of the Suffering Servant of Isaiah 53. In so doing He showed how far love would go. The extreme pouring-out of nonresistant love became for His followers a paradigm of the love of God. The cross, which symbolized complete sacrifice, became the central symbol of Christianity.

However, we must distinguish between the nonresistance of the cross and what led to the cross. What led to the cross was an aggressive confrontation with the Jewish authorities in which Jesus criticized the status quo and presented Himself as the legitimate Ruler of Israel.

His entry into Jerusalem was provocative, and the cleansing of the temple was a most audacious, coercive act. Turning over the tables of the money-changers is, to be sure, not an instance of injurious violence, but it can hardly be said to be the expression of pure nonresistance.

During much of His ministry, Jesus was in conflict with the rulers of Israel, and He deliberately cultivated conflict by healing on the Sabbath and criticizing the Pharisees. Appparently, Jesus did not think that His aggressive dealings with the authorities violated the law of love. Rather, it would suggest that love can take certain forms of resistance.

In our attempt to understand the fullness of Christ's life and teaching, it is necessary to see that there are many sides to His life. All too often, Christian spokesmen have emphasized one side to the exclusion of the other.

It is evident that Jesus was tender and forgiving. He taught peacefully in the countryside and on the mountaintop, but He also stirred up the nation. For this He was crucified as an insurrectionist. To be sure, He was crucified unjustly, but the charges leveled against Him had some basis insofar as Jesus confronted the nation as a political alternative.

The main issue in Jesus' approach to the nation was the issue of violence. That Jesus was tempted to use violence in the tradition of Holy War is clear from the account of Jesus' wilderness temptation. The possibility of using divine military power was probably the crucial issue of His life.

Many people in His day advocated a military solution. The country was rife with so-called Zealots, who sought to liberate Israel by the sword. Several of Jesus' own disciples were Zealots. What was at stake was the nature of God and His way of dealing with a sinful world. Will God bring in the kingdom by might or by a spiritual power?

Jesus rejected destructive power. He would suffer defeat of His purposes before He would use the sword. The sword is the way of the devil (Mark 8:33). Hence, Jesus devoted His life to a reinterpretation of the conception of the Messiah as One who is nonviolent.

We must not draw from this, however, that the decision to be nonviolent was a decision to be nonresistant in the sense that there is no place in the service of God for resistance. Jesus resisted the authorities by use of various ways and by various means. *This leads then to the main point of this essay: namely, that the issue is not between nonviolence and nonresistance, but between violence and various forms of nonviolence.*

Nonviolence is the way of God, but nonviolence can take the forms of resistance in certain circumstances, and it may take the form of nonresistance in others. When Jesus was apprehended in the garden before His crucifixion, the only alternatives left were violence or nonresistance. There was no use in resisting even nonviolently. Hence, He chose to be absolutely nonresistant.

We would gather from this that nonresistance is not the substantive principle of the Christian life as some have tried to make it. It is, rather, the extreme to which one may suffer ill at the hands of one's enemies. Apparently, Jesus decided to die rather than to destroy other people. The healing of the high priest's slave's ear in the garden symbolized in a dramatic way His decision to do no violence.

This would suggest that both nonviolent resistance and nonresistance are genuine alternatives to violence; they belong together in the same life. The danger of making nonresistance into an absolute is that it leads logically to a lifestyle that is so withdrawn from the conflicts of the world that the real cross is seldom encountered.

The "cross" that is encountered is more likely to be a psychological one. This, however, is a cross without nails—a cross like that of Simon of Cyrene. It is carried and it is heavy, but it is a burden, not a cross. The cross of Christ is one that is imposed by the world upon those who confront the world and try to change it.

Only those who really disturb the peace bear the cross. Had Martin Luther King, Jr., not resisted the world through various forms of moral and political intervention, he would probably be alive today. The people who bear the cross today are those who try to change things. Ironically, those who withdraw from world conflict as the "way of the cross" seldom die on a cross.

If the above analysis is correct, the question which faces the church is how to use power in a Christian way. This is a difficult question. It is far more difficult than the question of how to be nonresistant. It means that we must learn how to relate love to the struggle for justice—a problem which was seldom faced positively by previous generations of Mennonites.

In our contemporary situation it is a search for the meaning of "Christian power." Can we develop both in theory and in practice a concept of power which will include certain Christian qualities which have been emphasized especially in our tradition—simplicity of heart, patience, openness, honesty, kindness, forgiveness, prayer, and a sense of the presence and power of God?

There are those, of course, who would see the attempt to mix love with power as futile as trying to mix oil and water. However, life is capable of mixtures in practice which cannot be set forth abstractly. Most of our relationships contain elements of power and love, law and grace, sternness and flexibility. Any businessman, college administrator, minister, or parent knows that somehow power and care for others can and must be mixed, albeit imperfectly. The point is that they cannot be mixed thoughtlessly.

In order to cope with the facts, those of us who respect and revere Guy Hershberger for his pioneering work in Christian ethics must now move into new and uncharted waters. We must incorporate into our ethical calculus such realities as power, complexity, relativity, tension, and compromise. These are all loaded with dangers. The specter of a fundamentally different ethic as a result of incorporating the language of ambiguity must be recognized as a threat. The long shadow of

Augustine, Luther, Calvin, Troeltsch, and Niebuhr lies near at hand. It would behoove us, however, to seek an ethic which stops short of violence but which at the same time makes a place for the necessities of personal and corporate existence. Good homework would include study of Tillich's *Love, Power, and Justice (1954)*. His ontological analysis of reality enables the new definitions and perspectives that our situation demands.

What is called for is a Mennonite ethic that will justify in theory what is generally accepted in practice. This really means that Mennonites must move in theory from an absolutist ethic to an ethic that engages honestly the relativity of a complex reality. It means the end of innocence and the beginning of a vast and troublesome quest for places to draw the line short of pure nonresistance. To be sure, if one accepts relativity into his system a thousand new questions arise. If nonviolent resistance is accepted, what are the limits of nonviolence? If, as some say, it is necessary to do evil in order to do good, how much evil and what kinds of evil may be permissible? If evil is used that good may result, in what sense is it evil? If ethical situations are ambiguous in the sense that they contain necessary and indivisible forms of good and evil, how do we correlate them with the will of God?

These are just a few of the issues that must be faced. But in responding to the acknowledged difference between the actual situation and the ethical ideal, let us hope that the enduring power of the original vision of discipleship may continue to inspire heroic efforts for righteousness, compassion, and justice. To turn from a nonfunctioning absolutism to a functioning relativism, with regard to some perplexing contemporary issues, is not to abandon the way of the cross, but to call for creative imagination, courage to face suffering, and a renewed commitment of faith to follow in that way.

8

Institutions, Power, and the Gospel

Calvin Redekop

Introduction

"You got power, I got power, all of God's children got power; when I gets to heaven, gonna use my power. . . ." But the problem with power may indeed be *whether* one gets to heaven rather than *when,* for any serious reading of the Gospels and the New Testament in general raises serious doubts about the availability of heavenly mansions for those who "lord it over others"; the mansions, according to Jesus, are reserved, rather, for those who came to serve others—"whoever would be great among you must be your servant" (Matthew 20:25 ff., RSV).

The sobering fact is, however, that Christians do become embroiled in human structures and order, that they do exercise power, whether they are aware of it or not. Christian groups, congregations, and denominations become involved in almost all the dimensions of institutionalization and power that any secular organization does and in some ways, to be discussed below, they do a poorer job than many secular groups in solving the basic dilemmas.[1]

Although the Christian exercise of power has been seriously neglected in scholarly analysis (Hammond and Johnson, 1970: 149), the Christian church itself has wrestled throughout its history with the problem of institutions and power. The establishment of a division of labor between the deacons and the apostles in Jerusalem, the lines of authority that developed into presbyters and the head presbyter (bishop), the establishment of the center of the church at Rome under the chief bishop, the development of the Roman Catholic ecclesiastical system, the emergence of monastic orders, national churches, the establishment of church boards and church colleges, the emergence of religious communes—these are examples from a rich and comprehensive stream of events in the struggle of the Christian church to solve the

Calvin Redekop is vice president of the college and professor of sociology at Tabor College, Hillsboro, Kansas. Formerly professor of sociology at Goshen College, he has published several books and has been active in the Church, Industry, and Business Association

question of how the sacred dimensions of the gospel can be made incarnate, without the church's becoming simply another secular movement.

The "Being-Doing" Dilemma

The basic problem regarding power and institutions in the context of the Christian church is that the gospel and the Christian movement, quite apart from their continuity with the Jewish tradition which already provided a complex institutional system, embrace two orientations that are in tension: the message of a new being (a new status) and the message of a mission (a goal-achieving system).[2] The former emphasizes a new state of things: "Therefore if any one is in Christ, he is a new creation" (2 Corinthians 5:17, RSV); this suggests a quality of existential being—not by works, but by grace—a gift (Tillich, 1951: 163 ff.). The second emphasis is on becoming and doing: "Follow me and I will make you become fishers of men" (Mark 1:17, RSV); "Do not be conformed to this world but be transformed by the renewal of your mind, that you may prove what is the will of God, what is good and acceptable and perfect" (Romans 12:2, RSV).

If the former element of the gospel were the total message, the problem of power and institutions would be irrelevant, for a state of being tends to be an existential ahistorical state, *i.e.,* nonteleological. But the Christian message is also historical, process-oriented, purposive (Kaufman, 1968: 258). It presents a new state of being or experience, but it also promotes a becoming—a striving toward a historical unfolding, a denouement. This dual emphasis is, of course, not restricted to Christianity, but underlies much of the philosophical musings in human history. There are many "fault lines" that indicate the tension between the two orientations; one of the most pronounced is the difference between the Eastern metaphysics, which has tended to be "being"-oriented (although, of course, with many contradictions and conflicts) and the Western, which has tended to be achievement—or "doing"—oriented.[3]

The dilemma for the Christian gospel is that the becoming or purposive orientation introduces questions of power and institutionalization, for one of the basic axioms of human experience is that in order to achieve something, humans have to exert power and effect organization! Thus in Acts 6 (RSV), we read, "Now in these days when the disciples were increasing in number, the Hellenists murmured against the Hebrews because their widows were neglected in the daily distribution. . . . Therefore, brethren, pick out from among you . . . men of good repute, full of the Spirit and of wisdom, whom we may appoint to this duty. But we will devote ourselves to prayer and to the ministry of the word" (vv. 1-4).

We find here a vivid illustration of the conflict between being and doing. While the new Christians were breaking bread together, fellowshiping together, and praising God (experiencing being), there was a dramatic development in the doing (organization and process). New disciples were added daily, and order had to be created, so bureaucrats were appointed, an event immediately differentiating them from the apostles, who apparently continued to do the more important things. The church was not only pure fellowship, "a spiritual communion with its utterly personal character," as Brunner characterizes it (1953: 77); it was also an organization of persons, ordered in a specific way to achieve further goals beyond the experiencing of the new being.

It is interesting to note that some church historians maintain that the transition from the "communion of persons" to an institution took place through the administration of communion (the sacraments) and its liturgy (Brunner, 1953: 76; Oetting, 1964: 40). It was ironically at the center of the new life, the fellowshiping with God and with each other, the most essential nature of the new being, that structure and organization began. When this process has been completed, according to Brunner, Christians "*receive* the body of Christ, instead of *being* the body of Christ." Brunner concludes by saying, "Institutionalism is produced by sacramentalism" (1953: 77).

Other scholars of the early Christian movement maintain that the concepts of power and institutions can be seen from two perspectives: (1) the functional view that emphasizes the need/response pattern illustrated above; and (2) the normative view, in which certain structures that emerged in the early Christian movement are seen as the essence of a Christian order. Thus the "spiritual order" of the Christian church includes the "offices" and institutions of the "Church itself as divinely instituted" (Dombois, 1963: 117). The gospel, the sacraments, and the ministry, the community in its responsive functions such as preaching and teaching, pastoral care, service to the needy, and social action are all seen as constitutive of the church. And even though power and institutions are present, they are not relevant or threatening to the church's essence.

Whether power and the institutionalization process in the Christian context began when the liturgy and the sacraments were first

administered, or are seen as being constitutive of the church or a combination of both, it is clear that the Christian church has had to face the
fact of power and the development of institutions, because it is involved in *doing* as well as *being*. The institutionalization of the church,
and its use of organization and power must therefore be ascribed, not
to some fatal mistake in the early experience, nor to the Jewish tradition out of which it came, nor to a concept of inherent spiritual order in
Christianity. If the Christian message includes a mission, it will by
definition take on the form of institutions and join with other movements or aspects of human culture, which are also concerned about
achieving certain goals (Kaufman, 1968: 378 ff., 479 ff.).

We have established the pervasive presence of institutionalism and
the exercise of power. The tension between these two concepts and the
essence of Christianity, which was postulated above, needs to be
examined more carefully, however, if the discussion is to have much
relevance. The best evidence for the continuing tension between the institutional nature of the church and its use of power, and the "being"
dimension, is the continual anti-institutional renewal that has taken
place in the history of the Christian church. Indeed, as has been
recently maintained, the history of religion can be seen as the development of organization and "anti-structure" (Turner, 1974). The continuing tendency for the Christian church to become a corporation
with all the dimensions of power and institutionalism has been
countered by movements to return the church to a state of simple being
or pure "communion." Church renewal, whether the reference is to the
monastic movement of the fourth century, or the Reformation, or the
contemporary Pentecostal movement, illustrates the structure-anti-
structure process. The Reformation thus needs to be viewed to a large
extent as the struggle over where the reality of the church resides—in its
experience, or in its structures (Peachey, 1956a:217).

The Nature of Power and Institutions

We need to define power and institutions before we can proceed
further in the argument. *Power* is defined scientifically as "the ability to
mobilize collective energies, commitments, and efforts" (Light and
Keller, 1975: 197). Individual power is the ability to choose, to mobilize
energy for personal objectives. Social power means the ability to mobilize others; it can vary all the way from *influence*, which implies voluntary compliance on the part of others, to *coercion*, which implies compliance without concurring. Influence normally derives from personal

characteristics in the relationship, while coercion normallly implies the use of force to achieve one's goals.[4]

Authority is the legitimate use of power—that is, a person can achieve behavior compliance on the part of another person because the one obeying assumes that the authority figure has the right to command others. An army officer, by virtue of his authority, can order his men to enter a "suicidal" battle, even though every foot soldier would rather not give up his life. Authority can be further subdivided into three subtypes: *rational authority*—"resting on a belief in the 'legality' of patterns of normative rules and the right of those elevated to authority under such rules to issue commands (legal authority)" (Weber, 1947: 328); *traditional authority*— "resting on an established belief in the sanctity of immemorial traditions and the legitimacy of the status of those exercising authority under them" (Weber, 1947: 328); and *charismatic*—"resting on devotion to the specific and exceptional sanctity, heroism, or exemplary character of an individual person" (Weber, 1947: 328).

Institution, the other important and integrally related concept, refers to the complex set of "norms that cohere around a relatively distinct and socially important complex of values . . ." (Williams, 1941: 29). It is the pattern of norms, symbols, roles, and physical facilities organized to achieve certain specified ends. Institutions normally find expression most clearly in organizations or associations; they can be illustrated by a specific family, or by an organization like General Motors. Institutions can vary from the very informal and unstructured, such as mate selection in our society, to a total institution such as a prison or mental hospital.

Institution, or the normative system which develops to achieve values, thus consists of the establishment of positions (specifications of persons in given relationships to others), norms (obligations and rights of persons in given positions), and the facilities (buildings, furnishings, symbols, and the like) that are necessary to achieve the goals. The Christian faith produced a growing complex of institutions as it grew and prospered in achieving its mission. The *problem* with institutional structures is that they tend to channel, limit, hinder, truncate, harden, and routinize human relationships in ways contrary to the intent of the gospel.

Institutions and power thus are particularly problematical for the Christian church, because its normative system is premised on the concept of *koinonia* (fellowship), where relationships are free of manipulative or coercive aspects. Institutions with their inherent necessity to use power, even though usually legitimate power, thus tend to militate against the *koinonia* or communal dimension of the Christian faith. To the degree that power and institutions tend to undermine the fellowship aspect of the Christian experience, they are problematical and in tension.

Institutions and power may be consistent with the Christian experience of being to some degree, but there comes a point where institutional process and power create conflict; ethical tension begins when more emphasis is put *on the job to be done,* than on the *relationship between the persons.* In the vast area of gray between the pure *koinonia* (fellowship) and the total coercive institution, the Christian church does most of its living, and here the greatest tension occurs.[5]

The personal influence exercised in ecstatic fellowship is also power, but it is presumably sanctioned by the Spirit. The social authority exercised over individuals in the giving of tithes is another form of power that has biblical legitimation. But what about the revival meeting practice, for example, of singing the last verse of "Just as I Am" *one more time?* Is this pure fellowship or is it a mixture of motives ranging all the way from personal style to mass manipulation? Other examples could be cited.

The question is not solved simply by suggesting that all legitimate power (authority) is Christian, and that all illegitimate uses of power are unchristian and hence sinful. The question becomes rather how we can know when legitimate power (legal, traditional, or charismatic) is consistent with the *being* nature of Christianity. It is not possible to answer this question without examining the being aspect of the Christian tradition; unfortunately, space does not allow us to develop fully this aspect. We will need to accept a viewpoint and proceed from there. One recent treatment states, "If peace is the message and mission of the community of the Spirit, its inner quality and dynamic is love (agape). . . . *Agapeic* mutuality calls for *koinonia*—fraternal relationship and responsibility which rests not on mutual ability to reciprocate but on an *agapeic* identification with the person in need which makes him, neighbor and brother," (Kraus, 1974: 81, 89).

Ideally, there should not be any distinctions between persons in the Christian fellowship, if the above statement is valid. But as has been indicated earlier, goal achievement demands that power be exercised in the Christian church, leading inevitably to considerable institutionalization in its life. Some dimensions of this process are:

1. The determination of the essence and goals of the Christian movement itself. Historically, various forms of leadership, beginning with the apostles, have filled this function. As long as the determination of goals is the work of apostles and prophets whose spiritual credentials are accepted, the problems of power are not as pressing, but when there is no prophecy, no charismatic gift, or when the people do not respond, then the issues of inequality and power emerge. The Christian movement's determination of its goals has tended to devolve upon persons who used position, inherited status,or sheer politics to shape the direction of the movement, for genuine prophets have tended to become increasingly scarce.

2. The division of labor in Christian life and action. The worship, fellowship, proclamation, and service aspects of the Christian movement could not proceed without the division of labor. It was not possible, for example, to continue to worship without some type of order, in which various persons were given responsibilities in leading the liturgy. Ideally, all Christians would be proclaiming the Word of God, but in fact, special training, abilities, and experiences were required to proclaim effectively. As the division of labor developed, it was necessary that coordination, levels of communication, and authority structures emerge. A division of labor, according to sociologists, tends to create unequal responsibility, authority, knowledge, and prestige, which in turn creates an unequal access to legitimate power. Placing persons in a structure with responsibilities and superordination and subordination thus assumes and necessitates the use of legitimate power—authority.

3. The emergence of tradition. Sociology has analyzed the development of customs and traditions, and has determined that what people customarily do over a period of time tends to receive the aura of rightness and sacredness. Individual behavior, group experiences, tribal activities, and societal actions tend to become habitual and routine, and finally serve as the source for continuity, identity, and morals. Thus individuals may desire to innovate, or to act in freedom, but it may be very difficult because of the "way it has always been done around here." This type of coercion could be illustrated by the parish priest who is not able to make changes because of the rule of the bishop, or by the young person who submits to baptism because it is assumed that he does so when he gets to be of age.

The Christian movement has developed a rich and profound tradition. Each element in it has been justified on the basis of its historical meaning, and usually makes sense when understood in its context. In fact the self-understanding of the religious movement (its theology) has in large measure depended on the interpretation of what happened and how it helped to explain what was happening at the moment of reflection. This process, of course, has acted to make even more important the past events and procedures so that they become legitimate, just, and holy (Kaufman, 1968: 85 ff.). But tradition can be the most oppressive form of institutionalism because it allows norms and positions to coerce individuals in a way not even physical force can.

The difficulty that legitimate institutional power poses for the Christian movement is that in almost all its dimensions it is contrary to the "being" dimension. That is, the values of "being," which include fellowship, love, joy, equality, spontaneity, and the like, tend to be undermined in the "doing" aspect which, as indicated above, is premised on the allocation of position, status, prestige, and power itself. Relationships based on *power differentials* cannot easily be harmonized with the Christian teachings on how persons are to relate to each other. What has complicated the problem even further has been the tendency to legitimize the different statuses through a "baptism" of holiness and mystery. Thus even though the role of preacher may be a power position, it is given the sanction of being set apart on spiritual grounds. Thus "sanctification" of status difference has been an effective way to harmonize the inherent contradictions of the nature of Christianity and its practice as it attempts to achieve its goals.

A Christian View of Power and Institutions

It is the central thesis of this chapter that the problem of institutions and power for the Christian church is not institutional and power per se, but the fact that institutional structures and power tend to create differences among persons who are to be bound only by the norm of love and peace. The Christian church has from its inception been institutionalized and has exercised power, as we have seen. Any denial of this fact indicates a misunderstanding of the history of the Christian religion. The gray zone between outright coercion (an illegitimate use of power that ought to be rejected out of hand) and pure fellowship is thus the zone where authority is legitimate, but it is also the realm of status differentials.

The Christian gospel teaches the equality of all men before God—all were sinners, but now have become sons of God; all differences of sex, nationality, race, and social status have been obliterated, and persons are all one in Christ. The Christian, if he were seriously to follow Christ, would love his neighbor as himself, and lay down his life for his friends. But in actuality, the goals of the Christian movement have not been achieved only by loving the neighbor or laying down one's life for the neighbor in the abstract, but by organizing people to get the task done—and that involves exercising power over others.

But before simply accepting this dilemma, let us look at institutional relationships and power a little more closely. In spite of all I have said above, it is important to note that institutions do vary in the degree and manner in which they allocate and use power.

Theorists have analyzed human relations along dimensions such as those made famous by Talcott Parsons.[6] He proposes that human relations can vary along four dimensions: (1) *Self-gratification versus Discipline*—gratifying selfish desires on the one extreme and subordinating selfish goals totally to the wishes of the collective society on the other; (2) *Universalistic versus Particularistic Values*—treating everyone on the basis of universal norms versus relating to others on a personal and subjective basis; (3) *Ascription versus Achievement*—determining the relationship on the basis of the intrinsic reality of the individual versus relating to him on the basis of his performance or achievements; (4) *Specificity versus Diffuseness*—relating to a person on the basis of a particular task or goal-oriented objective versus relating to him on the basis of his whole being (1951: 57-67).

Most theorists conclude therefore that human relationships in institutional settings can be evaluated, in fact, need to be evaluated, along a normative or value dimension. That is, human interaction can be judged from a value/ethical point of view; each society has a value system that indicates what types of behaviors and interactions are desirable and should be supported. Institutions therefore *can* be less or more humane in terms of the particular society's own values!

The power symbolized by coercion is generally repudiated in most societies and hence is not supported in social institutions. Legitimate authority is at the basis of institutions; it is present in religious institutions as well. All three forms of authority defined above have been exercised in religious and Christian institutions, depending upon specific times and places.

From the specifically Christian perspective, it is difficult to insist categorically that one of the three forms of scientifically defined authority is most in harmony with the Christian gospel, for all three are present in the development of the Christian movement. Certainly Jesus used all three types: (1)*Charismatic authority* was expressed in statements such as "It has been said of old, but I say unto you. . ."; (2) "Not one jot or tittle shall be removed until the whole law has been fulfilled . . ." typified the *legal authority;* (3) "Think not that I came to destroy the law and the prophets: I came not to destroy but to fulfill" expresses solidarity and support for *traditional authority.*

It would seem therefore that the *type* of legitimate power (charismatic, legal, or traditional authority) is not the basis for the determination of the degree to which institutional structures and process contradict the Christian gospel, but rather the *degree* to which the power is used to continue the implied status differential and domination inherent in the situation. Power itself is not the issue, for the New Testament assumes it at every turn ("But you shall receive power when the Holy Spirit has come upon you . . ."), but what is immoral is the use of power to perpetuate or even entrench the status differences and domination that power enables. In a positive vein then, it is the assumption of this author that power is a vital force in human society, and that when it is used to assist others to become powerful also, it is in line with social values and the Christian tradition.[7]

Christian denominations, district or regional organizations, retreat centers, publishing houses, mission boards, Sunday school boards, young people's organizations, men's groups, women's groups, committees, study conferences (the list could go on and on)—all are institutional structures of the church that exert power. But the effects of power and institutions must be judged on the basis of whether they are consistent with the general system of Christian teaching. On this level, many Christian institutions and uses of power might be found inadequate and wanting.

In the Christian context the judgment of the use of power and institutions thus becomes critical: do the institutional structures and their possession of power tend to perpetuate the power differentials and even enhance them, or do they act as enablers to allow all persons to become brothers, "one in Christ," where there "is one body and one Spirit, just as you were called to the one hope that belongs to your call, one Lord, one faith, one baptism, one God and Father of us all, who is above all, and through all and in all" (Ephesians 4:3 ff., RSV)?

The normative Christian use of power, defined as increasing the power of all, is presented in the same passage as that cited above: "And his gifts were that some should be . . . for the equipment of the saints, for the work of ministry, for building up the body of Christ . . ."

(Ephesians 4:11 ff., RSV). It is clear that Paul assumes that gifts are a form of power but that they must be used for the edification and building up of the saints—the body of Christ which is one without distinctions, where power differentials will ultimately disappear as all are sanctified.

The liberating fact, therefore, is that the consequences of the use of power can be evaluated and sanctified. Thus, if a committee which is pursuing a desirable objective is actually helping others achieve more power either in relation to the committee's objectives or others, then the power use is justifiable and to be encouraged. If a young person who attends seminary and is installed as a pastor literally helps others become equipped to become powerful in the Spirit, if a church official (often called a bureaucrat) actually empowers others to become more free to be Christian disciples, then power has been used in the Christian manner. It is significant that the gifts of the Spirit as described in Ephesians and 1 Corinthians, as well as other places, are all of the kind that provide for the dissemination of power—for example, teachers. If knowledge is power, then a teacher is actively engaged in a distribution of power, for he helps others achieve as much power as he has (and if he is fortunate to have a few bright students, may be making them more powerful than he is).

Conclusion

There is really no way in which a treatise on institutions, power, and the gospel can be concluded. It is an ongoing dilemma, emerging and resolving itself in the daily process. Religious persons who become alienated from organized religion because of institutional power and its misuses are not more realistic about the nature of human existence than the individuals who exploit the institutional power opportunities for their own gain. A more reasonable stance is to accept the fact that religious movements must use power and create institutions—it is *how* they are used that makes the difference. This becomes one of the most profound challenges for the Christian movement.

But what makes the situation so disheartening is that Christians have often failed to acknowledge that the Christian movement needs to organize if it is to achieve its goals. Patterns of evasion have included millenarianism—Christ will return imminently and rule in person, thus we leave the problem of organization up to Him! Other evasions have been the Spiritualist-Pietist emphasis that ignores or downgrades the significance of sociological forces. But the most evasive and problematic response, one which has been used for many years in many Christian groups, is the denial of the problem's existence.

In one of the few specific studies of power and institutions, Harrison observes that "Baptist experience with autocratic associations indicates that congregational policy does not automatically prevent an inordinate concentration of power even at the local level" (1959: 196). One of the central conclusions of his study is that even when a theology does not allow institutional concentration of power, it is created nevertheless. He maintains that "it is impossible to think of any category of activity in which the local churches are engaged which is not significantly affected by the work and character of the denominational organizations" (203). But Baptist theology continues to deny the fact.

The theology of the Free Church tradition attempts to interpret the Scriptures as faithfully as possible and then to live by them.[8] It is especially antagonistic to those aspects of power and institutions that degrade, exploit, and dominate God's children. It has therefore rightly stressed the importance and reality of community. Hence the stress on communal living which has evidenced itself in various forms among Anabaptists, Brethren, and Quakers. Mennonites have been people of the land, where relationships were simple and democratic. The contemporary communal movement is in many ways a derivative of, and indebted to, the Anabaptist movement and the Free Church movement.

But the basic problem has been that members of this tradition have tended to ignore or deny the reality of institutions and power within its own borders. Thus in their internal life, Free Church groups like the Mennonites have used institutions and power to achieve their ends, but have tended to admit this reality only in hushed whispers in the hallways, while power is being "brokered" in the assembly. Hence the Mennonite church's use of excommunication and the ban has produced paradoxical situations that have never been fully examined. And there is little straightforward analysis of institutional structures and power in the scholarly or ecclesiological literature.[9]

In its relationship with institutions and power in the world, there is even more ambiguity and lack of clarity. The response of the Free Church to the institutional power of a Pentagon or State Department is at best cautious, unsure, and tentative. It has been stated that the only time nonresistant peace churches speak to institutional power is when "their own neck is in the noose," as, for example, the lobbying the Mennonites, Brethren, and Quakers exercised during World War II for achievement of exemption for "our boys." We can "speak truth to power," but that is the extent of our involvement with institutional power.

There is, of course, a good reason for the Free Church position regarding institutions and power, for institutions and power are not inherently regenerative or redemptive; in fact, as Lord Acton has reminded us, "Power tends to corrupt; absolute power corrupts absolutely." But institutions and power are the means to get things done; there is no other way. None of us, Christian or secular, is willing to relinquish power totally, even though we all espouse ideologies which decry its misuse and dangers. What is often done, however, is to sublimate the nature of power, for example, rejecting the power of the sword for the pen, as this author, however feebly, has tried to do as a life orientation. Most of us, whether members of the Free Church tradition or not, convince ourselves that we are sanctifying the fact of power by resorting to moral persuasion or the power of love and nonresistance. But if this essay has accomplished anything, it has made the point that "all of God's children" have *and use* power. The question is *how* is it used, and *what* is the outcome. A pacifist nonresistant ethic such as the one espoused in *The Way of the Cross in Human Relations* is undeniably faithful to the gospel, but a sociological analysis of the way this ethic (or any other ethic) is implemented reminds us that the institution and power question cannot so easily be thought away.

9

A Perspective on Mennonite Ethics

John Richard Burkholder

The various contributions to the present volume are testimony that the work of Guy F. Hershberger represents the major twentieth-century effort to synthesize and shape Mennonite ethical thinking. Hershberger, however, has not operated as an intellectual individualist, as the chapters by Gross and Schlabach demonstrate. His approach reflects continual sensitivity to the actual situation of the church—the peoplehood purporting to embody the Anabaptist Vision. For Guy Hershberger, history and community have always been decisive elements.

Other currents of thought in Mennonite ethics have of course appeared over the past three decades.[1] With Hershberger's work as a reference point, it seems appropriate on this occasion to examine some of these views, in an effort to clarify and redirect ethical discussion in the Mennonite context.

The Problem of Mennonite Ethics

In his classic essay, "The Anabaptist Vision," Harold S. Bender, after delineating the concepts of discipleship and the voluntary church, stated that the "third great element in the Anabaptist vision was the ethic of love and nonresistance as applied to all human relationships" (1944:51). It was in 1943 that Bender composed this presidential address to the American Society of Church History, using the occasion to make his case for the uniqueness of the Anabaptist perspective in the Reformation setting. At about the same time, Guy Hershberger was completing his substantial work, *War, Peace, and Nonresistance.* In his preface, Hershberger expressed the hope that the book would enable a better understanding of the faith and life of Mennonites. He emphasized that "nonresistance is a biblical principle, and a way of life, espoused by the Mennonites from the beginning of their history" (1944c:ix).

J.R. Burkholder, professor of religion and director of peace studies at Goshen College, is a member of the Assembly in Goshen. His writing and research interests include ethics, peace studies, and church-state issues.

Nonresistance, then, surely represents a key ethical category in Mennonite thought. J. Lawrence Burkholder has written that "nonresistance is the form and expression of love which has become almost synonymous with love itself for Anabaptists and Mennonites" (1958:85-86). Hershberger, in his mature work, has linked nonresistance, the love commandment, and the way of the cross as basic to the ethic of the Christian disciple. "Complete nonresistance," he has declared, is "pouring out one's love without reserve, even as Christ poured out His life completely on the cross for His enemies" (1958d:41).

Surely such words spell out a rigorous and demanding commitment. The "way of the cross" assumes the ever-present possibility of sacrifice. Hershberger writes: "When Jesus commissioned the disciples to live the good life in an evil world, He gave them a task which He frankly informed them would not be easy. . . . The Christian is called to endure hardness as a good soldier of Jesus Christ" (1958d:vii). But recognizing the high cost of faithfulness does not in itself make an ethic problematic. What, then, is the problem?

It is not difficult to accumulate evidence that Mennonites have not lived up to their strenuous ethic. Translating ideals into action is usually less than successful; even *assent* to the ideals has not been complete, as the recent Kauffman and Harder study of Mennonite members' attitudes has demonstrated (1975: chapter 8 especially). A survey of conference and committee proceedings, periodical literature, and pulpit denunciations could multiply examples of discrepancies between ethical statements and actual performance.[2]

So much for the practical questions of moral performance; our more basic concern is the theoretical adequacy of the ethical principle itself. The distinction between matters of theory and practice is not always clear, even in sophisticated ethical discourse, as John H. Yoder has observed in dealing with the concepts of "impossibility" and "necessity" as they have been employed in the thought of Reinhold Niebuhr. Yoder responds to Niebuhr's assumption of the impossibility of fully loving action by analyzing various kinds of impossibility. Some of these he has judged to be spurious, because real freedom of choice does exist (*e.g.,* the individual is unwilling to sacrifice or intentionally opts for a value other than absolute love). But where no existential freedom exists, there can be no guilt; "the existence of a moral imperative is meaningless if its accomplishment is excluded by definition" (Yoder, 1955: 113).

Similarly, "necessity" is instrumental rather than absolute; "there is no necessity of abandoning love as an ethical absolute unless something more important than love stands to be lost. This is in turn possible only if there is a moral absolute higher than love, and for a Christian such an absolute is difficult to imagine" (Yoder, 1955:113).

But the problem in ethical theory comes when the demands of love in themselves appear to be contradictory, so that they cannot be carried out without compromise. If love as nonresistance is an absolute ethic, apparently without limits, how does the disciple respond to competing neighbor claims that make contradictory demands? And if nonresistance seems to provide insufficient criteria for evaluating legitimate neighbor needs, how can it deal with the additional threat of an enemy—not just the disciple's enemy, but the neighbor's enemy? How does the disciple make love meaningful in a complex situation? Is nonresistance an adequate interpretation of love?

These are the questions that critics of absolute nonresistance raise. The critics object to the narrowing of the New Testament love commandment to a single principle presumed to be adequate for all instances. Paul Ramsey has put the issue succinctly and typically:

> Love, which by its nature would be non-resistant where only the agent's own rights and the perhaps unjust claims of a single neighbor are involved, may change its action to resistance by the most effective possible means, judicial or military, violent or non-violent, when the needs of more than one neighbor come into view. . . . Love not itself self-defensive . . . nevertheless will impel men to develop an ethics of protection lest injustice be done to innocent third parties. (Ramsey, 1950:165)

Ramsey affirms the absolutism of Jesus' nonresistant ethic in the person-to-person situation, but argues for a multilateral "ethics of protection" in relation to two or more neighbors. He finds support for this view in Jesus' harsh attitude to perpetrators of injustice, as found in such texts as Matthew 11:20-24; Matthew 18:23-35; Matthew 23; and Luke 20:45-47. But whether or not a preferential ethics of protection can be grounded in Jesus Himself, "beyond question Christian ethics soon developed such a view, the primitive pacifism generally practiced by early Christians so long as they were in a minority giving way to what were judged more effective means for assuming responsibility for the whole of organized society" (Ramsey, 1950:171-172).

Here is the fateful word: *responsibility!* What does it mean to be "responsible" to competing claims of neighbors, or to "the whole of organized society"?

Mennonite Ethics and Social Responsibility

Social responsibility has been the central challenge to Mennonite ethics in the twentieth century. No longer isolated either socially or geographically from the mainstream of Western "Christian" civilization, Mennonites have had to come to terms with the meaning of their nonresistant ethic for people now intimately involved in world affairs. On the practical level, sustained interaction with complex social and economic forces has tested the range and relevance of the nonresistance norm; the chapters in this volume by J. L. Burkholder, John Redekop, and Don Smucker illustrate the problem. And at the level of ethical theory, Mennonite thinkers have engaged in debate with the prominent voices of mainline Protestantism.

In the midst of World War II, Guy Hershberger was aware of Reinhold Niebuhr's critique of Christian pacifism; indeed, the index to *War, Peace, and Nonresistance* indicates that Niebuhr is the most-quoted source. Hershberger endeavored to meet accusations Niebuhr had made that Mennonites were parasites. He did this by way of an apology for nonresistance that was not only grounded in biblical obedience, but that also claimed more pragmatic justification. He argued that the nonresistant Christian community, modeled on the biblical "salt" and "light," provides a creative resource, bringing healing to human society in a manner that is beneficial, not parasitical (1944c:298-301).

Accusations of social irresponsibility were not new to Mennonites; the earliest charges against the Anabaptists of the sixteenth century emphasized the threat to the social order that the new movement represented. J. Lawrence Burkholder has observed that, although it was not their intention to promote revolution, "when a body of Christians such as the Anabaptists insists upon the higher righteousness as a consistent pattern of life, they may become not only a neutral quantity, but even a threat to society. This is one of the main reasons that the early Anabaptists were persecuted so severely" (Burkholder, 1958:31).

Among historians of Anabaptism, Walter Klaassen has written frequently on the revolutionary potential of the movement, as it was viewed by its contemporaries (1969:334; 1971:309-311; 1973:48-63). "The authorities, civil and ecclesiastical," he has said in a summary, "saw in Anabaptism a conspiracy against the social order" (1971:310).

Klaassen concludes that the Reformers were wrong in their certainty that the movement must turn to violence, "but it was a threat even in its basic nonviolent stance" (1971:311). Claus-Peter Clasen also emphasizes this dimension: "ironically, these meek people, who endeavored in the name of Christ to establish the kingdom of love, in reality seemed to be bent on destroying civilization" (1972:475).

From the viewpoint of the magisterial reformers, nonresistance was the prelude to chaos. Thus, the authorities who were charged with maintaining the social order saw Michael Sattler's refusal to take up arms against the Turks, the nemesis of Christian civilization, as both blasphemous and subversive. His subsequent martyrdom "reveals the dilemma of Christianity and social responsibility. Sattler was utterly irresponsible from the standpoint of the normal interests of the state" (Burkholder, 1958:96).

Political irresponsibility is still a central point for critics of Anabaptism. In a recent essay intended as a commemorative tribute on the 450th anniversary of the movement, Calvinist Lester DeKoster underlines the threat to the state that Anabaptism continues to represent. Ruling out the use of force, he believes, will unleash illegitimate violence. "The lawful use of force, in war, as well as in other ways, is the only alternative a society has to submersion in violence. . . . The Anabaptists were apprehended as seditious. At issue then, and now, is always the continuation of that order essential to social survival" (1975:77).

How have Mennonite ethicists responded to the charge of irresponsibility? John Howard Yoder, in his 1954 essay, "The Anabaptist Dissent," challenged the issue head-on. Utilizing classic church-sect terminology, he identified the basic sectarian dissent as "its refusal to assume responsibility for the moral structure of non-Christian society" (1954:46). Yoder argued that the fundamental shift in Christian thinking at the time of Constantine was not simply the establishment of a state church, but the identification of church and society that resulted in the "responsibility" assumption. Throughout the massive changes in other aspects of theology and church practice during the intervening centuries, neither Catholics nor Protestants ever questioned this assumption. Only sectarian groups such as the Anabaptists did so.

For Yoder, responsibility is God's problem, not the disciple's. He sees a clear dichotomy in God's dealing with the world in history, "with the Christian's conscious obedience limited to the realm of redemption, and God's providence working in the realm of conservation without the help of the Christian's compromising" (1954:51). "Because the work of the church is what gives real meaning to history, we need not be ashamed of our 'irresponsibility' in giving our attention as Christians to the church's particular tasks, and thus leaving to the 'good heathen' the functions, necessary but nonredemptive, which fail to accord with our particular mission" (1954:56).

Although the bold contrasts of this statement suggest a strategy of social withdrawal for the faithful church, Yoder's later writings deny this. Instead he calls for voluntary commitment to following Christ in meeting human need, for being both conscience and servant within society, witnessing against evil through involvement in the social order. What the Christian withdraws from is the temptation to run society from the top down—the form of responsibility that has been conventional ever since Constantine. There *is* a Christian responsibility to the social order, but it is based on an ethic shaped by a distinctive view of history and eschatology (see, for example, Yoder 1964:8-27; Yoder 1972a:55-88).

Guy Hershberger drew heavily on John Yoder's work in his 1958 critique of the "social responsibility" doctrine of the Christian Action group—Reinhold Niebuhr, John C. Bennett, and others. Hershberger found that their acceptance of the general social order as a basic frame of reference makes the task of the Christian harder than necessary, because their viewpoint "assumes social responsibility beyond that which God Himself has assigned to the Christian" (1958d:109). Their ethical preoccupation with the tragic necessity of compromise, coupled with a failure to lay hold of the redemptive power of the cross, leads to a human predicament with no escape. With a twist of irony, Hershberger, the proponent of strenuous discipleship, suggests that "they are making it more difficult to be a disciple of Christ than our Lord intends it to be" (1958d:110).

Two other Mennonite scholars addressed themselves to the responsibility question in 1958, offering perspectives that take us beyond Hershberger's position. Gordon Kaufman's provocative essay "Nonresistance and Responsibility" appeared in *Concern No. 6*, one of a pamphlet series published by a group of younger Mennonite thinkers concerned with questions of Christian renewal. Kaufman's thesis provoked replies in later issues of the series and was further developed in his 1961 book. But the most thorough study was one that received little attention, because it was buried away in the form of a doctoral dissertation: "The Problem of Social Responsibility from the Perspective of the Mennonite Church," submitted to the faculty of Princeton Theological Seminary by J. Lawrence Burkholder.

Burkholder examines the challenge for Mennonites, caught between a tradition of nonresistant noninvolvement and the pressures of modern societal and cultural trends, that the ecumenical doctrine of the responsible society poses. The conceptual categories he employs owe much to Ernst Troeltsch, Reinhold and Richard Niebuhr, and ecumenical church pronouncements. He accents the dilemma of the love ethic in a manner reminiscent of Paul Ramsey's statement above:

> Love itself demands responsible participation in society for it is in the social order that the Christian meets the neighbor. . . . If the corporate neighbor is to be the recipient of Christian love, the way to help him . . . is to engage in the struggle for justice through the use of social and political power. (Burkholder, 1958:33, 34.)

Burkholder accepts an interpretation of the ethic of Jesus that is purely religious, absolutist, and perfectionist—one that makes no concessions to the conditions of human sinfulness. Thus, he says "the clash between Christ's ethic and the facts of social existence are simply inescapable" (1958:47).

Following this acute positing of the problem, Burkholder reviews in substantial detail the theology and practice of classic Anabaptism under the heading of "Christianity as discipleship." He focuses attention on the development of the Mennonite Church community and the programs of missions and service that resulted from a combination of historical circumstances and the working out of the inner logic of discipleship over against the *corpus christianum* and the changed conditions of the modern world. The persistent challenge of responsibility ethics underscores the fundamental conflict between the absolutism of the way of the cross and the relativities of the social order. By way of conclusion, Burkholder states that Mennonites must come to terms with the inevitability of power and coercion, the necessity of compromise, the presence of ambiguity, and the ethical demand for justice. Nonresistance simply cannot serve as a comprehensive norm; rather, "love must take the form of justice if it is to be effective" (1958: 351). (In his chapter in this book, Burkholder expands one aspect of this position—the need to include nonviolent resistance in the Mennonite ethic.)

Burkholder's critique of traditional Mennonite formulations gives primary attention to phenomena external to the Mennonite position. On the one hand, he takes account of the actual social, cultural, and economic forces impinging on the semi-isolated Mennonite community; on the other, he takes seriously the ethics of justice and responsibility expressed by ecumenical churchmen. The movement of history and the wisdom of the "world" shape the Mennonite ethical dilemma. In contrast, Gordon Kaufman's argument claims to be rooted in the implications of the love ethic itself. He rejects the usual assumption of both pacifists and nonpacifists, that the nonresistance stance leads inevitably to withdrawal from social responsibility, for such withdrawal, he claims, negates the very nature of Christian love.

> Love is not that which keeps out of trouble, a means of remaining above and secure from the conflicts of this world. Love is precisely that which goes into the very heart of an evil situation and attempts to rectify it. . . . Christian love, as perfectly exemplified in God's act in Christ, sacrifices itself for and to sin; Christian love gives itself to its own enemies. (Kaufman, 1958:7, 8)

Thus, love must take responsibility for the sinful situation, for the sins of fellowmen and of society. This responsibility has three aspects: witness to the truth and right of the gospel as we understand it, full acceptance of the other's integrity to decide in freedom the form of his own response, and the obligation to support the other in his commitments even when we think him to be wrong. The "other" may be an individual or a society; in any case, love's radical self-giving concern for the other means involvement, not withdrawal. We dare not forsake those who take a course contrary to our convictions; indeed, we must identify with them. Love must support the other even in his wrongness, just as God remained faithful to erring Israel (Kaufman, 1958:18).

Kaufman emphasizes the responsibility of love to enable others to live up to their own best insights, rather than imposing our convictions on them. In practice, this may produce contradictions, such as the "paradox of a Christian writing to his Congressmen to vote in favor of a given conscription bill as the most adequate for the nation as a whole, but himself finding it necessary to refuse to register under that same bill in order to bear his witness to his deepest Christian convictions" (1958:25). This is not compromise, but a necessary consequence of love's freedom and adaptability.

In his later book, *The Context of Decision* (1961), Kaufman carries further his view of love as radical freedom:

> Love, in seeking to serve the *other,* must always *relate itself to that other in his actual situation.* . . . This requires that we take account of love's demand for justice *and* redemption *and* the fulfilling of our special responsibilities. (Kaufman, 1961:112; italics in original.)

For Kaufman, those special responsibilities are illustrated by the hypothetical case of a pacifist secretary of state in a nation with a majority of nonpacifists. The moral demands of the office determine the limits of his responsibilities and thus prevent him from exercising a pacifist foreign policy. But far from being ethical compromise, "it is precisely the radical demand of the Christian ethic to love without self-concern that may require one to serve his fellows through government position" (1961:112).

Albert Meyer and David Habegger responded to Kaufman's views in the pages of *Concern,* and John H. Yoder (whose sharp church/world dichotomy was criticized in Kaufman's essay) replied to the essentials of the Kaufman position in a lengthy review of *The Context of Decision.* All the respondents agree with Kaufman's rejection of the forced option of "withdrawal or responsibility"; they accept his claim that love must lead to active engagement in human affairs. But they question the absolutizing of "love" so that it seems to become an ethical abstraction distinct from the normative authority of Jesus Christ, and they challenge his apparent acceptance of secular society as the locus for defining responsibility.

Habegger suggests that Kaufman "so separates love and justice that love becomes amoral" (1959:35). The admonition simply to love the sinner, accepting his own ethical evaluation of his calling, leads to dangerous ambiguity. "Righteousness without love is unredemptive, but love without righteousness is mere sentimentality" (1959:34).

Yoder, recognizing that the gospel supports the claim that love must indeed risk entering even the most sinful situation, nevertheless asks just what should be done there. Does Kaufman imply "the sacrifice of one's moral commitments and the acceptance for oneself of ethical obligations which in themselves are in some sense 'sinful' " (Yoder, 1963:134)?

For Meyer, the crucial problem is the choice of loyalties that determine the Christian's priorities. In urging support in the name of love for either individuals or societies whose ethical stance is considered wrong by gospel standards, Kaufman in effect makes the ethic of the other ultimately determinative. But the Christian cannot be on all sides at once; his commitment "means a certain unavoidable separation from all societies but that unique society, the church of Christ" (Meyer, 1958:37).

This brief discussion of Kaufman's position, and the replies to it, help to illuminate the central problem with the ethic of social responsibility, as it is usually advocated by mainstream Christianity. Responsibility begins by assuming a necessary involvement in the course of events in the world arena—government, economics, culture, and the like. To remain outside the main currents of history is to be irresponsible, withdrawn, even parasitic. But when one inquires about the ethical judgments to be applied within this realm of responsibility, the advocates of involvement usually reject the stringent ethic of Jesus— whether the issue is pacifism, economic sharing, the exercise of power, or whatever. "Responsible" Christian ethics seldom questions the secular criteria for defining the requirements of the vocation; in effect, this reduces Christian love to pastoral and personal dimensions. As for structural and social issues, the ethics of responsibility offers little substantive difference from an enlightened humanism. Why should sectarian Christians be criticized for noninvolvement, if Christian participation makes so little difference in public policies and programs?

But perhaps there is a mode of involvement other than the uncritical acceptance that Kaufman's examples suggest. John H. Yoder, as noted above, is concerned with the *how* of involvement. He compares Kaufman's test case of the pacifist secretary of state with the political stance of Jesus Himself. "He not only chose not to defend *himself* violently; he chose as well not thus to defend Israel and the law of God. He not only entered the realm of politics; he remained utterly nonresistant within it" (Yoder, 1963:135).

In this appeal to the example of Jesus, we find the leverage to move forward the discussion of social responsibility, without abandoning the radical love ethic of Anabaptism. The new step is the rediscovery of the biblical career of Jesus as politically relevant, yet totally nonviolent in obedience to the will of God. Nonresistance as the sole principle embodying the love ethic is inadequate; it is subject to distortion as in some of Kaufman's examples, or more often it leads to withdrawal from social conflict and need, as Burkholder has demonstrated. But the "politics of Jesus" offers fresh possibilities.

The Politics of Jesus and His Church
John H. Yoder in his epochal book *The Politics of Jesus* (1972b)

has synthesized a series of exegetical biblical studies in order to establish a solid foundation for proclaiming the sociopolitical significance of the historical Jesus. The figure of Jesus that emerges is neither an ascetic perfectionist whose ethic is marginal to basic human issues, nor a proponent of a one-dimensional nonresistance that ignores the weighty question of justice. In Jesus' words and deeds, the ethic of the kingdom of God takes form in a social program grounded in the Old Testament year of Jubilee. Thus Jesus is not merely a teacher of spiritual principles, or a sacrificial lamb fulfilling a plan of salvation; He is the leader of a movement rooted in the history of Israel and directed to concrete historical needs and expectations. That movement is the messianic community, a foretaste of the coming kingdom of God, actualized in the eschatological claim that a new order of existence is a present possibility (Yoder, 1972b:11-114; 1971:122-27).

The politics of Jesus, however, as a strategy for social action, goes beyond the traditional range of options. Jesus does not line up with the politics of the temple establishment, nor straddle the issues with the dualism of the Pharisees, nor escape to isolation in the wilderness. Most significant, He rejects the Zealot path of revolutionary violence (Yoder, 1972a:18-27).

> The one temptation the man Jesus faced—and faced again and again—as a constitutive element of his public ministry, was the temptation to exercise social responsibility, in the interest of justified revolution, through the use of available violent methods. Social withdrawal was no temptation to him; that option (which most Christians take part of the time) was excluded at the outset. Any alliance with the Sadducean establishment in the exercise of *conservative* social responsibility (which most Christians choose the rest of the time) was likewise excluded at the outset. We understand Jesus only if we can empathize with this threefold rejection: the self-evident, axiomatic sweeping rejection of both quietism and establishment responsibility, and the difficult, constantly reopened, genuinely attractive option of the crusade. (Yoder, 1972b:98)

What then does He do? In line with the prophetic message of the Old Testament, Jesus proclaims the good news of the kingdom, a new order of priorities and relationships in the social and political and economic life of mankind. The mission of the Messiah is to bring good news to the poor, to proclaim release to the captives, to set at liberty the oppressed, to preach justice to the Gentiles (Luke 4:18, 19; Matthew

12:18-21). This program carries forward the social critique of the Old Testament prophets and posits a clear alternative to both the ethics and the politics associated with the "responsible" status quo of society.

The radical ethics of the kingdom calls for deliberate social commitments. To identify with Jesus is to take the side of the victims—the poor, the oppressed, the powerless—because God Himself is the Savior of the helpless. This is not withdrawal but involvement. And since to stand with the oppressed in most cases means to stand against the oppressor, it leads to confrontation with power—the power of injustice and violence.

Here then is the point where nonresistance becomes relevant—*after* one has taken sides in the social arena. It is not the neutral bystander who is likely to be faced with violence, but rather the one who is recognized as a threat to the perpetrators of injustice. Nonresistance by itself does not offer a social strategy, but in the politics of the kingdom, it becomes the only appropriate response for those who have chosen to follow their Lord faithfully in the way of the cross.

To follow Jesus politically therefore calls for making judgments, for taking sides, in conflict situations where there is obvious injustice. Guy Hershberger, whose emphasis on nonresistance has often been interpreted as simply avoidance of conflict, recognized the obligation to stand with the victims of discrimination in his qualified approval of Martin Luther King's Montgomery bus boycott (1962b:7-8). In 1965, Hershberger's sympathy with the civil rights movement was such that he could say with regard to racial discrimination: "Christians must engage in demonstration against this moral wrong. How else can we testify to its evils?"[3] Nonresistance, thus, is *not* noninvolvement.

Two qualifications, however, are necessary. First, there are conflict situations where choices are not clear. Thus, a family squabble, or a labor-management dispute, or an international border clash, may demonstrate blame on both sides, and victims in both camps. Judgments based on careful analysis may not lead to a simple choice. Second, even where there is a clear choice, to say with the Bible that God takes the side of the poor and oppressed (Psalm 72:4; Isaiah 11:4) does not make the victims of injustice automatically into saints of the kingdom. While the Bible consistently proclaims God's bias on behalf of the downtrodden, it does not equate them with the company of the redeemed. One must avoid a naive identification of God's purpose or people with one side of a particular historical conflict.

Our point is simply that nonresistance, in the light of the politics of Jesus, is not uncommitted neutrality, it is not just an umpire role, nor an uninvolved quest for reconciliation (although efforts at reconciliation are of course appropriate). Reconciliation implies prior conflict, even antagonism; persons who stay out of fights don't need to be told to turn the other cheek! Only those who engage in the controversial and dangerous work of the kingdom are likely to face a situation calling for a nonresistant response.

The point of reference for such involvement is not the total social order, but the messianic community. The social strategy of Jesus deals with the injustice of the old order, not by destroying it, but by replacing it with the new order of the kingdom. In Yoder's words:

> This is the original revolution; the creation of a distinct community with its own deviant set of values and its coherent way of incarnating them (Yoder, 1972a:28).

> The primary social structure through which the gospel works to change other structures is that of the Christian community. (Yoder 1972b:157)

> The foremost political action of God is the calling and creation of His covenant people, anointed to share with Him as priests, prophets, and in the servanthood which He revealed to be the human shape of His kingship. The church is both the paradigm and the instrument of the political presence of the gospel. (Yoder, 1974:102.)

Guy Hershberger chose to call this community the "colony of heaven," a theme derived from the figure of speech in Philippians 3:20 and developed in his contribution to the present volume. In his 1958 book, he set forth this concept as the link between the strenuous cross ethic of Jesus and the human social order (1958d:43). "The New Testament colony of heaven was planted in the very midst of the pagan social order for the purpose of challenging its evil, and of calling its members to repentance and to the acceptance of a new social order which is based on the way of the cross" (1958d:195). The colony of heaven is, thus, in effect, an ethical countercommunity, or as Yoder puts it, the political presence of the gospel.

Grounding the cross ethic of radical love in a visible community of called-out disciples provides an alternative both to the threat of absorption into the wider society with the consequent loss of a distinctively Christian ethic, and the charge of social irrelevance. Stanley Hauerwas in his analysis of John Yoder's thought titled most appropriately "The Nonresistant Church" (1974: chap. 11), emphasizes the crucial role of the Christian countercommunity: "the church fulfills its social responsibility by being an example, a witness, a creative minority formed by its obedience to nonresistant love" (1974:212). In short, the real responsibility of the church is to be itself. "This discriminating social ethic does not justify withdrawing from society," says Hauerwas, "but rather attempts to free us from the assumption that the church's social ethical task is synonomous with compulsive programs for improving society" (1974:7).

In John Yoder's words, the truly responsible church is freed from the "old pattern of seeking in the name of God to make history come out right" (1969:278); instead, its responsibility is carried out in the posture of servanthood. A Christian community that takes seriously its calling to sacrificial service may begin to answer the problem of multiple and competing neighbor claims posed at the outset of this essay. Such situations are no longer the problem of the isolated individual, with limited resources in the face of contradictory demands. They become the responsibility of a community organized and empowered to give form to kingdom justice. The needs of the neighbor, even of the enemy, become the goals of the servant church. Such a stance may be costly, but, as Hershberger wrote of the colony of heaven, "it is the entire Christian community, the body of Christ as one unit, which pours out its corporate life in redemptive living, and if need be lays it down in obedience to Christ the head" (1958:196).

Admittedly this ethic of the nonresistant servant church—the countercommunity of the cross—does not provide an answer to the full range of the criticism directed against sectarian ethics. This is so largely because the view set forth here does not accept the assumptions that the responsibility critique takes for granted. The politics of Jesus calls into question the axiom of responsibility for the survival of the existing social order and the need to make history come out right for God's sake. In Yoder's words, "the calculating link between our obedience and ultimate efficacy has been broken, since the triumph of God comes through resurrection and not through effective sovereignty or assured survival" (1972b:246).

Conclusion: The Church as the Context of Decision
The nonresistant ethic, therefore, requires embodiment in a com-

munity of faith, if it is to begin to meet the challenges of its critics. If the way of the cross is to become a social ethic, it demands the existence of the disciplined church. E. L. Long, in his comprehensive study of contemporary Christian ethics, recognizes this dimension of the sectarian approach, and uses Paul Peachey's treatment of the Christian community (Peachey, 1962) as a prime illustration of the distinctive character of Mennonite ethics (Long, 1967: 279-282). John Yoder, in his elaboration of the Believers' Church, has provided a comprehensive rationale for the role of the Christian community as both ethical resource for the moral development of its members and as a model, a city set on a hill, for ethical witness in society (1969:263-265, 274-278; 1974:94-104).

Thus there is no lack of testimony to the importance of the church for ethics. But simply stating this point in general terms provides no direct guidance for specific issues in a nonresistant social strategy, or for the day-to-day decisions of the disciple community. Building on this recognition of the church's crucial ethical function, we must give attention to the church's necessary role in developing concrete ethical guidelines.

Lawrence Burkholder has noted that, for Mennonites, "Christian ethics are really church ethics when viewed from the standpoint of the ethical agent as well as the context of decision-making" (1959:1080). Beginning with a key essay by Franklin Littell (1960), a number of significant writings have focused on the recovery of the church as a locus for ethical decision (Burkholder, 1963, 1965; Redekop, 1970; Yoder, 1967). Although the scope of these studies is broader than a strictly ethical agenda, they present a rationale and a method for moving ahead on the necessary task of making the foregoing ethical perspective relevant to specific issues and problems.

The obvious next step must be a sustained effort to make these findings functional in the life of the church. That concern will no doubt meet resistance. For the Mennonite past is cluttered with debris from detailed regulations for lifestyle and behavior, so much so that for many present-day Mennonites the very thought of church-sponsored ethical discussion is distasteful. Consequently much of the brotherhood has adoped a *"laissez faire"* attitude toward such issues and has accepted what in effect amounts to an individualist, situational ethic.

Surely both the method and the assumptions of the older church discipline statements deserved criticism, however commendable the effort to provide guidelines for the faithful. Rules made by a minority who assumed that deduction from principles was a self-evident and timeless process, obviously appear dated, static, and legalistic. But the alternative—acquiescence to the spirit of each doing what seems right in his own eyes—leads only to apostasy.

The challenge is to develop and activate an approach that avoids both the problems of rigorous adherence to fixed formula and the faithless refusal to search together the mind of Christ on important matters of action in the world. The quest for a new form of social responsibility, rooted in the way of the cross, requires for its fulfillment a church that is ready to take seriously its calling. It requires a church ready to believe that if God has committed Himself to His people on their pilgrimage in history, then His will can and must become specific in the decisions of the gathered and visible church. "Mennonites," John Yoder has written, "have suffered from too little, not too much of the faith that the Spirit of God truly works here and now in the fellowship to bind and to loose" (Yoder, 1963:137).

Kingdom Citizens
and the World

Kingdom Citizens and the World

An integral connection between faith and life has been a central motif of the Anabaptists and their descendants. Much of the renascent study of the Anabaptist Vision has pointed to discipleship as an all-embracing concept for interpreting the essential character of the Radical Reformation. The early confessions stress the quality of life that should distinguish true disciples, marking their distinctiveness from the world.

At the same time, Anabaptists recovered a sense of mission to the world that had been largely neglected since apostolic times. Their evangelistic fervor drove them out into the world to preach and to persuade. The call to ethical absolutes on one hand, and the commission to witness on the other, set up a tension that has been in precarious balance ever since that first Reformation generation. Holiness suggests withdrawal; mission demands involvement. Can they be held in creative tension? Is the "world" a problem or an opportunity for the disciple?

The chapters that follow explore some dimensions of this constant dialectic in Mennonite life. James Juhnke asks some hard questions about the behavior of Mennonites in wartime. He suggests a sobering reassessment of actions and pronouncements that may have been products of more complex patterns of motivation than has usually been recognized.

The next two essays offer complementary perspectives on the relation of the free church to the public political realm. John Redekop argues that the contemporary church-state scene must be viewed in a new light; the old simple dichotomies are not adequate for today's realities. He urges selective involvement in government, for the sake of effective witness to kingdom values. John A. Lapp sees both continuities and new problems for the Believers' Church in the current attention to civil religion. The Christian community must remain alert to seductive efforts to use the symbols of faith for unworthy ends. Together, these chapters represent the kind of necessary reflection about current issues that realistic faith demands.

Emma LaRocque articulates some of the inherent ironies in the missionary effort of a presumed "colony of heaven" that has become in many respects an ethnic people. With keen sensitivity to culturally rooted problems in bridging the gaps, she calls for acceptance of plurality and diversity within the community of faith, if it is to be true to its calling.

Ranging widely over time and space, Donovan Smucker catalogs the variety of socioeconomic models that have marked four centuries of Mennonite history, and asks which of them are viable vehicles for carrying the vision into the next century. His concrete examples illustrate vividly the continual tension of isolation or absorption that challenges the church.

10

Mennonites in Militarist America: Some Consequences of World War I

James C. Juhnke

The experience of Mennonites in North America in the twentieth century was profoundly shaped by the world war which rocked Western civilization in 1914. At the Anabaptist origins in the sixteenth century, the explosive symbol of church-state confrontation had been rebaptism. In a twentieth century dominated by international militarism, the flash point was refusal of military participation. Because they rejected warfare, Mennonites in World War I were outcast. No set of relationships is more important for understanding Mennonite life and identity in the twentieth century than those which flowed from the Mennonite encounter with their warmaking national communities.

The Mennonite historical understanding of the meaning of their encounter with twentieth-century warfare was fashioned by historians who knew the world wars and the interwar years as primary experience. Guy F. Hershberger and his generation wrote from the inside about a people whose sufferings and triumphs they deeply shared. Their fathers, uncles, and cousins had been drafted and persecuted in military camps in 1918. Their relatives and friends had been scorned for speaking German and for opposing the war bond drives. The brotherhood they loved had been fractured by theological disputes in the post-war period.

The framework and assumptions of Mennonites of the Guy F. Hershberger generation were a product of their effort to define a distinctive witness and mission for Mennonites in the post-World War I era. There was a need to fashion a doctrine of Mennonite nonresistance which would be separate from, and more reliable than, the unsteady pacifism of some elements in the American Protestant churches. There was a need to carve out a middle ground in the destructive debate

James Juhnke is associate professor of history at Bethel College. He has served with Mennonite Central Committee in Germany and Africa; his writing and publications include musical drama and American Mennonite history

between the Fundamentalists and the modernists. There was a need to conceptualize the Anabaptist Vision in a way that would support the development and growth of Mennonîte institutions of social maintenance and identity—colleges, missions, relief agencies, and alternative service programs in World War II.

The success of Hershberger's generation in focusing the Anabaptist-Mennonite identity and task in the generation after World War I was remarkable indeed. The very phrase, "Anabaptist Vision," had become a code word for that which was good and right for Mennonites to be and become. Almost no one doubted that Mennonite Central Committee, Mennonite Mutual Aid, Civilian Public Service, Mennonite Mental Health Centers, and other Mennonite institutions were in fact the embodiment of the vision. By 1970 Hershberger could confidently claim that the "Anabaptist Vision of mission and service . . . was approaching maturity" (Hershberger, 1970a:213).

How does one write history in an age of "maturity"? Mennonite historians of the final quarter of the twentieth century, grateful for the focused vision and institutional vigor within which they were themselves nurtured, will see the recent Mennonite past in ways that fit their own needs and perceptions. The views of the Hershberger generation will inevitably be revised and reshaped, as certainly as the fact that each generation writes its own history in the light of insights from its own experience.

Mennonite historians in the waning decades of the twentieth century will probably reflect a more distinctly Americanized view of their past. Mennonite history will be seen as closely woven into the fabric of American social and intellectual life. The national context of Frank Epp's 1974 volume, *Mennonites in Canada,* may well be a harbinger. The dust jacket promises that Epp's book teaches "something of what it is to be Canadian" (Epp, 1974).

The perspective of several decades may well reveal that the Mennonite twentieth-century experience in many ways is profoundly reflective of American culture. Mennonites were Americans. They chose American ways of asserting and maintaining their identity as Mennonites.

Several lines of inquiry may be suggested for the interpretation of Mennonite experience in the first half of the twentieth century, with the distance of several decades for perspective. One avenue for investigation is the relationship of Mennonite benevolence to Mennonite wartime experience. The burst of benevolent activity symbolized by the establishment of the Mennonite Central Committee is one example of how Mennonites developed resources within the American cultural framework at the very time they endeavored to establish a witness and identity separate from prevalent American ideology and practice.

The great crusade of 1917-18 was for the United States a noble exercise in human benevolence. President Woodrow Wilson and his idealistic friends saw the American contribution to the war as a species of self-sacrificial altruism. America had no imperialist ambitions, no territorial claims. America was only giving of herself to make the world safe for democracy.

Some American Mennonites did find their spirits lifted by the grandeur of Wilson's crusade, most notably a group of talented young intellectuals who had drunk the heady wine of progressive education in graduate schools such as the University of Chicago or Columbia University. At Bethel College in Kansas, for example, teachers Samuel Burkhard, J. F. Balzer, and C. C. Regier, who had sat at the feet of the likes of John Dewey and Shailer Mathews, were ready to abandon the doctrine of nonresistance and enlist in the war effort. Not long after the armistice, Burkhard wrote to Balzer of "the new chapter that had been added to Genesis. It was the second and third day of a new world order" (Burkhard, 1919).

One did not have to attend graduate school in the Progressive Era to be affected by the vigorous confidence in human reform which characterized those days. It is in such a context that we should understand Mennonite embarrassment as their young men were persecuted and court-martialed in military camp, their leaders were tarred and feathered, or as they were insulted for their German accents. Mennonite wartime suffering had profound psychological implications. They had been brutally rejected by a national community whose high ideals and altruistic benevolence seemed quite undeniable.

What could Mennonites do in such a situation to reestablish themselves as acceptable citizens in America and as worthful, productive people in their own eyes? Part of the answer was to fashion an alternative nonmilitary form of benevolence on their own terms. In a country that was giving of itself to a holy cause, the Mennonites began giving money to their church agencies. The contributions came so fast that Mennonite leaders were hard put to find avenues for disbursement. When the pattern of handing out such funds through non-Mennonite relief agencies proved unsatisfactory, the Mennonites banded together and formed their own central committee to carry on the work.

The Mennonite Central Committee, then, can be seen as a child of World War I, the Mennonite moral equivalent for participation in war (Juhnke, 1970).

The link between Mennonite war experience and the rise of Mennonite benevolence remains adequately to be documented and explored. Many questions need to be pursued. For example, at what point and in what language did Mennonites begin to conceptualize their relief efforts as an outgrowth of Anabaptism? To what extent were they aware that their efforts were a reflection of new forces in American life? How can Mennonite benevolence be related to their varied responses to the war? Did the absolutists on the questions of military service and war bond drives tend to be more interested or less interested in relief efforts than those who took a more moderate position? Where on a continuum of Mennonite acculturation from the most separated to the most acculturated does one find the most enthusiasm for postwar relief?

A second area in which it may be fruitful to examine the consequences of Mennonite war experiences as an American phenomenon relates to the debate in Mennonite circles between the so-called Fundamentalists and modernists. This controversy, which sapped the leadership and creative energies of a generation of Mennonites and which left sores still festering in the 1970s, reached its destructive climax in the years immediately following Warld War I. The crisis which closed Goshen College in 1923, as well as the purge of the Bethel College faculty in 1919, were in some sense related to the war. Without denying the multiple causes and the prewar roots of the Fundamentalist-modernist split, it can be suggested that the war-induced trauma contributed significantly to the intensity and destructiveness of the controversy.

Leaders of Mennonite churches and conferences had had to accommodate themselves to a bewildering succession of changes already before the war crisis. There had been the impact of the Sunday schools, the rise of missions programs, the shift from German to English in many homes and congregations, and the impact of higher education. The very shape of Mennonitism was being transformed, as surely as new technologies and patterns of organization were changing American social and economic life generally around the turn of the century.

The coming of the war produced a defensive reaction among leaders who had already been beset with bewildering change. The underpinnings of a stable social and religious order seemed to be giving way. The prevailing climate of opinion in postwar America contributed to this sense of malaise. The holy war crusade soured almost overnight. The war produced not only its harvest of death on European battlefields, but also the rise of communism in Russia, the disruption of European state relations, and a wave of intolerance and fear in North America. The early twenties were scarred by urban race riots, the A. Mitchell Palmer "Red Scare," the rise of the Ku Klux Klan, and the enactment of immigration restrictions. The war that had promised the world safety for democracy had made the world ripe for bigotry and dictatorship. President Wilson was ill and discredited. The dream of human progress and goodness lay in shambles.

In such a national context it is not surprising to find Mennonite leaders reflecting the climate of disillusionment and fear in their own words and deeds. In the *Gospel Herald* of March 27, 1919, for example, editor Daniel Kauffman noted in one column the latest news about the 358 religious conscientious objectors who had been court-martialed and imprisoned at Fort Leavenworth. In the next column, Kauffman printed a list of things "most to be feared" under the title, "Christianity's Greatest Foe." Kauffman's assumption that *fear* was the natural and normal response for times such as these, an assumption he shared with non-Mennonite Americans, is as important as his list of bogies, which included "Prussianism," "the curse of Romanism," "the curse of strong drink," and others. But Kauffman's own nomination for the most ominous movement—the thing most to be feared—was "modern LIBERALISM" (Kauffman, 1919: 921). Members of Bethel College board of directors, who quizzed Samuel Burkhard on the virgin birth and the theory of evolution before offering him a contract in 1919, had something in common with Kauffman's sentiments and analysis.

The climate of fear produced irrational responses on the part of both conservatives and liberals in the brotherhood. The conservative leaders, who had seen so much change which seemingly threatened Mennonite identity, lost their capacity to embrace the younger people and to admonish them in love. The war had somehow destroyed a center of confidence which is necessary for effective brotherhood functioning. Some of the most talented Mennonite leadership in the 1920s and 1930s was alienated as a result.

Some have speculated that a more balanced and confident leadership might have led the Mennonites through this conflict with much less pain and loss. What if M. S. Steiner, who died in 1911, had been spared for another twenty-five years of leadership among the Mennonite Church (MC)? What if C. H. Wedel, who died in 1910, had lived to remain at the helm of Bethel College through World War I? Was the great tragedy of these two groups of Mennonites the premature deaths of their most enlightened and capable leaders? Such questions probably imply too much faith in the influence of heroic figures in Mennonite history. Men like Steiner and Wedel would themselves surely have been affected by the World War and the psychology it imposed upon other Mennonites and Americans.

The agenda for Mennonite historians in coming years should include an effort to uncover the extent of the correlation between nonresistance and orthodoxy among articulate Mennonites of the World War I generation. Could it be that those who were accused of being weak on general orthodoxy (*i.e.*, liberals or modernists) tended to be those who were weak on nonresistance (*i.e.*, accepted noncombatant service and war bonds, or showed interest in Wilsonian militant progressivism)? And could it be that the perception of this correlation contributed to the strenuous efforts of conservative Mennonite leaders to defend the faith by purging the brotherhood of its liberal taint?

It would be surprising if the war issue and the Fundamentalism issue did not intersect in significant ways, particularly in the light of the exchange between modernists and Fundamentalists reported by Ernest R. Sandeen in *The Roots of Fundamentalism.* The war fostered a resurgence of millenarian interest, which was vigorously combated by liberals Shailer Mathews and Shirley Jackson Case of the University of Chicago Divinity School. Sandeen writes: "Rancor had existed in previous decades, but the spirit of open hostility, so characteristic of the twenties, seemed to find food for its soul in the First World War" (Sandeen, 1970:237). Would this not have been especially true for Mennonites whose self-conception had received such a wrench during the war? The need for scapegoats had seldom been more urgent in Mennonite history. Historians should read the documents of the postwar period with this dynamic in mind.

A third area which deserves further attention in understanding Mennonite experiences in the context of American nationalism-militarism relates to the diversity of Mennonite responses to the changes brought by war. The Mennonite experiences have contained much more variety than one would gather from the reading of Mennonite history books.

The agenda of Mennonite historians and leaders in the post-

World War I period was to define the distinctiveness of the Mennonite peace tradition and to gird the brotherhood for the possibility of future war experiences. In this effort to focus a distinctive peace vision and program, Mennonites held up certain wartime positions or experiences as normative. The *true* conscientious objectors, it was assumed, were those who refused noncombatant service and suffered the consequences. In the same way, the Mennonites at home who refused to buy war bonds were held to be those who really carried out Anabaptist-Mennonite peace principles.

One consequence of this focus was subtly, or not so subtly, to read out of the Mennonite tradition proper those Mennonites who had taken up noncombatant service or purchased war bonds. This position was most natural for the Mennonite Church (MC) on the military question, since their official position against noncombatant service had been clear during the war and their young men had been more consistent than some other groups, such as the General Conference and Mennonite Brethren. (It is notable, however, that the majority of Mennonite draftees who were court-martialed and imprisoned were from General Conference churches.)

But the war bond issue was more fuzzy, since large numbers of Mennonites from all groups had bought war bonds under the wartime pressures. The Mennonite capitulation on the war bond issue was, by and large, not treated forthrightly in Mennonite historical writing. For example, the stories of Walter Cooprider and Daniel Diener, who were tarred and feathered in McPherson County, Kansas, for their refusal to buy bonds, were told without mentioning that these men did in fact eventually buy war bonds to get the superpatriotic Americans off their backs. The submerging of the evidence on this point even led some historians to the erroneous assertion that Mennonites rejected bonds in World War I (Dyck, 1967:296).

The Schowalter Oral History project at Bethel College, which has conducted interviews with about 300 Mennonites who told of their experiences in World War I, uncovered an astonishing variety of human experience. One person tells of the inspiring witness of draftees who bore up patiently under persecution, while another says the Mennonite draftees were foolishly sullen and uncooperative in camp. Some reacted against the war with conservative separatism, while others joined the American Legion in the 1920s. The variety of Mennonite experiences, which cuts across a very wide range of attitude toward American culture, is a daunting challenge to historians who look for unity and common themes in their subject matter. But the challenge needs to be accepted. It will not do to create an artificial unity by high-lighting only the experiences of Mennonites whose behavior fits into a predetermined norm. Nor is it fully satisfactory to find the unity in the subject by writing only about one particular Mennonite conference or institution. We need ecumenical Mennonite histories which do justice to the rich and confusing variety in the Mennonite experience.

Mennonite historical work in the coming decades will probably build upon the institutional and conference-oriented studies of the past by moving into examinations of Mennonite social, intellectual, and cultural life in relationship to its American setting. The need for a focused vision, and for a historical framework grounded in New Testament values, is as great today as in the post World War I era. But the challenges are new. Mennonites today must contend with the consequences of their acceptability in American society. Mennonite non-resistance, missions programs, relief efforts, and historical quest for Anabaptist roots have become highly popular in America. This new situation, which is in part a product of American reaction to the Vietnam War, will produce historical writing with different shadings from that which emerged after the trauma of World War I.

11

The State and the Free Church

John H. Redekop

Introduction

Anabaptists have traditionally defined and redefined church and state in a way which emphasizes their fundamental differences. Having experienced harsh suppression by the state in the early years of their existence as well as in subsequent centuries, our forefathers were hardly inclined to view government as an arena for any type of cooperative Christian activity. The notion that the more authentic the church, the less it gets involved with government has understandably had broad support. Consequently, and sometimes properly, citing theology as well as history and experience, we have focused on the sharp differences between the ideal form of the love ethic Jesus taught and practiced and the worst, most corrosive expressions of selfishness commonplace in sub-Christian society including governmental structures.

However, in continuing to contrast extremes we have minimized the effect and significance of major political and social changes, especially in recent decades, and have largely overlooked the extent to which the concerns and actual activities of the faithful church and the concerns and actual activities of certain types of government now overlap. Even more important, we have hardly begun to probe the extent to which they could or should overlap. Thus our theology and sociology has lagged behind reality and largely ignored potentialities.

The standard Anabaptist emphasis on church-state mutual antipathy is an important one, perhaps even a crucial one, but it is not the only way of looking at today's complex relationships. This essay constitutes a plea for a broader, more inclusive orientation. Guy Franklin Hershberger's suggestion in 1958 that Anabaptists could be characterized as people who are "indifferent toward the state" (1958d:156) may have been descriptively adequate at that time but it

John Redekop is professor of political science at Wilfrid Laurier University, Waterloo, Ontario, Canada. He is active in the Mennonite Brethren Church and has published books and articles on church-state relations, labor problems, and both American and Canadian politics.

cannot be accepted as a sufficient prescription today or at any time, for that matter. To be indifferent to the policies and practices of the greatest concentration of human power, to suppress all judgment of government policies, and to neglect all opportunities for Christian impact in the governmental apparatus constitutes an unacceptable restriction of the Great Commission which Jesus gave His church.

In the following pages I wish to set forth a free church view of governments, especially modern governments, to suggest some general guidelines for possible Christian impact on government, to show why it is incumbent upon obedient Christians to generate such an impact, and to delineate important problem areas with special reference to Canadian and American situations. By the term "free church" I mean any organized group of Christians not having any formal economic or political ties to state or government (as the Anglican Church does in the United Kingdom), or informal ties (as most denominations have in the United States), but accepting only the lordship of Christ. I am assuming that at least theoretically Anabaptist groups belong in this category. By the term "state" I mean a politically organized group of persons occupying a definite territory and living under a government entirely or almost entirely free from external control and able to secure general obedience from persons residing in that territory. "Government" refers to the political and administrative activities of the state by means of which its powers are exerted and its policies implemented.

God, State, and God's People

Any defensible analysis of church-state relations requires a balanced reading of biblical and related history. For many of us this may produce a new awareness of the extent to which God has continually worked through the political structures of the day. In Old Testament times, for example, the life of God's people was closely interwoven with the policies and activities of generally secular governments. This held true for the period before the Egyptian captivity, during the Exodus and the conquest of Canaan, throughout the time of independence, captivity, and the subsequent restoration, and during the various periods of later colonial subordination right to and beyond the time of Jesus' birth. In other words, not only were affairs of temple and temporal rule meshed during the Hebraic theocracy, but the entire history of God's people involves continuous interaction with secular authorities of various kinds.

When Jesus was born the political situation was clearly of great significance. We are inclined to say that in a sense the sociopolitical climate made Bethlehem and early Christian expansion possible. The Pax Romana made census-taking feasible and the impressive communication and transportation systems, especially the vast Roman road network, facilitated the dissemination of the good news. Presumably the efforts of Hebrew (and other!) road-building crews as they worked their stone-cutting shifts helped bring about the rapid dispersion of believers whose feet were shod with the gospel of peace.

In New Testament times and the intervening centuries the situation did not change and has not changed. Government has continued to loom large in the development and activity of the church. To argue the opposite is to ignore the persecutions and Constantine, the Crusades and the holy wars, the state churches and Christian nationalism, as well as modern missions and the chaplaincy roles of various kinds.

For our Anabaptist forebears, specifically, civil authorities clearly played a major role. Church-state interaction, albeit largely related to suppression of the "radicals," was intensive and extensive. Indeed, we can say that to at least some degree the first Anabaptist groups emerged as a response to church-state fusion, that they were persecuted because of civil decrees, and that one of their key assertions was that so-called Christian leaders of the day had misunderstood the proper role of the state (Menno, 1956:549; Hillerbrand, 1958:86-87). They criticized the state for trying to coerce beliefs but, at least by implication, did not deny it humanitarian and other service roles (Menno, 1956:604). In at least some of his writings Menno Simons perceived a definite and positive role for government and if he had lived under an enlightened, democratic system he would probably have argued for the propriety of considerable cooperation (Sanders, 1964: 75-88). In any event, only in the last half century or so has it become commonplace to find broad segments of the evangelical and Anabaptist communities asserting that cooperative interaction between church and state was somehow unnatural and undesirable. Theories about "a wall of separation," especially as set forth in early American history, have their root in political, constitutional, and juridical thought, not in theology or the assertions of early Anabaptist theologians.

While part of this recent negativism arose as a critical response to blind Christian patriotism, no doubt part developed also out of the false notion that God works only through His church. Some of us have forgotten that even unregenerate man is made in the image of God, has

a God-breathed soul within him, and may be commanded or utilized
by God to carry out His will, doing good as well as ill. That non-Christians, in and out of government, may not be aware of their role in
God's plan in no way minimizes the effect of that role. What does this
mean for the church? On the one hand it means that we dare not cate-
gorize all governmental pursuits as somehow being juxtaposed against
God. On the other hand, and more positively, it means that we must
assess, or reassess, in what ways the discipleship activities of God's
people relate to that part of God's will which is expressed through
governments and what roles, perhaps supportive or participatory,
Jesus' followers in modern times might have in that phenomenon. Let
us not limit God. Who is so bold as to set narrow strictures on the ways
in which God might desire His disciples to function as salt and light?
Who among us has the authority to prescribe the bounds of the un-
leavened environment in which God might want His leaven to work?

But a consideration of history and speculation about how God utilizes secular agents to effect His will are only the backdrop for our
further analysis. Our basic concern is straightforward—to ascertain
why and how it happens that in God's divine economy church and state
are not necessarily and not always placed in antagonistic juxtaposition.
In presenting the various arguments we must keep in mind that in order
for conclusions to be valid they must have general applicability. Too
often our thinking turns out to be culture-bound or even nation-bound.
Thus we tend to consider free church activity either in terms of a framework of Western-style liberal democracy or as a Western-based creed
penetrating alien communist or other authoritarian regimes. The free
church, we must ever remind ourselves, originated in an authoritarian
environment, flourished under authoritarian governments, and has as
much relevance to a closed as to an open society. The political
vicissitudes within any specific country or within any political party
within a country do not validate, invalidate, or determine what state-
free church relationships should be.

The recently published commentary on the significant Chicago
Declaration illustrates such parochialism by asserting, for example,
that "Watergate is forcing evangelicals to reexamine many fundamental assumptions about the supposed justice of governmental policy
and practice at home and abroad" (Sider, 1974:18). Similarly, "Watergate revelations have hopelessly tarnished the image of trusted
political heroes and their slogans, Watergate may free the evangelical
community (which, by and large, has been a part of middle America) to

take a new, far more critical look at all aspects of American society" (Sider, 1974:19). But Watergate must be viewed in the larger perspective. It is only an American phenomenon, admittedly of considerable political significance, but was greatly disillusioning as far as the ethics of politics and church-state relations are concerned only for those believers who placed the American system on some superior pedestal or who persisted in their belief that Richard Nixon was saintly long after he had demonstrated the opposite. Honorable political heroes should and will still be trusted to a considerable degree.

What we require in the first instance are basic propositions which have validity for free churches everywhere. Then we can derive specific expressions of these propositions having applicability in the full spectrum of political environments. One of these propositions is that the free church, by definition, does not see itself as constituting component building blocks within a series of discontinuous nation states. Functionally, the free church is above and beyond any particular state or even a state system. Another is that the state as a secular entity evolved because of the Fall as a device to control evil, but that its qualified jurisdiction now extends to all.

In developing these and other ideas we must avoid becoming issue-bound. Preoccupation with a military draft, with a recent or current war, with the Christian professions of political incumbents, or with favored governmental treatment of Christian schools or other church-operated establishments will blur our thinking about basic roles and relationships. We need to deal in specifics but not before we have clarified a general orientation and a theoretical position based on biblical theology. The point is that while church-state relations never exist in the abstract we need to think about them that way, at least initially, if we hope to gain a clear understanding of general roles. Also we need to be aware at the outset that given the contemporary pervasiveness of governments, any church interaction with government, but especially a consistent free church stance, cannot avoid coming to grips with economic systems, labor-management problems, ecological dilemmas, educational systems, mass media content, and a host of other secondary questions beyond the traditional areas such as civil liberties, special religious privileges, and military service.

In all of this the free church accepts a strategy of influence—not exploitation or manipulation (even if it be Gandhian in style) but only influence. Depending on one's definition such influence may perhaps be described as coercion, especially psychological coercion. It may be termed that because the free church has an unalterable mandate to make God-rejecting individuals and institutions feel uncomfortable and guilty about their rejection. Thus, when governments exploit minorities, enforce religious practices, forbid voluntary religious practices, rule arbitrarily or inconsistently, ignore pressing moral problems, waste our money, practice racism, or cultivate jingoistic militarism, all of which are expressions of God-rejection, then the free church is bound by the social thrust of its Christian commission to speak up (Yoder, 1972b: especially chapter 10; Yoder, 1964: chapters 5 and 6).

Such prophetic witness by the free church to the state has a threefold purpose: (1) by addressing itself to specific major problems, to the extent that a government permits it to do so, the church helps the government to recognize its role and its limitations in God's universe; (2) by speaking in the manner it does, concerning the kinds of other-oriented issues it selects, the free church helps the government and society in general to comprehend the ethical thrust of Christianity; and (3) by being faithful in this fashion the free church may, in fact, facilitate the resolution of specific grievances or problems. Naturally, in the exercise of this part of its mandate the church will itself constantly be rediscovering its uniqueness and reassessing its own authenticity.

One reason why we can properly speak of free church coercion is that the church has a biblical directive to exercise selective resistance as well as selective nonresistance. An emphasis on one without reference to the other is unscriptural and cultic. Love is a basic trait of God but nonresistance is not! God resists evil (1 Peter 5:9), God resists the proud (James 4:6), and from Genesis to Revelation God resists the evil one. We can say that God is love but we cannot properly say that God is nonresistance. Consequently, Christian disciples likewise must not make a fetish of nonresistance but in the realization that love is the root and that selective resistance and selective nonresistance are both fruit, we must let a consistent implementation of the love ethic determine the nature of our response.

If we keep our theology and our thinking straight on this matter we will not only realize that on certain occasions the church must interact with government, even taking the initiative, but we will also be able to avoid a new kind of Constantinian church-state synthesis. As Professor Hershberger often has reminded us, the state lies "outside the realm of God's perfection" and God has selected His church, not the state, as the primary realm of His manifestation and operation. What still needs to be stressed, however, is that the sharp distinction between church and state as power centers in no way undermines that part of the church's mandate which in a positive or negative way involves the state. Nowhere are we instructed to turn away from non-Christians whether viewed as individuals or groups; we are only instructed to shun evil. Certain values rather than certain people ought to be the objects of our avoidance, resistance, or even derision. And besides, Christian saints have no corner on insight as Jesus noted when He said that "the children of this world are in their generation wiser than the children of light" (Luke 16:8).

The above view assumes, of course, the acceptance of a qualified "two-kingdom" thesis. Granted, there is only one Christian ethic and when we seek to influence government we always point to that ethic, even when we suggest strategies for less evil, but because the bulk of mankind rejects God's claim we can speak of a duality derived from human response. Such a duality is reflected in Jesus' assertion that His kingdom was "not of this world" (John 18:36). the corollary truth, of course, is that while we strive for justice, humanitarianism, freedom, and respect for human dignity, and urge governments to do likewise, we are not justified in demanding that governments abide ipso facto by the love ethic.

While the general orientation briefly summarized above is valid in all political situations, its expression will obviously vary from one country to another. The Christian guidelines are constant; the nature and conduct of the government in any given situation will determine the extent and specific nature of Christian involvement and the thrust of church-state interaction in that situation.

Transformation of the State

A major reason why we need to broaden our view of church-state relations is that during the past several generations governments in both open and closed societies have generally been altered so greatly that we may properly speak of transformation. Admittedly this transformation has not been primarily or even substantially ethical, but the changes in size, scope, function, and processes have impinged in new ways on voluntary groups such as the free church and have also created vast new opportunities. With reference to size alone the changes are staggering. A century ago the typical ratio of governmental employees to the total population was one government employee for each 150 or more people. Today in the United States and Canada one out of every seven people works in one capacity or another for government at some level. In many Western European countries the ratio is substantially higher. As governmental services increase—and they still are—and as more professions and vocations such as teaching (at all levels), the healing arts, and social services come under governmental jurisdiction this ratio is bound to rise. The growth of government in regulatory, proprietory, and welfaristic undertakings has not yet reached its zenith in the Western world and certainly not in the developing countries. In the communist and other closed societies the percentage of the work force employed by governments is already high varying, in the main, between 30 percent and 70 percent and rising slowly. In the future more and more of us will be working for the government.

Fiscal measurements point in the same direction. At one time it was considered extraordinary for governments to levy taxes and other imposts totaling more than 10 percent of the gross national product; now, in Canada and the United States, that figure has passed 40 percent and continues to rise. In many countries more than half the total wealth produced passes through government coffers. "Does Christian stewardship and accountability terminate with reference to the almost 50 percent of our total income in the U.S. and Canada which is channeled through government once this money is in government coffers, coffers of a government we helped select?" (Redekop, 1972: 16). Matthew 25:34-46 has taken on a whole new meaning in our time, a meaning whose impact will become compelling as the percentages inch upward.

It thus becomes clear that flight into agricultural enclaves or foreign lands—if such flight ever was theologically adequate is a question in its own right—no longer offers escape from entanglement with government. With urbanization and the new government pervasiveness, the option of fortifying ourselves in ideological or sociological compounds has come to an end. Like the New Testament churches which were organized in the cities we will have to put our witness to the test in urban settings, modern urban settings where government bureaucracies thrive and tentacles of government penetrate everywhere. Once having accepted the notion that the community of believers does not require and can no longer flee to isolated, more or less self-sufficient, rural enclaves, with or without ethnic props, we are forced to come to terms with the state. There is, thus, no alternative to accepting the significance, even preeminence, of modern government and our involvement with it.

In fact, ever since Pentecost the church has been politically significant whether by conscious involvement or attempted noninvolvement. Irrelevance has not been an option. Any church which advocates and tries to follow total withdrawal may well be aiding and abetting the triumph of evil. As in Nazi Germany, silence may functionally be the twin of support. The more likely result, however, is that a quiescent church will slowly become an uncritical chaplain to the existing political system and appear to be in complete agreement with the status quo. Silence and inactivity may thus serve to ease the conscience pangs of evil rulers, or at least seem to sanction specific evil policies, but they certainly do not reflect Christian integrity. For us in North America this point is especially relevant because our corporate Christianity has been moving up the socioeconomic ladder rapidly and we know that the higher that any group climbs on this ladder, the greater the temptation to endorse the established systems.

We need to keep in mind also that the staggering growth of government has invalidated any simplistic monolithic stance toward it. Today government is millions of people, a myriad of policies (sometimes contradictory), and a bewildering array of services and projects at national, state or provincial, and local levels. The United Nations organization, its related agencies, and other supranational bodies also function in at least quasi-governmental ways. Accordingly, while keeping the theoretical orientation clear, free church interaction with government must now be spelled out with reference to specific roles or segments of government. Our response to a burgeoning military budget or flagrant corruption will no doubt be different from what we have to say about enlightened treatment of racial minorities or rigorous enforcement of legislation to eliminate child battering.

Complex government has also become diversified government. While agreeing with Hershberger's frequent assertions that, by and large, modern states are enmeshed in a tangle of legitimate and illegitimate activities, I suggest that it is equally important to acknowledge that most governmental endeavors, especially in liberal democracies, are no longer primarily negativistic. Next to military expenditures, health and welfare and education funding usually consumes the bulk of government spending and involves the bulk of government personnel. Indeed, in Canada and some other Western countries the broad category of military funding has actually slipped into second place and continues to decline as a percentage of total government expenditure and personnel utilization.

True, the state continues to function outside of "the realm of God's perfection" (which, of course, hardly implies that the church is perfect!) but many of its more recent ventures bear a striking likeness to the humanitarian concerns that Jesus expressed and that have always characterized the true church. That is really not surprising—for two reasons. In the first place civilized non-Christians and Christians have always shared many values and aims. Such diverse efforts as campaigns to terminate slavery, to eradicate diseases, to promote literacy, to ensure freedom of beliefs, and to provide assistance to destitute people in foreign lands often involved the combined efforts of Christians and non-Christians alike with the latter not infrequently taking the initiative. Such sensitivity and social responsibility on the part of many non-Christians persists to this day. The atrocities perpetrated by Nazi Germany, or by Soviet Russia, or by racist South Africa, or by the American military in Vietnam shocked society at large precisely because they were not typical of usual government activity.

In the second place much of what governments now do closely resembles what socially aware Christians have always done, for the simple reason that governments have taken over many humanitarian projects first initiated by Christians. The operation of hospitals, of various kinds of schools, of orphanages, of homes for the blind, of emergency relief projects, and assorted other welfare activities fall into this category. In other areas such as subsidized housing, public compensation in no-fault personal injury accidents, preventive health care, and the rehabilitation of alcoholics and other drug addicts, government agencies have exhibited the church's earlier sensitivity and leadership. Not infrequently they have come to be competent pioneers, even in those situations where Christians have been hesitant, reluctant, or in opposition. The fact that essentially unchristian societies and governments now sometimes express more concern for the total needs of others and are capable of greater moral indignation constitutes no small indictment of the free Christian church. In some respects the salt has obviously lost its saltiness.

A particularly thorny problem involves the state's role in counteracting evil. To what extent should the free church support the state in its counter-evil policies, particularly when the methods employed are sub-Christian? Since doing nothing may in itself be a significant determinant of government behavior, the group will have to make choices. In general the free church, recognizing that the state has a right to use force to control violent evil, ought to urge that no more force be used than absolutely necessary and to object to the taking of human life. This means that while we support a responsible law and order stance, we will frequently find ourselves in situations where we cannot offer support but where we make it clear that some practices or policies, while still sub-Christian, are less objectionable than others. After all, killing two innocent children is worse than killing one!

Frequently one hears the argument that citizens of "the heavenly colony" ought to resist evil wherever possible but not if doing so involves any association with governments. The problem with this stance, aside from its confusing arbitrariness and the naive assumption that the bounds of government are easily discernible, is that much large-scale exploitation and oppression in our society can be alleviated only by government intervention and that in some important instances the government, at one level or another, is itself the culprit and must be confronted if the evil is to be challenged at all.

A further aspect of state transformation involves democratization. Obviously the social role of the free church in any society rests on the fundamental moral imperative given the New Testament churches but that does not mean that in our democratized society the free church must use methods appropriate in first-century Palestine, a vassal territory rigidly controlled by a totalitarian empire. Government in the Roman provinces was remote, impersonal, and unresponsive. Opportunities for influence were severely limited.

But our sociopolitical situation is drastically different. If we consider all facets of government at the various levels we can easily see that in many countries the distinction between government and governed has become blurred. By means of elections, media influence, pressure group activity, and general citizen reaction, governments have become both responsible and often responsive. This situation, coupled with public freedom and knowledge, has created much opportunity. And opportunity with ability creates accountability. Consequently we have to ask ourselves, "How can we be Christian in such a situation?" Our North American political systems have provided us with much freedom—what do we do with it? The elemental question for us is not simply making sure that the discipleship imperative takes precedence over citizenship activity—that much ought to be assumed—but to gain an understanding of the broad and permeating dimensions of responsible discipleship.

One result of the advanced democratization of a political system, especially in an industrialized society, is the growing significance of interest groups. For the free church, particularly the Anabaptist church with its emphasis on group activity, this situation presents additional opportunity. The basic exhortation to "love thy neighbour as thyself" takes on an additional corporate significance. The biblical observation, "Therefore, to one who knows the right thing to do, and does not do it, to him it is sin" (James 4:17), now assumes group relevance as well. The traditional group conscientious objection, which is but one side of the coin, acquires new meaning and new credibility in the light of group conscientious participation.

The Nature of Free Church Involvement

On one point there can be no misunderstanding: the church has not been commissioned to speak out on every political issue. On most matters the church has nothing to say either because the issue has no important moral dimension, or because the church is divided (in which case individuals can still speak for themselves), or because in view of the church's overarching mandate the issue simply falls below the priority cutoff line. We cannot deal with everything; we have to decide what is important and what is not.

Having made certain that its own example does not countermand its words, the concerned church normally makes a strong plea for justice whenever it sees substantive injustice prevailing. In an open society such a plea will rarely fall on totally deaf ears. At least in Western Europe and North America, politicians are not usually willing to get the reputation that they or their employees ignore the protestations or intercession of Christian spokesmen. Since election campaigns normally elicit assurances that candidates will give fair treatment to all with special favors for none, we have a ready-made approach at our fingertips. To the call for justice we add a call for humanitarianism, to the call for humanitarianism we add integrity and honesty, to the call for honesty we add receptiveness, and to the call for receptiveness we add sensitivity. If politicians are themselves Christians or at least identify openly with the Christian ethic—and most do in North America—then we have an additional basis for our input.

In no case should the free church crusade for superficial Christian sloganeering, formal externalities, or strictly ritualistic exercises. The state's contribution to Christian activity consists of providing the climate of freedom and granting such favors as it sees fit in gratitude for those activities of the church which benefit society, not to coerce compliance to any creed whatsoever, even the biblical one! If a government, however, in seeking to garner votes or generate good will makes a show of promoting Christian symbols or values, the church should speak out in opposition, but only when the promotion becomes sacrilegious. In other words, we have more urgent matters to tend to than clamor for external symbols, but if others choose to employ these, we should not be too hasty to be critical. What may be of no value for us may still have meaning for others. In any event our concern is more with what governments do than with what governments say.

Nor should our political activism, be it individual or corporate, be primarily self-centered. Traditionally, despite repeated protestations of political aloofness, we have usually not hesitated to seek justice or even special privileges for ourselves. The potential of political participation has not been lost on us as we have repeatedly sought political favors such as special tax and school exemptions for the Amish, for example, or waivers of immigration regulations (provided the applicants are our relatives), and preferred treatment concerning many other problems. Some fraternal critics see such a stance as praiseworthy selective involvement; I suggest it can be more aptly and honestly described as stunted and self-centered civic consciousness. It implies an unjustifiable redefinition of Jesus' concise summation of the law which then reads; "Thou shalt love the Lord thy God with all thy heart, with all thy soul and with all thy mind, and with all thy strength, and thou shalt love thyself." As far as interaction with government is concerned—as contrasted with our private sector assistance efforts—the reference to our neighbor has been conveniently ignored. For too long we have doubly deceived ourselves: we have told one another that pressuring governments to further Christian causes does not constitute political activity and we have supposed that interaction with governments becomes political only at the point where our own individual or corporate self-interest is not immediately and obviously at stake. In the former instance our mistake has been to believe that motives and ends, rather than means, determine what is political, while in the latter instance we have bought the standard pressure group argument that pork barrel politics is what others get—what we seek for ourselves is deemed to be uniquely justifiable and praiseworthy.

A further component of the free church relationship with government involves the blending of praise and criticism. As in the past, we must continue to criticize forcefully but responsibly, always seeking to be helpful and constructive. The temptation, as long as we are not the ones being disadvantaged, will be to say nothing. But who of us familiar with the righteous indignation expressed by Jesus can remain silent in the face of injustice, exploitation, deception, or barbarism? There comes a time when we must remind ourselves and others that opposition can be the highest form of true patriotism.

When government action warrants support and praise let us convey these sentiments openly and strongly. Not only will such reinforcement encourage the civil authorities to rule more wisely, but it will also make more credible our subsequent criticisms. Given the usual ethical vicissitudes of governmental actions it follows that for a segment of society committed to the way of the cross, cooperation mixed with criticism, and participation tempered by rejection, need not be opposites but can form part of an ethically consistent whole, each part reinforcing the other.

At all times we must be fully clear on one basic fact—the options, from attempted total noninvolvement to unqualified endorsement, which the free church faces in any political environment and concerning any issue, are always all imperfect. That is simply the nature of the situation. Therefore it is highly advisable not to rush in with a so-called Christian response to every problem and doubly important that as much as possible our response to important moral matters evolve out of brotherhood or at least congregational consultation and consensus. Of course, at times sensitive individuals will speak out even when they stand alone.

For those fellow Christians who for one reason or another cannot accept my overall description and prescription concerning selective and limited involvement of the free church in political affairs, may I point out that a political witness, provided it is thoroughly Christian, does not increase but in fact decreases our responsibility for unfortunate policy outcomes. In this connection I should emphasize also that in no way does my prescription imply that the free church should unreservedly throw in its lot with any government, even a liberal-democratic government which may provide an excellent environment for the people of God to be about their business. Nor is the orientation I have set forth rooted in optimism about the extent to which we can expect good works from civil authorities even when prodded by faithful Christians diligently fulfilling their gadfly role. It is based, rather, on an acceptance of reality, recognizing the self-serving tendencies of all sub-Christian civil authorities, as well as the awesome demands arising from an unqualified readiness to carry out the Christian mandate in our contemporary setting. In most situations the effect of even an optimum Christian witness to the state may be minimal but in itself that is not reason to abandon the task. In the political expression of discipleship, as in all facets of Christian obedience, the criterion of adequacy is not objective success but diligent faithfulness.

Specific Problems

The preceding pages still leave us with many problems but at least we now have the general outline of a recognizable and fixed framework. Good men may differ on the level and degree of involvement—and in most instances quite properly so—but it is surely impossible to deny the fact of free church relevance in contemporary political settings. The problems which remain and which defy easy resolution include the following

1. How can the church be politically responsive without becoming partisan, especially petty partisan?

2. How can we speak clearly in opposition to capital punishment, racism, the exploitation of women, and other matters on which we believe the biblical directive is clear, when a significant segment of the free church community opposes the perspective we believe to be biblical?

3. How can the church find ways of assessing laudable government programs such as Social Security, public health insurance, and various other welfare programs, without investing undue effort and resources in such assessment or allowing it to divide the brotherhood?

4. How can the church retain an awareness of its own responsibility to perform welfare work and at the same time urge government to use its great tax revenues to meet pressing social needs?

5. In view of the sharp disagreement among members, how can the church maintain a spirit of openness and toleration about which government positions Christians should be ready or even eager to accept, from social work to law enforcement, from tax collecting to food inspection, from routine typing to intelligence gathering, and from teaching to running for high elective office?

6. How can we ensure that Christian political involvement, of whatever stripe, will not become an end in itself, especially in view of our failure in preventing wealth and fame from becoming ends in their own right?

7. How can we learn to live at ease with the perpetual tensions and risks which invariably accompany prophetic Christian interaction with sociopolitical authorities?

8. How can we become politically informed and sensitive without becoming narrowly nationalistic or cynical?

9. How can we combine exhortations about ethical improvement with the evangelical commission to invite all ungodly men to become transformed Christian disciples?

10. How can we discipline ourselves to be critical without becoming filled with hate and to be supportive without accepting unqualified allegiance to the state?

11. How can we learn to persevere in prophetic politicking with good will, humility, and Christian grace, if the result turns out to be success or if it is perpetual rejection, ridicule, and even persecution?

12. In light of the fact that for many people the ideas and actions of government have already replaced the ideas and actions of the church as the integrative, direction-giving influence on their lives, how can Christians present government and its bureaucracy as a major locus of humanitarian service and agent to restrain evil, at least potentially, as well as an arena of Christian responsibility and service, without generating undue allegiance to it or dependency on it?

13. Finally, how can the free church as a whole learn to take politics seriously without giving it the status of ultimate seriousness?

Conclusion

In striving to terminate the impotency of sociopolitical drift and indecision the free church must come up with something other than mere chaplaincy or flight, something more than a superimposition of accommodation or compromise upon separation. We require a carefully thought-through and consistent orientation which can be readily understood, communicated, and applied in concrete situations. It is impossible, of course, to prescribe in detail what we should be saying to governments in specific situations, but the orientation presented in this essay attempts to show how we should view governments in general, and how we should act or react when governments become what they now are in much of Europe, North America, and elsewhere.

We need to adopt it or something similar without delay, because if we fail to do so, a haphazard, highly individualistic accommodation will by default become rooted in our constituency. In times past a failure to assess where we were and where we should be with reference to governments has brought about situations in which the heirs of Anabaptism widely acclaimed Hitler (Wagner, 1974: especially 205 to 210) and became adamant boosters of the most extreme, least Anabaptist, far right agitators in North America (Redekop, 1968: especially chapters 16 and 17). If we fail to broaden the definition of responsible discipleship we may slip into a new cultic Fundamentalism, probably camouflaged in Anabaptist rhetoric, but in fact firmly rooted in civil religion.

Why must we extend our sociopolitical horizon? Not to prove loyalty, not to counteract taunts of being peacetime parasites or wartime slackers, not even to become model citizens but because Christian discipleship, Christian stewardship, and the Good Samaritan ethic require it.

12

Civil Religion Is But Old
Establishment Writ Large

John A. Lapp

Religion plays a very political role here. By acquiescing in the standards of our rulers, the churches give them tacit endorsement.... Thus is religion trapped, frozen, in its perpetual de facto accommodation of power. It becomes a social ornament and buttress, not changing men's lives, only blessing them.... Religion is invited in on sufferance, to praise our country, our rulers, our past and present, our goals and pretensions, under the polite fiction of praying for them all. The divine is subordinated to the human—God serves Caesar. This is what Americans quaintly call "freedom of religion," and what the Bible calls idolatry. (Wills, 1972: 259-260.)

Such an assessment by the Catholic commentator Gary Wills stands in stark contradiction to the popular notions regarding religion in America. The man in the street, the woman in the pew, the scholar in the library generally concur that in some form or other there is a "wall of separation" dividing the religious and political orders. The secular Thomas Jefferson made much of this phrase long since hallowed by time and usage. Actually the notion is deeply rooted in Christian thought; it was stated classically by the free church leader Roger Williams 150 years before Jefferson. Williams described "the hedge or wall of separation between the garden of the church and the wilderness of the world" (quoted in Howe, 1965: 5-6).

From another angle Gary Wills contradicts the contemporary notions regarding the secular character of American culture and politics. He seems to reject the "secular city" and instead suggests the important role of religion in sanctioning and supporting the political process. Perhaps this is a clue that society needs a faith to provide meaning and order values for its survival. Indeed Jacques Ellul sees "a massive invasion by the sacred" in the twentieth-century West. The nation-state, ac-

John A. Lapp is professor of history and dean at Goshen College. Formerly secretary of the Mennonite Central Committee Peace Section, he is active in church and community affairs and has published numerous articles and several books.

cording to Ellul, is a prime example of a sacred order which "presupposes adoration, communion, abandon, self-dedication, and a glorification of the sacralizing power" (1975: 64, 79).

It is in this context of the political realities of religion in America and the legal separation of religious and political institutions that the term "civil religion" has emerged as one of the more provocative concepts for understanding the American situation. The term "civil religion" is derived from the eighteenth-century French philosopher Rousseau. Robert Bellah, a sociologist of religion, delineated the concept in a now famous article first published in 1967. [1]

Civil Religion or Civil Religions

The problem of understanding is compounded by the complex role of religion in American society and the equally complex self-understanding of religious groups regarding this role. The multiplicity of church buildings and denominational nomenclature raises real questions about any generalizations regarding religion in the United States. Add to this the regional and cultural diversity within American culture and society.

Perhaps the most difficult aspect of defining civil religion is knowing how to cope with the behavioral qualities of both the religious and civil orders. The terms "church" and "state" suggest institutionalized structures identified with certain spheres of influence. Terms like "political" and "religious," however, emphasize the dynamic quality of methodologies and the all-embracing character of a viewpoint. Religion is not simply a creedal and organizational structure, but includes the notion of value systems and ways of life. Similarly "political" refers not only to governmental activity but also to the process of organizing society and the value system which makes government possible.

The discussion of civil religion grows out of these understandings of both politics and religion. Neither can be compartmentalized. The questions are then in what way is religion in America "political" and conversely, in what way is American political life "religious"?

Some recent commentators illustrate the problem. Theodore White in his retelling of the fall of Richard Nixon titled *Breach of Faith* says the "true crime of Nixon was simple: he destroyed the myth that binds America together." In describing the myth he adds that "politics in America is the binding secular religion, and that religion begins with the founding faith of the Declaration of Independence" (White, 1975: 322-323). The novelist Norman Mailer, commenting on the 1972 political conventions, observed: "In America the country was the religion. And all the religions of the land were fed from that first religion which was the country itself" (quoted in Novak, 1974: 105). Michael Novak in a more direct analysis states that the American presidency is "the nation's most central religious symbol, and that American civilization is best understood as a set of secular religious systems" (1974: xiv).

These uses of the term "religion" compel us to look for a sharper definition. The cultural definition of religion that underlies the concept of "civil religion" sees religion as "a sense of reality, a way of structuring consciousness" or "what a people takes to be real, gives significance to, permits to dominate its imagination" (Novak, 1974: 12). Peter Berger has used the metaphor of the "sacred canopy" to describe the way in which a sacred cosmos is established (1969: 25-28). Religion can also be understood as "a pathway of life, a symbol system primarily concerned with man's coming to terms with questions of ultimate concern" (Hutchinson and McDonald, 1965: 7).

Each of these definitions looks at religion as a set of beliefs, rituals, and symbols organized in a manner that attracts loyalty, makes behavior legitimate, and supplies meaning. Given this definition, nearly everyone has an "ultimate concern"—something around which he lives and dies. This is why anthropologists and sociologists tell us "every functioning society has, to an important degree, a common religion. The possession of a common set of ideas, rituals, and symbols can supply an overarching sense of unity even in a society otherwise riddled with conflict." (Quoted from Robin Williams in Herberg, 1974:76).

Based on this concept of religion, White, Mailer, and Novak see the country as the religion. Robert Bellah observes "certain common elements of religious orientation that the great majority of Americans share . . . a set of beliefs, symbols and rituals that I am calling the American civil religion" (1974: 24). Other scholars label this national religion "the American way of life" (Will Herberg) or "the religion of the Republic" (Sidney Mead).

No matter who makes the analysis, there is a focus on commonalities which together make up the national religion: symbols such as the flag; symbolic public figures, especially the President; holy days such as Memorial Day, Independence Day, and Thanksgiving; liturgies with hymns such as "The Star-Spangled Banner," "Battle Hymn of the Republic," " America the Beautiful"; poetry and oratory; a creed extolling freedom of the individual, education, democracy, free enterprise, and the defense of the nation; a language with frequent reference to God, prayer, faith, commitment; saints such as Washington as the father of the nation and Abraham Lincoln as the supreme redemptive figure; an understanding of history which sees the United States as providentially created with a special role in the world to defend and expand freedom and inevitably triumph. Each of these is intrinsic to legitimating and sanctioning American culture, especially the political enterprise.

The content of the national faith varies from time to time. Certain common themes are always present: the uniqueness of this nation and its superior way of life, the need for national unity and defense, the glorious past and the boundless future, providential direction of the American experience, a mission to expand freedom and the American-style of government to other nations less fortunate. There are volumes of material illustrating the national faith (for example, Hudson, 1970). Perhaps no one summarized it so succinctly as Senator Albert Beveridge early in the present century.

> God has not been preparing the English-speaking and Teutonic peoples for a thousand years for nothing but vain and idle self-contemplation and self-admiration. No. He made us master organizers of the world to establish system where chaos reigned. He has given us the spirit of progress to overwhelm the forces of reaction throughout the earth. He has made us adept in government that we may administer government among savage and senile peoples. Were it not for such a force as this the world would relapse into barbarism and night. And of all our race He has marked the American people as His chosen nation to finally lead in the redemption of the world. (Quoted in Tuveson, 1968: vii.)

These ideas are expressed frequently over the pulpit, at political rallies, and in a rich accumulation of patriotic literature. The public educational system and the Americanization process for new immigrants have been major instruments for socializing new Americans into the value and thought patterns of the civil religion.

One of the major problems in defining the American civil religion is its relationship to Christianity and the churches in America. Bellah declares at the beginning of his famous essay that civil religion "exists alongside of and rather clearly differentiated from the churches." In the concluding paragraph he observes that "behind the civil religion at every point lie biblical archetypes: Exodus, Chosen People, Promised Land, New Jerusalem, sacrificial death, and rebirth" (1974: 21, 40). It is this feature that has made it easy for secular Americans to use Christian motifs and for pious Christians to use American sentiments. The resulting confusion means that it is not always possible to distinguish what is uniquely Christian from that which is uniquely American. Some persons would insist that the nation is Christian and hence the American civil religion is simply another denomination in the Christian pantheon. The opposite question is just as real: Is there any difference between civil religion and American nationalism?

One way out of this imbroglio is to observe varieties of civil religions. Richey and Jones see five ways of viewing civil religion: (1) as a folk religion; (2) as the transcendent universal religion of the nation; (3) as religious nationalism; (4) as the democratic faith; and (5) as Protestant civic piety (1974: 15-17).

Michael Novak, on the other hand, finds Protestant culture permeating the nation's public life. The American civil religions are all variants of Protestantism. There is a populist Protestantism of the Bible Belt and lower classes; a denominational, commerce-instructed moralism of the heartland churches; the mainline Protestantism in the high church tradition; a reformist Protestantism with revival and sectarian roots; and finally a black Protestantism. Each of these traditions, Novak says, has its own view of America, its own metaphors, aspirations, thought patterns, and forms of celebration (1974: 131-134).

Emphasizing the diverse types of civil religion helps to unravel the problem. There does appear to be an amorphous but definable civil religion that affects all other American religions and is in turn molded by them. But it is also important to recognize the profound identification of the Christian mission with that of the nation. Sometimes when civil religion is mentioned it refers to this deep Americanizing of the Christian tradition. Sometimes this identification appears more like an attempt to Christianize some deeply held Americanism.

Civil religion, however problematic, is a reality. If the Christian message is to have integrity, one must understand the role of civil religion in the American situation. The question can be focused sharply. What does it mean to be a biblical church, authentically incarnate and authentically universal, in a regional society which has its own faith?

The Appeal of Civil Religion

Civil religion has a strong appeal; one can hardly be neutral. Robert Bellah, while not uncritical, nevertheless doubts that "the leaders of the churches have consistently represented a higher level of religious insight than the spokesmen of the civil religion" (1974: 33-34). He along with Sidney Mead (1975) generally puts this religion of the republic in a positive light.

Other analysts are sharply critical. Will Herberg, while recognizing the American civil religion "as probably the best way of life yet devised for a mass society," nevertheless insists that it cannot be seen as authentic Christianity or Judaism. If viewed as such, it is "idolatry" (1974: 86-87). Some of the most sustained criticism has come in the periodical *Post American* (now known as *Sojourners*) and in a hard-hitting critique by Herbert Richardson. Richardson asserts that whenever we "ascribe finite characteristics to what is infinite we also claim infinite characteristics for what is finite." Civil religion for him is an idolatry that must be confronted by the church at every point since "there is nothing the church believes which cannot be woven into the state's mythology." The church must stand as an organized "alternative to civil religion" (1974: 164, 182). Senator Mark Hatfield said much the same at a Presidential Prayer Breakfast in 1973 when he compared the "small and exclusive deity of the national folk religion" and "the biblical God of justice and righteousness" (1976: 58).

While rejecting neutrality, we must seek to understand the pervasive appeal of civil religion; why is this faith so conspicuous in the American environment, compared to many other nations?

First of all it is important to observe the way the nation has been "endowed with churchly attributes." Civil religion developed in the womb of "Christian America." Robert Handy has described how even though the colonial established churches lost their prerogatives, the idea of a Christian society became deeply embedded in the broader American mentality (1971: 64). This reality permeated nearly every denomination in the American spectrum. The denominations founded as a result of revival enthusiasm seemingly had the clearest evangelical vision of a Christian America. Though the notion of a Protestantized America has been buffeted severely by new immigrant faiths (especially Catholicism and Judaism) and by secularization, the idea continues to persist strongly into the twentieth century. Close investigation of the language of many Christian spokesmen, as well as political leaders, suggests that this dream continues to have great appeal.

John Smylie in a provocative essay pointed to three energizing concepts of the Christian nation, formerly considered to be functions of the church. Each of these ideas emerged as the power of the denominations waned, giving more focus to the nation. The nation became first "the primary agent of God's meaningful activity in history" (1963: 4). The nation instead of the church was seen as the chosen people of God, or the New Israel. What the nation did and hoped for was God's work, with the goal of Americanization or Christianization of the world.

Second, the nation "became the primary society" in which "individuals, Christian and non-Christian alike, found personal identity" (1963: 7). The new man was not the Pauline man in Christ but, as Crevecoeur put it, the American was this new man. "American" became the primary identity rather than "Christian" or "Jew " or "Roman Catholic" or any other denominational label.

Third, "the nation became the primary community in terms of which historic purpose and identity were defined." The American nation rather than the Christian church became the community of righteousness and sanctification (1963: 9). Winthrop Hudson went so far as to say that by the time of Lincoln "the ideals, the convictions, the language, the customs, the institutions of society were so shot through with Christian presuppositions that the culture itself nurtured and nourished the Christian faith" (1953: 108). For most Americans, a civil religion apart from the church was and is simply inconceivable, for this interlacing of religion and culture has become a social fact.

One of the interesting phenomena in the American experience is the pressure for the various denominations to conform to a series of religious platitudes and to develop religious styles very similar to their neighbors. Part of this is the natural desire to be like the Joneses. Part of it is due to the democratic pressure to create a common front. The desire for respectability and acceptance has meant that self-conscious and often persecuted minorities—Mormons, Seventh-day Adventists, Hard Shell Baptists, and Mennonites among others—cease to be critics and challengers to the prevailing faith. If they don't become an establishment they tend to accommodate their eccentricities to the majority faith.

Thus the second appeal of civil religion—its substantial social integrative role–is not an unusual historic quirk. People appear to need a sacred vision to legitimize, integrate, and make historical experience itself meaningful and livable. Most of man's worlds, says Peter Berger, have been sacred worlds. Religion or sacralization has been and is the way people harmonize their objective and subjective definitions of reality. Social institutions have status and public support to the degree that they represent the "sacred cosmos" (Berger, 1969: 27 ff.). This desire for meaning, being, and truth—the essence of the "sacred"—explains the attraction of civil religion.

From this viewpoint, the American tradition of the separation of church and state never really meant a secularized state. If anything, the church was secularized—compartmentalized—as the nation carried on the sacred mission in the world. The "Battle Hymn of the Republic" translated the apocalyptic imagery of a militant church to the militant state. American wars were successful to the point that they became crusades for righteousness and not simply politics by another means. Recent scholarship has shown how already during the American Revolution, preachers adapted a millennial view of history to commonly held political ideas. "American liberty was God's cause, British tyranny was antichrist's, and . . . sin was failure to fight the British" (Hatch, 1974: 408). Similar sentiments have been repeated in every war since!

If social institutions need a sacred quality (is this not why so many Christians feel so deeply about Romans 13 as a biblical justification for government no matter what it does?), civil religion serves as the religious justification and sanction for the American body politic, or as Robert Bellah says, "a transcendent goal for the political process." The issue then is not simply a struggle between religious and political orders, but a fundamental clash between two religions—Christian and civil.

Seeing the religious character of political culture should not strike us as a novel idea. Did not Yahweh regard the desire of the Hebrews to have a king not only as a new politics, but as a rejection of His own kingship and a worshiping of other gods? (1 Samuel 8). [2] The New Testament language of principalities and powers likewise reminds us that the Christian struggle in the world is against cosmic powers and superhuman forces of evil which energize the structures of human society.

Civil religion in America thus should not be considered as unique, but rather as the natural, normal situation. It is perhaps a measure of our secularization and our deception to think that political structures could serve simply as functional realities for organizing society without a sacred dimension to inspire and preserve loyalty and obedience.

The recent discovery of the American civil religion is no accident. Indeed at the very moments of deepest national anxiety, due to racial unrest at home and an unwise war abroad, civil religious ceremonies and language became more conspicuous than ever. Presidents Johnson and Nixon displayed more public piety and used more religious language about faith and God than any other presidents (excepting perhaps Eisenhower).

This leads to a third appeal of civil religion—the modern politicizing of all human activity. Politics refers to the organizing of public life in a given geographical community. It is essentially a means to achieve that which is corporately necessary for a smoothly operating society. Politics can refer to governmental organization at the local, regional, national, or international levels. Every institution has a political aspect, for someone must decide "who gets what, when, where, and how."

Modern analytic tools have broken human activity into numerous parts—social, economic, political, cultural, religious—with numerous subsections. Yet the interrelationships are such that in recent years interdisciplinary approaches are developing as a recognition that human endeavor is a complex organism both in space and time. In this sense modern scholarship is returning to the organismic models of human behavior of an earlier epoch.

This explanation is necessary to put the politicizing of human behavior in context. During the past three centuries organized religion has generally been in retreat in the West. The nation as a spiritual reality filled the place earlier taken by the church. Politics as the process of social organization similarly developed from simple process into more spiritual or ideological forms. Politics both as process and idea has by the twentieth century permeated all of life. Jacques Ellul, the Christian French social theorist, has put it strongly: "All problems have, in our time, become political" (1967: 9). At the same time the nation-state has become the most important reality. The "state directly incarnates the commonweal. The state is the great ordainer, the great organizer, the center upon which all voices of the people converge and from which all . . . solutions emerge." Political considerations are likewise "the preeminent value, and all others adjust to them." (Ellul, 1967: 13, 16-17.)

It is not necessary to accept the total accuracy of Ellul's analysis to recognize the power of political organizations and ideas. Our point in this analysis is that civil religion is another sign of politicization. Were there a total secularization and no established church tradition, the modern nation-state would need ideological justification simply to survive.

So for the United States the symbols and activities of civil religion have increased as on the one hand Christian influence has waned and on the other hand the tensions of war and social conflict stimulated more public religiosity. It is no mere accident that prayers at presidential inaugurations began as recently as 1936 or that the phrase "In God We Trust" was put on coins only in the 1950s. Perhaps worship services in the White House under Richard Nixon reflect the anxieties of the times and the need to wrap the power and prestige of religion around the increasingly sordid politics of the 1960s and 1970s.

The Dissenting Community

The title of this essay is an obvious paraphrase from John Milton's sonnet "On the New Forcers of Conscience Under the Long Parliament." For that doughty dissenting Christian "New Presbyter [was] but old Priest writ large." The paraphrase suggests the stance conscientious Christians might adopt vis-á-vis the phenomena of civil religion.

Civil religion as described here is an American variant of political religion (Moltmann, 1974: 11). All societies, as we have noted, are tempted to sacralize their institutions and to use religion to provide an ideological sanction for political activities. Ancient religions were so central to the political arena that the early Christians were called atheists for not worshiping the god of the city-states. It was the kingly claims of Christ that challenged both Jewish and Roman political religions and led to the cross.

The temptation of the Christian church has continually been to become a religion sanctioning and supporting a particular regime. Just as the Hebrews succumbed to a politicized faith under David and Solomon, Christianity became the political religion of the Roman Empire under Emperor Constantine. This establishment continued into the twentieth century at various places, in spite of the protest of sectarian free churches and the onslaught of modern secularism. Civil religion in the United States is a unique form of political religion because it represents a syncretism of Christian and American elements in a new style establishment. The temptation is not simply to bow down to Baal but more importantly to legitimatize Caesar.

In this context the first task of renewing faith is to catch a glimpse again of the church as a dissenting institution. The biblical motifs of wilderness, remnant, suffering, and nonconformity suggest that the norm for the faithful church is not triumph and worldly power. Such dissent is not the cultivated oddity of an outsider but results rather from obedience to a way of life which continually challenges majority opinion. This faith is not a mystical apoliticism but indeed a political stance where Christ is truly King and the ethic of Jesus is practiced by the peoplehood of God.

The way to cope with civil religion is to recover the tension which grows out of a genuine alternative. Instead of a faith linked to a particular time and place, there is the mandate to be a peoplehood that transcends ethnic and national boundaries. At the same time this vision is deeply rooted in local cells of belief and principle. Part of the appeal of civil religion is to provide identity and belonging in an age when older centers of loyalty—family, village, congregation, factory—no longer command the respect of participants. If the appeal is to be withstood, it cannot be by lonely heroic effort, but by an alternative community of faith where meaning is rooted in the Bible, Christ, and the fellowship of like-minded believers.

The dissenting community will be a perpetual witness against the misguided and inadequate claims of civil religion. The tendency of civil religion to sanction the actions of the government must be challenged. Inevitably there will be the dehumanizing impact of the majority toward minority groups, the distorted priorities of using wealth for national glory and power rather than the building up of the arts of civilized life itself. It has been political religion that has justified discrimination and segregation, supported wars and the arms race, and sanctioned perpetual inequality and injustice at home and abroad. The witness of dissent must include a reproof of all idolatry and an appeal to organize political life in order to sustain a vigorous plural society. The incarnated transcendent faith of the church becomes a witness against any attempt to deify or sacralize any government or public policy.

Will Campbell has urged Christians in the United States to again "think sect" (1970: 49). On the one hand this means the "Yes" of total commitment to Christ and His kingdom. On the other hand there is a vigorous "No" to any alliance of religion with any worldly power.

The tradition of dissent has as much dignity within the Christian tradition as within any state. In nearly all cases—medieval heresies, sixteenth-century Anabaptists, seventeenth-century Quakers, eighteenth-century Baptists, nineteenth-century nonconformists, twentieth-century Pentecostals—the struggle has been neither solely theological nor primarily political, but rather the struggle against an alliance of church and culture.

Christians in the United States have expended enormous energy struggling to maintain the separation of church and state. But the issue is broader and deeper. Indeed the issue finally becomes one of recognizing two views of politics and two views of religion. The question is less one of institutions in conflict, and more a matter of asking "Which religion?" and "Which style of politics?" Both the old establishment and the new civil religion have distorted the biblical message and the political order by giving "ultimate meaning and direction" to a particular human activity. The issue was clearly perceived by the person in whose honor this essay is written:

> Since no nation, not even Judah itself, is Christian, we must ever bear in mind the fact of the two social orders in our world, the Christian order and the pagan disorder; and the individual Christian must find his place and his work with the Christian order. The Christian order must live in the midst of the pagan disorder, and must ever serve as a goad and a challenge to that disorder. The order must never be identified with the disorder, however, nor adopt its ways and its means. (Hershberger, 1958d: 198)

13

The Ethnic Church and the Minority

Emma LaRocque

They walked down the aisle slowly with their heads bowed as the brown, heavy-set preacher with straight black hair, mixing English with Choctaw, paced up and down the aisle coaxing his listeners to "accept Jesus as your personal Lord and Savior." And those already saved he invited to "commit and consecrate your lives to Jesus Christ." As two convicted souls walked to the humble altar, the congregation intoned, "Just as I am without one plea; but that thy blood was shed for me. . . ." They sang the first verse more than once; finally, all was quiet, including the animated preacher whose face was streaked with perspiration. Then, his voice slightly cracking with emotion, he added the evening flock to the week's harvest, and with a mighty "Praise the Lord," he dismissed the service.

It was a hot Mississippi evening in the summer of 1973, and by invitation I had come to visit this tiny Choctaw Baptist Church. The building was made of plywood, with few windows. The benches were cramped and unpolished. Dizzy bugs buzzed around three bald bulbs. The church was by no means a spired, Southern Baptist cathedral, yet the service had been an "ole fashioned," Bible-thumping, Southern Baptist revival complete with soul-counting—a sort of service that has been popular in the Southern Bible Belt ever since the Great Awakening of the mid-1700s.

To me, it all seemed a bit incongruent. The Choctaw Indians of Mississippi are, generally speaking, unassuming and unobtrusive. Historically, they were not necessarily religious, although they were devoted to their ancestral homeland. They had danced according to agricultural cycles, and now they were confined to a boxlike construct ornamented with a twangy piano and enlivened by an intense Choctaw preacher whose voice echoed the "Hour of Decision" broadcast.

Emma LaRocque, a graduate of the Associated Mennonite Biblical Seminaries, has worked with Mennonite Central Committee. She is presently a graduate student at the University of Manitoba and has written and lectured on native American and cross-cultural topics.

No less unforgettable were the ruins of a former General Conference Mennonite Church in Oraibi, Arizona. The church had been made of bricks with the very familiar frame of most German-white churches in North America. Apparently, the church had had a spire. The thing that impressed me most was that the ruins were on a high bluff isolated from the clustered, earthy, adobe homes of the Hopi Indians.

Several hundred miles east of Oraibi, among the various buildings of a Brethren in Christ Navajo Indian Mission, a church with a steeple glints against the sun. The windows are large and the pews varnished. The walls are painted pastel and the pulpit stands on a carpeted platform. Bulletin boards frame either side of the pulpit. It is a church that would be at home in any middle-class, suburban town. Perhaps this is why it seemed odd to watch modestly clad Navajo people—many of whom tend sheep, weave rugs, and know the feel of the desert sand—come there for Sunday worship.

One could go on and describe similar steepled churches in the wilds of Northern Canada—and there are many. But the point of the above examples is to show the obvious distance between externally-imposed church constructs and the authentic life ways of indigenous peoples.

Since it has been my lifetime experience to observe such vast differences between Christian missions and native inhabitants, I have been plagued with many questions. For example, what part of the Christian movement is cultural and what part is "Christian"? Or, since Christianity ultimately consists of various groups and individuals, and since groups and individuals are inescapably linked to human cultures, how does one discern the difference between "Christ and cultures"? Put in more experiential terms, does becoming a Christian mean that one has to worship in a four-walled, sky-reaching construct, sing music to the tune of revered but ancient European melodies complete with patriarchal and medieval imagery, as well as sit in straight rows, eyes and ears attuned to one leader up front? In other words, the church has developed cultural characteristics.

If we hope to begin to discern the difference between prophetic Christianity and the "seductive culture," it is undoubtedly wise to trace *how* a church develops cultural characteristics. For our frame of reference we will look at the Anabaptist journey from its beginnings as a Radical Reformation movement to the modern-day ethnic group. We will then explore how this ethnicity has affected its mission and service and relationship to outsiders, especially from the vantage point of the minority.

However, before we go on with Anabaptism and ethnicity, it must be pointed out that it is not only the Mennonite church that is vulnerable, neither is it just her that displays her ethnic colors (as we shall see). From the perspective of the minority communities, most, if not all, missionaries, whatever their denominations, have come with cultural baggage. They have superimposed their ethnic schemes upon their listeners. The Choctaw service—Baptist-style—and the Brethren in Christ Navajo Indian Mission are just such examples. And, of course, there are significant ethnic differences even among the Western Christian churches. While this may not always be clear to Westerners,it is quite evident to cultures radically different from Westernism. H. Richard Niebuhr's problem of "Christ and Culture" is a classical and universal dilemma. The picture becomes even more complicated when Christ and culture is taken beyond the Western context.

Anabaptism and Ethnicity: Peoplehood

There are several ways one can trace Anabaptism and how it acquired distinct traits. One way is to look at it from the angle of sect development, which Calvin Redekop does in his article "A New Look at Sect Development." He lists three steps: Anabaptism as a sect had its origins in dissidence; it then gained a "minority status" from which it developed a sense of specialness that began to express itself ethnically. Redekop points out that his usage of "ethnic group" goes beyond the "traditional identification of a collectivity marked by a common language, nationality, or religion and refers to a collectivity of persons who have developed a 'sense of peoplehood.' " (1974a: 349-350).

A related way of viewing Anabaptist ethnicity is in terms of nonconformity, or separation from the world. H. S. Bender in his classic essay, *"The Anabaptist Vision,"* explains:

> An inevitable corollary of the concept of the church as a body of committed and practicing Christians pledged to the highest standard of New Testament living was the insistence on the separation of the church from the world, that is nonconformity of the Christian to the worldly way of life. (1944: 48)

The logical outcome of this separation is a feeling of being different, being called out or, in theological terms, becoming a "peoplehood."

Whether the sense of peoplehood is included within ethnicity, or as the outgrowth of nonconformity, it seems that the peoplehood concept is basic to Anabaptism. Theologically, it is understood in terms of a covenantal relationship with God. This understanding is rooted all the way back to Israel's belief that they were the chosen people of God. Ross T. Bender links the Jewish experience with Anabaptism:

> Behind that sixteenth century commitment stands the biblical tradition of the people who were called into a special relationship of faith and obedience to God. Millard Lind has demonstrated that the roots of the Free Church tradition are already implicit in the Old Testament teaching on the covenant. The church in this view stands in direct continuity with Israel; she identifies herself with the long history of the people of God and sees herself in the perspective of the fulfillment of the promise of God to Abraham. The New Testament traces the continuing fulfillment of the promise of God in the history of the church. (1971: 136-137)

The Marks of Peoplehood: Chaco

Assuming that the concept of peoplehood is established in the Anabaptist tradition, the logical question remains: what are the marks of peoplehood? Perhaps another way to put it is: what characteristics develop in a people who believe themselves to be a community of believers called away from conformity to the world? Or, to get back to our original question: how does a church develop ethnic characteristics?

From the theological perspective H. S. Bender succinctly sketches the central teachings of Anabaptism which include discipleship, brotherhood, and the "ethic of love and nonresistance" (1944: 42). However, the crux of the matter (for our purposes) is how these teachings were actually expressed in daily life.

Whatever the theological ideals, it behooves any group to attempt to concretize such visions by giving them distinct social forms.

As a frame of reference from which we can make comparisons it may be helpful to look at the Mennonites in the Paraguayan Chaco. In an insightful essay, "Anabaptism and the Ethnic Ghost," Calvin Redekop shows how this modern-day Mennonite group's ideal of being the people of God takes on a sociological shape.

Although these people migrated to Paraguay in three waves from 1926-47, Redekop finds that they are still separated from the rest of the world geographically, economically, socially, culturally, and religiously. In other words, the Mennonites are a commonwealth unto themselves trying to realize a kingdom of God on earth. However, they are faced with serious problems. While "the New Testament was rather clear on the structure of the fellowship," Redekop notes that the New Testament "is silent on what is to be done with the sociological or non-ecclesiastical aspects of a 'people of God.' " Since it is left to the Anabaptists (or any other group, for that matter) to find their own way in the socioeconomic sphere, it is not surprising that they have confused "the sacred and the secular," and consequently have emerged as an "ethnic group" (1974b: 17).

Some highly interesting (and problematical) dynamics happen in any ethnic process. By its very nature, any ethnic group is vulnerable to ethnocentrism, and the Mennonites in the Chaco have been no exception. As a further illustration of such vulnerability these Mennonites have had "the tendency to be closed so that no mission work is carried on . . . for the degree of ethnic solidarity is inversely proportional to their missionary outreach" (1974b: 18).

The problem becomes more acute when an ethnic group identifies itself as living in the kingdom of God. The first thing that happens is the tendency of the community to equate itself with the kingdom of God, "so that the critical, refining, or purifying nature of the gospel tends to cease operating. In other words, an ethnic group formed on the basis of an attempted obedience to the gospel can become blinded by its own forms, assuming that these are an expression of the ideals or goals of the gospel blueprint" (1974b: 19).

Redekop goes on to show that the religious ethnic society tends to interpret any "differential treatment" or hostility from the outside world, as proof of its faithfulness to God. Faithfulness thus achieved, "all criticism and suspicion that there might not be some unfaithfulness or apostasy in the group" tends to be subverted (1974b: 19). This is further reinforced in the in-group mind by the fact that there is little or no communication with outsiders, "which ends in a fully involuted ethnic group which may be justifying its existence on the basis of religious principles, but which is a full-fledged ethnic group, with very little religious dynamic remaining in the basic ideology or ethos" (1974b: 20).

North American Mennonites Transport Ethnicity

The Mennonites in the Chaco help us see how difficult it is to try to realize a kingdom of God on earth. The thorn in the flesh lies in the inevitability of the ethnic process. And since no one of us escapes this cultural dilemma we can be sympathetic to these people in Paraguay. Well, what about the Mennonites in North America? In this essay, I am particularly thinking of the "Old" Mennonites, General Conference Mennonites, and the Mennonite Brethren. Are they any freer from the ethnic process? How do they handle such factors as ethnocentrism, self-criticism, and communication with outsiders? Do they blindly equate their communities and their outreach programs with living the kingdom of God? Is the concept of Mennonite peoplehood confused with the ideal of being the people of God? And against what can these questions be tested? With what or with whom can we compare these North American Mennonites to check the nature and the extent of the ethnic process present in them as a group?

We have seen how one group of Mennonites committed to being a people of God have developed ethnically. This becomes more clear as we look at how Mennonite ethnicity affects its outreach to, and relationship with minority groups and other outsiders.

Unlike the Mennonites in Paraguay, most North American Mennonites have not closed themselves off from the rest of society, nor is their ethnic solidarity woven as tightly. This is attested to by the fact that they are engaged in missionary work and voluntary service on an international scale. This does not mean, however, that the ethnic process is absent. While they have not formed enclaves totally separated and independent from the larger society, North American Mennonites have usually transported their ethnicity along with themselves to mission fields and VS units. Many examples can be cited to show that this does happen.

At the outset, it seems necessary to emphasize that the following analysis is not merely an emotive-expressive one. Its purpose is not to harangue or be judgmental; neither does it imply that the Mennonites are malicious. It only seeks to point out some of the dynamics between the minority groups and a church vulnerable to ethnicity. Also, it must be pointed out that my examples are primarily from the Indian perspective and experience rather than from the often generalized "minority" point of view. It has been my observation that the greater the cultural difference between the Mennonite Church and the minority group, the clearer the ethnic process. To be sure, there are great differences between white Mennonites and American black and Latino peoples. However, an even a wider gulf separates white Mennonites and the Indian peoples because of language, religion, customs, and a world-view and heritage that dates back at least 10,000 years!

Ethnic Groups Meet

The first thing that can be said about the ethnic church and the minority is that it is usually a meeting of *two* ethnic groups. This, it seems, has been the most difficult thing to understand and to accept on the part of missionaries or VS workers. If ethnicity refers to a social group with a common past and identity in the areas of religion, nationality, or language, then it follows that the blacks, the Chicanos, the Puerto Ricans, the Indians, and the Mennonites are all ethnic groups.

This becomes especially evident when Mennonite missionaries go to Indian communities. The differences are clear with respect to architecture, dress, language, customs, and of course, religion and values. Many examples can be cited from various places. For instance, the architecture of the Mennonite church ruins in Arizona point to significant differences between the missionaries and the Hopi. The Nanih Waiya Mennonite Church services in Philadelphia, Mississippi, show differences in language, dress, and customs between the Choctaws and the white leadership. The American flag in the Mennonite Brethren Church in Pine Ridge reservation indicates there is probably some difference in world-view between the Sioux and the pastor of that church.

The Power Factor

These illustrations also hint at something else that happens between the ethnic church and the minority, that is, the monopoly of power traditionally exercised by missionaries and some VS workers. Undoubtedly, the statement sounds unorthodox in light of the pacifist stance of the Anabaptist tradition. However, a close look at most mission and/or VS units has revealed this to be the case. Perhaps the greatest evidence of this lies in the fact that so few minority church leaders and congregations are independent of white leadership and funding. Although there have been dramatic changes in leadership in the black and Latino churches within the past decade, such changes have been few and minimal in the Indian communities. White Mennonite leadership remains tenaciously in control, in many instances.

Even those Indian congregations that have their own leadership have maintained Euro-American patterns of worship. It is fair to say that the most glaring weakness of most missionary endeavors has been the failure to train indigenous peoples for native church leadership. Surely, this speaks of power on the part of missionaries.

Voluntary Service can also be a power structure. Again this may sound startling because it is taken for granted that the program exemplifies a posture of servanthood rather than power. Ideally, of course, VS is based upon the notion of servanthood; in reality, however, volunteers have often had the upper hand in minority communities. They have come in as teachers, social workers, agriculturists, recreation directors, youth leaders, counselors, and the like. Sometimes, especially in the past, they have even come unannounced!

Even today VS orientations sketch (to a certain extent) the needs of the outlying communities, send in volunteers and resources, and usually define the conditions upon which these resources are used. This very process elevates the servant to the role of master. And this of course, can limit, or diminish the relationship between the server and the recipient. If this process is carried out persistently through many years it can emasculate the recipients and imbalance the perspective of the servers to the extent that they confuse their services with the kingdom of God. However, the greater tendency seems to be to form parasitic relationships between VSers and minority communities. Both need and feed on each other.

If the above discussion on the matter of power is not convincing, perhaps we need to turn our attention to the Mennonite organizations where crucial decisions are made. Where are the minorities at Akron, Elkhart, Newton, Hillsboro, Scottdale, and Winnipeg? And what about the Mennonite educational institutions? These issues are not purely rhetorical.

The task presently facing the Mennonite church is to come to terms with its own power with respect to minority peoples and its potential power within the larger society. We may wish to dismiss the notion of power on a theological level, but we must own up to its existence in the socioeconomic realm. There is a power-powerlessness relationship between the Mennonite churches and minorities. Somehow we must grapple with this; we must seek to understand how it operates and then take steps to balance the situation. It seems fruitless and abstract to speak of nonresistance or voluntary subordination when white (Mennonite) churches are in a power position both in minority communities and in the larger society, while minorities are basically powerless in both areas.

A word must be said about the minority status of the Mennonite church. While it may have gone through that phase in historical development, and while it may still hold sectarian status (numerically and intellectually) in comparison to the larger society, it is by no means in a minority position in relation to the racial minorities in North

America. Redekop defines "minority status" as "the inability of a group to determine its own way of life because it lacks the power to achieve its ends in the larger society . . . or, because it rejects the type of power needed to achieve its own ends" (1974a: 349). Although this twofold definition may converge intellectually, I would like to point out that there is a world of difference between the former and the latter. In other words, actual powerlessness is not the same as having the choice to reject the use of power.

The Change Factor

Certainly not all the dynamics have been negative between Mennonites and minorities. Things are changing--social gaps have been closed, cultural understandings have developed on both sides, and both groups have benefited each other for different reasons. Sometimes the relations between Mennonites and minorities have offered models of reconciliation and peacemaking. Cross-cultural retreats, seminars, and conventions have provided opportunities for dialogue. Organizational headquarters have become more sensitive to the *real* needs of minority communities as Mennonite horizons have been expanded through exposure and contact with minority people. The Mennonite press has gradually recognized the minority presence in the Mennonite church. Nevertheless, we have miles to go before we sleep. . . .

An independent Mennonite publication recently featured an intriguing forum entitled "I Am Not a Cultural Mennonite." That title reflects a collective consciousness-awakening among minority peoples across the North American continent beginning in the 1960s. It was a bittersweet awakening to self-identity distinct from plain clothing, coverings, borscht, shoofly pies and "Gott ist die Liebe" in four-part harmony.[1]

Although we could and indeed have had to shed external Mennonite trappings, many of us could not throw out the ideals of the Anabaptist Vision. Slowly we began to perceive a difference between Anabaptist theology and Mennonite culture. The difference is not the awareness of discrepancy or hypocrisy, but rather the realization that we minority peoples, with ethnic backgrounds distinct from German or Swiss Mennonitism, could nevertheless also claim the Anabaptist Vision, because such a vision is found in the New Testament and in other great traditions. And so we can say, "I am not a cultural Mennonite." To say this is not a put-down of Mennonitism; rather, it is an affirmation of our own uniqueness.

The Ethnic Impasse

There is always tension when two ethnic groups meet. It becomes even more interesting when the church is involved! Such an encounter is fraught with risk and possibilities. As we have seen, the encounter of the ethnic church and the minority is really a meeting of two peoples. Not surprisingly, we have experienced clashes and creativity. In some ways we have reached an ethnic impasse—and that may not be as bad as it sounds. It is not bad for the simple reason that, try as I may, I can never be a cultural Mennonite. That is, I can not claim the Germanic heritage with its own architecture, clothing, foods, customs, and even modes of worship. My own origins are rooted in the North American soil, with its own brown rhythms in language, customs, and values.

As white Mennonites must come to terms with—and eventually embrace—their own uniqueness, so we also must be doing likewise. We have both discovered—with great pains—that we cannot be other than who we are, in the best sense of the phrase. As long as we continue to affirm our respective identities, we are at an impasse—but it is an impasse of a positive sort.

There is of course, an ethnic impasse with negative tones. It is when ethnocentricity gets the best of us, and we close ourselves off from each other. We do not dialogue or fellowship together, neither do we listen to each other's admonitions. We have been vulnerable to such tendencies. And sometimes we have also confused God's leading with our respective eccentricities.

Toward Interrelatedness and Diversity

Perhaps the most creative way out of this ethnic impasse is twofold: it seems that it should be possible to respect each other's cultural peculiarities and still meet at the point of a commitment to God which entails discipleship, mutual aid and service, and the ethic of *agape* love. The ambiguity will not altogether disappear, because each ethnic group will still interpret and work out the ideals according to context and sociological reality. However, as brothers and sisters on the journey toward truth, we can covenant together to dialogue. And in the process of covenant and dialogue we can be lovingly watchful for each other. In other words, the gospel may be most prophetic under cross-cultural scrutiny. Or to put it in the vernacular, if rubbing shoulders with each other brings out our cultural cobwebs, it is equally feasible that it could also enable us to mobilize "the critical, refining, or purifying nature of the gospel." The gospel gains when there is more than one correct understanding and interpretation.

We may also dip into sociological and psychological insights on this matter. Reisner has said, "We can never understand something if we know only that thing." Elizabeth O'Connor presents a psychological perception: "In the writings of Nicoll and Ouspensky the instructions stress the importance of self-observation in a man's inner journey. The first thing one is told to do is to divide oneself into two— the observer and the observed. . . . Unless a man divides himself into two he cannot shift from where he is" (1971: 8).

In the inner journey of the church this means that she suffers if one cultural group monopolizes, whereas with a variety of perspectives, we will take turns as observers and the observed. As the ecosystem depends upon interrelated diversity for its very existence, so the church will only gain when her members are interrelated and diverse.

14

Gelassenheit, Entrepreneurs, and Remnants: Socioeconomic Models Among the Mennonites

Donovan E. Smucker

Against the background of the Russian catastrophe, the power and the sickness of American culture, the rage of the minorities, the new Canadian nationalism, and the explosions in the Third World, North American Mennonites must discover models for community, and, therefore, answers for the perennial problems of economic life.

This must take place in a strange new environment full of paradoxes. Never have the scholars retraced the biblical and historical origins with so much clarity. We know whence we have come, but some of us are still afraid of whither we are tending, because of the cultural whirlwinds swirling around our heads. Never has conference life been better organized, staffed, and financed. Yet, an apocalyptic time makes one ponder whether this organizational finesse is an adequate match for massive economic and social malfunctioning, or, in Toffler's phrase, an "eco-spasm." Never before has optimism reached the status of scientific fact as in the sociological studies of Leland Harder, J. Howard Kauffman, and Leo Driedger. The computers tell us that we are coping quite well with the twentieth century. Though the computers may be reading the face of the sky correctly, our hearts ask if they discern the signs of the times. What would the computers have said in Russia several decades prior to the revolution? Except for the cloud of Russification, everything looked fine in the commonwealth. Then the army collapsed, Lenin was sent home in a sealed car, and Machno's marauders marched down the lane prior to banging on the front door.

Even if the reader does not have the agony of *Angst, Weltschmerz,* or the demonic, it is obvious that a socioeconomic strategy in this time of crisis must be resilient and formidable. Trying to stand alone with a kind of Western capitalistic creed of "I-can-do-anything-if-I-work-hard-think-well-and-worship" will not suffice.

Donovan Smucker is professor of social sciences in Conrad Grebel College, University of Waterloo, Ontario, Canada. He has been active in peace and theological education in the General Conference Mennonite Church and was formerly president of Mary Holmes College, West Point, Mississippi.

When a situation bristles with paradoxes it suggests that there are contradictions within the system. When there are contradictions it further suggests that the polarization is due to different perspectives which fix on one pole of the paradox: one affirmation or one denial of that affirmation.

At this time the pessimists have their eyes on a seductive culture (to use C. Redekop's phrase) which looms formidably because culture is the building block in modern social science—a building block which is a sophisticated equivalent of the biblical idea of "the world" which we are bidden to overcome. Culture is the overarching thrust of unredeemed life which provides both the natural setting for Christian community and the opposition to that community. It is this seductive culture, not the aberrations of Fundamentalist theology, that is the enemy for the social realists. Proof of this is that an individual or a group may be wholly extricated from Fundamentalism and still be overwhelmed by cultural forces.

The optimists, on the other hand, focus on the impressive life *within* the church: historical, theological, and biblical insights and guidelines. A rich array of educational and service institutions supported by affluence and good stewardship. Exciting options for young people through Voluntary Service, camping, and assemblies. A flood tide of superior publications supplemented by radio and television. Diminishing conference isolation, growing ecumenical cooperation. Creativity in the fine arts. All this and more bringing a good feeling in a once-static church. To the optimists continued fear of the world seems like dyspepsia of the spirit, unwarranted by the realities of church life in the last quarter of twentieth century.

The realists believe that this glow of good feeling ignores the ways in which we are perceived by the victims of injustice and institutional violence in the twentieth century. Further, students of history believe that enormous discontinuities come periodically to rend the hardest monuments of human pride and to shatter the finest hopes of good people. In any case, the least that this demands is a hard look at the economic situation within and without the church, in a way that takes us beyond the present levels of discussion.

Four years *before* Harold Bender published his watershed essay on the Anabaptist Vision, Roland Bainton sent forth what may have been the first revisionist essay by a major American church historian, "The Left Wing of the Reformation" (1941). A Yale scholar utilized a Chicago publication to inform the academic community that there were rich insights among the Reformation radicals, insights that, in fact, had more influence on the shape of Christianity and culture than did the main-line Reformers. That historic essay of Bainton included a disclaimer: it was his conviction that the left wing had made only a small contribution to the place of economics in the context of the Radical Reformation, granted the enormous achievements elsewhere.

An obvious reply to Bainton is that persecution and martyrdom did not permit this contribution to come forth as it did later, in many countries and in varied contexts. A critical reading of two recent books—Peter James Klassen, *The Economics of Anabaptism* (1964) and Claus-Peter Clasen, *Anabaptism: A Social History, 1525-1618* (1972)—suggests that the previous social historians lacked the scholarly materials now available to include the left-wing Reformation and its subsequent developments. Max Weber's *The Protestant Ethic and the Spirit of Capitalism* (1930) and R. H. Tawney's *Religion and the Rise of Capitalism* (1926) gave primary emphasis to the rise of capitalism against the background of Catholic medievalism (monasteries and guilds) and to the major role of Lutheranism and Calvinism in the development of the new entrepreneural system. Larger social forces brought forth capitalism. Protestantism baptized it. Much needed now is a Weber or a Tawney to study the current economic scene, using but going beyond the work of Klassen, Clasen, and Peachey (1954). No gap is bigger than this one, yet some spadework is being done already.

An example of this spadework is James Juhnke's *A People of Two Kingdoms: The Political Acculturation of the Kansas Mennonites* (1975). After locating the four requests of the Russian Mennonites to the United States government—exemption from military service, closed settlements with German language, good land, and financial assistance for the migration—Juhnke asks:

> Why did so many Mennonites come to Kansas where their two foremost requests were not guaranteed? Could it be that free land outweighed all other considerations, in spite of Mennonite insistence that they came for religious reasons? To say that the Mennonites talked like religious men but acted like economic men would be to substitute a simple slogan for a more complex reality. . . . But the experiences of the Mennonite official delegation in touring the prospective settlement areas demonstrate that it was not the American government but rather the American railroad that played the decisive role in settling the Mennonites on the frontier. (1975: 15)

In any case, the powerful role of economic considerations is a basic part of past and present situations. Later the writer will utilize the work of Weber and Tawney to make an important point regarding the economic outlook of Mennonites.

Before outlining a series of economic and community models with which we must struggle, it is important to note that considerable distortion is introduced in most discussions of large economic issues in the church because most North American Mennonites know only one of the two economic systems operating in society as a whole. The planning system of the big corporations we do not know. The market system of small businesses and small agriculture we do know. The world of the billion-dollar corporations like Esso and General Motors (now the number 1 and 2 companies) is a world apart from the DeFehr or Miller-Hess operations in Winnipeg and Akron. In the world of the small business there is still a personal element among ownership, management, worker, and consumer. The power of the small businessman does not propel him into the elite power structure of the region, province, or nation. Correlations still exist between work, discipline, and brains on the one hand, and achievement on the other. Older workers will not be summarily fired after years of service. Unions are rarely if ever a part of the small businesses of the Mennonite entrepreneur. Monopoly is not possible even if it were desirable. It is neither possible nor desirable for the small businessman.

The last paragraph describes the world symbolized by Archbold, Ohio, in Guy Hershberger's writings. Since this is the world of the dynamic businessman of the market, it is hard for him (and for those of us who know him and need him as a generous steward) to resonate with that other world of campaign contributions, mass advertising, price fixing, cartels, CIA deals, war work, lobbying, country clubs, and posh expense accounts. Yet that world of Madison Avenue, Detroit, and Washington produces the major material goods that even the small businessman needs to run his own marginal but dependent operation.

To express one's faith in the last outposts of the free market leads in the direction of a conservative politics that uses much of the rhetoric of the small-town businessman while following *de facto* policies in the opposite direction. Talking of fiscal responsibility, for example, while spending money recklessly on the sacrosanct defense budget. Talking of the simple virtues while living the high life of men and women in the corridors of power. An almost inescapable myopia comes from seeking to understand economic realities from an operational base in the small sector of business and agriculture in league with conservative politics.

By the same token, the churchman with a base outside the world of business may respond to the neo-Keynes economic analysis of deficit financing and welfare programs, and then realize with disillusioning despair that the political options here are only a veneer of social compassion wrapped around the same old demons of defense, war, big city machines, and programs which constantly flirt with rip-offs and shoddy administration. There is a slight advantage in the analytical approach of the liberal and left-liberal Keynesian thinkers who start with a more realistic knowledge of the planning systems. When this is yoked with an antimilitary posture, as in the writings of John Kenneth Galbraith, it provides what, to this writer, is a sounder perspective. Yet it remains dangerous territory full of agony and ambiguity.

Meanwhile, millions of people are succumbing to the blandishments of Marxist political parties and their socialist economic systems. This includes many Christians, some of whom are Mennonites in the USSR, East Germany, Latin America and other parts of the Third World. The writer's colleague, John Rempel, studied for two years in a Protestant theological seminary in East Germany where the question of Christianity and Marxism was one of the basic questions in the school. These developments are particularly difficult for Christians of North America, especially in the U.S.A., where a vigorous faith in the market economy of free enterprise exists more fully than anywhere in the world. This persists despite the realities of the military-industrial complex of huge interlocking institutions, a far cry from free enterprise!

Canadian Mennonites also operate in the same orbit of small market businesses in a national economy dominated by the big American corporations with much less involvement in the military support system and, on the other hand, a tradition of populist politics which has led to three socialist governments in Manitoba, Saskatchewan, and British Columbia. These socialist governments are in the tradition of British liberalism rather than the Russian or Chinese models. A final difference in the western provinces of Canada is a much larger involvement of Mennonites in the cooperative movement, a secular version of mutual aid in the churches.

Models for Economic Life and for Community

Given the paradoxes, ambiguities, and problems of the economic situation in the North American environment, the Christian brotherhood must struggle with different models of economic and community life. The following are offered in fear and trembling:

A. *Of the two models developed in the sixteenth and seventeenth centuries, only the Hutterite model remains.*

1. *The Hutterite model combines Gelassenheit* (yieldedness, surrender of the will) *with community of goods.* Severe restraint, if not indeed obliteration of individual gain, yoked to a communism of production and marketing, has brought brotherhood affluence and individual poverty. In North America the embrace of advanced technology made possible the brotherhood affluence. Variations on these basic themes by the Society of Brothers in three American communities and the Community Farm of the Brethren (Hungarian Nazarenes) in Ontario offer adaptations on the original model principally in the break with a rigid tradition; and, in the Society of Brothers, acceptance of higher education, musical appreciation, and books.

The Society of Brothers at Rifton, New York, is a particularly interesting case for Mennonites since they have sent musical groups to Mennonite churches in Ontario, received visitors from Conrad Grebel College regularly through the arrangements of J. Winfield Fretz, and have Mennonite and Church of the Brethren people in the community. The rejection of cultural primitivism by the Rifton community, along with the presence of members who are similar in background to the college-trained Mennonites of North America, raises the question whether this model is not an option for that persistent minority of Christians who want a form of Protestant monasticism, that is, a communal life which accepts marriage in contrast to the Catholic monastics. Moreover, this persistent minority now knows that the hippie communes, although large in number and frequent in their rise and fall, have a self-destruction mechanism in their romantic subjectivism, transiency of commitment, and anarchy of purpose and meaning. The price which must be paid, according to Hutterites of all stripes, is the loss of individual freedom, since the novitiate must pledge to obey the judgments of the community without question.

If the Rifton model is accepted it need not operate in the particular context and discipline of the Society of Brothers. It could operate, *de novo*, in an independent Christian setting or, preferably, with the blessing of one or more conferences related to the Mennonite Central Committee. Like Rifton, any community of this sort must find a source of cash income such as they have developed in the manufacture of Community Playthings, the brand name for a fine line of educational toys. The hippie communes quickly discover to their dismay that a cash flow is a crucial necessity.

Other variations of the Hutterite theme are Koinonia Farm in Georgia, Reba Place in the Chicago area, and the Reba outpost at Plow Creek near Tiskilwa, Illinois. Koinonia retains the involvement in communal production and marketing while Reba Place enjoins the common purse in a variety of vocational and professional pursuits, a less radical step.

Outside of Protestant Christianity there is the long tradition of Catholic monasticism which has never been seriously considered by Protestants, since it implied an ethical dualism and was often condemned for alleged abuses within the four walls of the monastery, though much of this is unexamined caricature. The Jewish kibbutzim are a mixture of Zionism, European socialist utopianism, and back-to-the-land feelings. War clouds in the Middle East have obscured the kibbutzim which, in fact, are one of the gems in the melancholy history of Israel.

The model of communal living in its various forms, then, is very much before us for those who are ready to make a more radical break with the dominant patterns in church and society. John Hostetler introduces his new book on the Hutterites by observing that these are communities of people "who live a satisfying, stable, and rewarding life" (1974: xvi). Bon Homme? Rifton? Koinonia? Plow Creek-Reba Place? Bright? Which variation of the model is best? Many will ask. Growing numbers will ask, answer, and join. A major portion will remain permanently in this powerful way of life.

2. *The second model* is from the main stream of the Radical Reformation; it rejected Christian communism by *combining the same Gelassenheit austerity* (expressed within the fellowship as mutual aid with unlimited liability) *with a posture of confrontation* with the religio-social-political establishment outside of the fellowship. But this model is no longer an option; *Gelassenheit* is incompatible with the highly motivated entrepreneur of the free market and confrontation is incompatible with Russian privilegiums or North American pluralisms. After outlining this model, the writer will describe the Amish, Holdeman, and Old Order attempts to preserve *Gelassenheit* without confrontation, and the effort of Art Gish to reunite *Gelassenheit* with confrontation in an appeal addressed to the middle-class peace church person with a base in simple congregational life.

If Henry J. Cadbury of the Quakers properly warned us of the peril of modernizing Jesus, we need to be sensitized to the peril of modernizing the early Anabaptists. Bainton writes of the *left-wing* Reformation. Williams writes of the *Radical* Reformation. Walter Klaassen writes of the Anabaptists who were *neither Catholic nor Protestant.* All of these terms suggest a sharp deviation from conventional religion and culture.

Gelassenheit was the climate within which a radical new approach to life developed; supremely it means complete self-denial and voluntary surrender to the will of God *(Gottesgebenheit).* Through it, suffering becomes the royal road to God in witness, martyrdom, and subordinating material and physical needs to the spiritual. From this self-surrender comes peace and serenity. Thus two great poles of Christian truth—the love of God and the will of God—are held together.

Robert Friedmann's survey of *Gelassenheit* in *The Mennonite Encyclopedia* relates the doctrine to the Middle Ages, the mystics, the Philipites, the Hutterites, *Martyrs Mirror,* and Menno Simons. He concludes by observing: "Present-day Mennonitism has lost the idea of *Gelassenheit* nearly completely; yet with the recovery of the ideal of discipleship also *Gelassenheit* may be revived" (1956: 449).

Gelassenheit was the perfect teaching for the conquering of egocentricity under the powerful impact of brotherhood in the midst of a hostile, even lethal environment. Much of the radicalism of the early Anabaptists stems from this total flinging of the self into the heart of a Spirit-filled fellowship radiant with Messianic Kingdom awareness. It is quite in the spirit of *Gelassenheit* not to pay war taxes, as Hut and Riedemann taught. It is in character to refuse all usury when investments were rejected out of hand. It is not surprising that the early brethren could interrupt worship services, call for disputations, develop an underground movement and, like Menno, remain in flight for several decades. This was an eschatological moment for a beleaguered Christian remnant. But if the radicalism of the Anabaptist heritage is to be continued, one must ask whether such a stance is possible over the long pull when the environment is not openly hostile and when the fires of renewal and revival die down.

Although the pioneer skills of clearing land and starting new settlements in a fraction of the time required by halfhearted settlers quite early demonstrated an economic flair to be applied by Mennonite immigrants during four centuries on three continents, the basic orientation at the beginning was antitrade and anticommerce. Claus-Peter

Clasen reminds us in his social history of Anabaptism that the common man in sixteenth-century Germany "bitterly resented" the great trading companies which dominated commerce, banking, and mining. The Tirolese peasant leader Michael Gaismaier (subject of a forthcoming book by Walter Klaassen) even demanded in 1526 that all commerce be abolished.

In any case, Mennonites could not retain *Gelassenheit* in the face of rising capitalism. Max Weber has described the movement from the earlier commerce of the guilds to the entrepreneur, who is an economic adventurer seeking to make large profits from the labor of workers employed on a wage basis. Weber's thesis is that Protestantism contributed to the rise of capitalism by providing morale for the entrepreneur.

The movement into the Protestant ethic, according to Weber, was aided by Lutheranism, Anabaptism, and Calvinism, in the following outline:

Lutheranism
1. Poverty degraded from the rank of virtues.
2. Secular occupations dignified as "callings."

Anabaptism
1. Transfer of monastic asceticism to callings: *inner-weltliche Askese* (inner-worldly asceticism).

Calvinism
1. Predestination allows the elect to proceed in the world with courage and a clear conscience.
2. The removal of the ban on interest, as distinguished from usury.

Weber placed a religious interpretation on the final result, whereby wealth was not to be enjoyed by Protestants but used for philanthropy or to augment capital. Later Wesley said: "Get all you can, save all you can, give all you can."

Long after the Reformation, the restraints on wealth were limited to voluntary stewardship. Soon the business ethic was tempted to equate prosperity with virtue and poverty with vice. More recently gatherings of businessmen and mutual aid societies have encouraged a reconstruction of the business ethic in the light of more independent and profound analysis of the Christian ethic.

Not only have we lost *Gelassenheit* in the blessing of motivation for investment and in the need for some status in the business community, but the vast array of church-related institutions supported by voluntary contributions now *demand* an affluent, business-oriented church. Consider three Mennonite colleges in the United States in 1974-75, for example:

Bethel College—$2,271,689 budget; $956,000 gifts.

Goshen College—$4,700,000 budget; $1,426,000 gifts and grants.

Eastern Mennonite College—$3,930,333 budget; $1,179,000 gifts.

Together the three institutions raised $3,561,000. Obviously, this level of money-raising for only a small part of the total institutional life of North American Mennonite churches is possible only in denominations which have successful farmers and prosperous businessmen, active in the marketplace, striving to expand, eager to innovate, always dissatisfied with present sales and service.

In the last quarter of the twentieth century the present educational, mission, service, artistic, and communications programs are marks of vitality and vision. They are possible only because we no longer need to restrain ourselves with the *Gelassenheit* of the sixteenth and seventeenth centuries. Indeed, if we did enforce such restraint the dynamism of the church in its present stance would be destroyed.

Harold Barclay of the University of Alberta has studied the Church of God in Christ, Mennonite (Holdeman), to show how they place capitalistic drives under severe restraints (1969). A dialectical relationship exists between mutual aid and capitalism in an agrarian setting, in an ethos marked by distrust of the city, restraint on expansion, and rejection of conspicuous consumption. At some point the Holdeman businessman must restrain his business or leave the church. A definite ceiling exists over the dynamics of the business enterprise. Barclay suggests that further studies are needed for the less strict Mennonite groups who have no restraining force, other than gifts from surpluses to church institutions. But, the gifts from surpluses are the financial lifeblood of the rich institutional life of the less strict groups, as over against the limited institutional development of the Holdemans with no schools and only modest beginnings in missions and hospitals. One can say that the Holdeman ceiling on expansion and conspicuous consumption characterizes the Amish and Old Order Mennonites as well, where cautious support of MCC and a tiny publication program constitute the small extra-congregational demands on the pocketbook. *The dilemma is obvious: capitalistic restraint plus limited outreach or large outreach supported by business surpluses.*

In a more sophisticated form, Art Gish of the Church of the

Brethren has promoted voluntary poverty in lectures he has given in the Mennonite "circuit," along with his two books: *The New Left and Christian Radicalism* (1970) and *Beyond the Rat Race* (1973). He presents simplicity as a lifestyle to free Christians from the pressures of competing in a complex society, a society giddy with affluence. Gish calls for a Christian counterculture with home industry, handcrafts, sharing, and mutual aid. General Motors need not be destroyed by direct attack. It will be bypassed with a new creative minority working from the grass roots, a minority with limited consumption of goods and services. Despite the freshness of approach in rejecting conventional liberalism, conservatism, and radicalism, Gish writes books based on his training in church institutions, sends forth the books with major publishers, rides to conferences in his automobile—in short, the rhetoric is more radical than his ability to extricate himself from the rich institutional life which nurtured him. The vision of voluntary poverty, however, continues to haunt the Christian prophet. The least this vision can do is to restrain and judge. The most is to create genuine alternate structures for the Franciscans and the Gishes as it did for the Huts and the Arnolds.

The Hutterite option is very much alive for a small minority in the Christian fellowship. The line runs from the sixteenth into the late twentieth century. The semicommunal or noncommunal model of *Gelassenheit* plus mutual aid plus confrontation has been dissolved by the Protestant ethic and the consumer-bourgeoisie society in order to finance a dynamic church in a sick society. Even the Protestant ethic is modified toward consumerism and free spending by that bourgeoisie society. The ambitious plans and fiscal needs of our schools and other institutions suggest we need more not less expansion in the market.

Let us consider other models.

B. *The commonwealth model of Russia, its brief appearance in Manitoba, and its adaptation in Paraguay and Mexico: Mutual aid under various Caesars meets Adam Smith and the Old Adam.*

When persecution ceases, when the land is fertile in quality and ample in quantity, when natural increase in population requires new settlements, what are the economic dynamics of Mennonites several centuries and more after the early Anabaptist beginnings? Look to the Russian commonwealth for the answer. It is impressive but fragile. It is an alloy of mutual aid and entrepreneural thrust.

1. *The Commonwealth of Russia.* Mutual aid launched the migra-

tions through a group-sponsored agreement with the czars. It was continued in the four mother settlements divided into 97 villages and the 52 daughter settlements divided into 320 villages. They used what Leo Driedger calls the European village system: a broad main street with even rows of houses on either side, the church and school opposite to each other at one end, and a common village pasture. Land was divided into strips so that all would share the good and bad land. Each village had common pasture and each family had several acres for gardening adjoining the house. These brothers and sisters in Christ were laced together not only by their common suffering in the past and common problems in the present, but by an intricate network of mutual aid practices in money, aid to widows, improvement of breeding stock, fire insurance, ferries, and land distribution. In this context the rejection of the Hutterite option was only a difference in degree.

But, *Gelassenheit* is not coterminous with mutual aid which always contains a measure of self-interest; the "trans-*Gelassenheit*" self-interest in mutual aid spilled over into the frontier psychology of a national situation overripe for the highly motivated entrepreneur.

In the Fullness of Time, 150 Years of Mennonite Sojourn in Russia, by Walter Quiring and Helen Bartel, was translated into English and reissued in 1974. It is a breathtaking picture of the greatest material civilization Mennonites have ever known. First the institutions of the colonies: superb church buildings, schools, welfare agencies, and places of service. The architecture conveys a functionalism modified by a handsome "meeting house" feeling like the Quakers and Puritans in the American Colonies. Not in just one place but everywhere one observes an impressive number of buildings housing the ministries of the church. Nothing in North America can equal these architectural symbols of an aggressive, prosperous people who were skilled practitioners of mutual aid and strong, even brilliant, community life.

Then Quiring describes "The Farm Nobility and Their Estates" as follows: "It was not only the proverbial hunger for land, which caused the Russian Mennonite farmers to break through the boundaries of their village communities and establish themselves alone and independently on landed estates. Neither was it the inherited driving force of experienced pioneers who looked for an occupation. *It was rather the only way out for most active farmers, and their only chance to get into a field of expanded enterprise which matched their vigour and abilities"* (1974: 15; emphasis is added).

The estates of David Willms, "Brodskij," and Heinrich Dyck,

"Rosenhof-Brodskij," would have been the envy of the landed gentry anywhere in the world. And they were only two among many. Before World War I there were 384 large estate owners among the Mennonites, one of whom had 50,000 acres. This group, which numbered only 1.9 percent of the Mennonite population, contributed 80,000 rubles or one third of the total funds for the alternative forestry service program for the young conscientious objectors.

The new entrepreneural vigor also was expressed in business and industry where 2.8 of the population owned three fourths of the total Mennonite capital (Krahn, 1959: 389).

A landless proletariat began to develop along with those in small businesses, very different from the factories and mills of the Niebuhrs, Hildebrandts, Koops, or Paetkaus.

When a disciplined, intelligent people permit unlimited economic expansion, when the juices of free enterprise begin to flow, a high materialistic civilization develops which can support enormous church-sponsored institutions, as well as conspicuous consumption. The setting aside of *Gelassenheit* for the Protestant ethic is the opening wedge for this powerful dynamism. Real human needs are met by the flour of the mills, the implements of the factories, and the credit of the wealthy. But the opening wedge also opens the doors to inequality, dissolution of brotherhood, and resentments which can feed movements as contrary as communism and counter establishment revivals such as the Mennonite Brethren.

This is nothing peculiar to Mennonites. The economics of Quakerism described in Tolles's *Meeting House and Counting House* (1963) portrays the same problem in another peace church. The William Penn of the countinghouse, idealist though he was, was the opposite of John Woolman, the prophet of restraint who worked only to have enough money for a mobile ministry of witness.

If the fires of revolution had not fallen on Russia the number of large estates, industries, and businesses would have led to even greater opulence. Neither the Dutch nor the North Americans had ever equaled the economic thrust displayed in Russia for 150 years.

But, this must not obscure the remarkable achievements in mutual aid, community development, and meaningful associations with close neighbors. Alas, it proved to be unequal to the dynamics of free enterprise and, later, revolution.

2. *The Manitoba Reserves: a lost opportunity for a semicommunal alternative to Hutterite Christian communism.* For a brief time it ap-

peared that the core of the Russian insight into Christian community might be reestablished in Canada, hence providing a semicommunal alternative to the totally common ownership of the Hutterites, and a partly communal alternative to Western individualism. It was an exciting prospect.

The East and West Reserves sought to recreate the Russian pattern minus the dilemmas and dangers of Russian imperial culture. Only the Hutterites seem to survive and recreate their classic patterns of communality. The semicommunal patterns of the European village qualify the impact of untamed economic forces without demanding the total conformity of the Hutterites. This is a desirable goal then and now.

But, as E. K. Francis pointed out in his many studies(1955), Manitoba, in 1870 to 1890, transformed its economy from fur trading, through pioneer and frontier economies, to high capitalism characterized by the cultivation of cash crops, extensive and largely exploitive farming methods, new technical inventions, and a struggle for money and profit.

In this context of high capitalism the Mennonites did not have a monolithic tradition which was solely one of mutual aid; they brought experience in the expanding Russian market, technical innovations, capitalistic finance, and a market economy. With the Manitoba context wide open for commercial farming, with the greater inflexibility of a solidaristic economic system, with the incorporation of many villages, the abandonment of the old tradition started with a few and gradually increased to the many. The Russländer immigrants added further movement in the direction away from the old peasant community. While mutual aid would persist in many forms, including the newer one of cooperative economics, North America lost an opportunity to see a semicommunal society persist into the twentieth century, a tragic loss.

Meanwhile, under commercial farming and then urban businesses like the Reimer Trucking Company and Block Brothers Real Estate, the Mennonite reputation for vigorous economic achievement was frequently praised when competitors were not smarting under the competition from these highly motivated, intelligent, disciplined people.

The high morale of the Mennonite entrepreneur in an environment offering opportunity and encouragement led to the collapse of the semicommunal option.

3. *The semicommunal model in Paraguay: a state within a church.*

Perhaps Paraguay provided a second chance for the Russian commonwealth, with a political covenant analagous to the privilegium.

With considerable assistance from North America, the colonies in Paraguay have shown characteristic motivation and ingenuity in a much more difficult physical environment than Russia or North America, hence retaining more of the frontier peasant society flavor.

The central problem is political and cultural: political in creating a state within a church, and cultural in learning how to relate to native peoples. The church-state becomes judicial, with all the problems attendant to that role. In Redekop's words: "The relatively new information that this thesis provides us with is that the Believers' Church, or sect, to use the classical terminology, can become secularized not by adopting or accepting the values of the world as it attempts to become respectable, but by becoming the world from within by remaining separate" (1973: 356-357).

Meanwhile, anthropologists are questioning the depth of Mennonite acceptance of the Indians nearby, sensing a real effort to reach them but facing cultural barriers which keep them as second-class citizens.

Paraguay, then, tests the Mennonite finesse in economic matters in a Third World country in the poverty belt; in a colony isolated from major urban areas; and with a "contract" with the government which leaves the colony people very much to themselves.

There isn't the slightest chance for the dazzling material civilization which developed in Russia and the one that has developed in North America. The economy is under natural restraints from the environment, natural and national. But, the problems of working with privileges no one else possesses, and of more advanced European culture clashing with native peoples, are agonizing.

Involuntary poverty can be induced by migrating to a country with limited resources which grants space in a remote area. But high capitalism seeks good land and good markets.

4. *Modern adaptations of the semicommunal models of the Russian commonwealth, the Manitoba Reserves, and the Paraguayan colonies.* Within the pioneering social patterns of the commonwealth we find a key insight still valid here in North America. It is the possibility of creating an intentional community based on proximity of living with people of a common faith bound together with structures of mutual aid. The prefix "semi" before "communal" preserves some privacy against the excessive collectivism of the commune. The "communal"

after the prefix creates collective strength against the adversaries of intimidation which single individuals or single families cannot resist. Fortunately, there are excellent examples of the semicommunal pattern and it is the opinion of the present writer that we have underestimated its use in more urbanized societies.

Caryndale is a semicommunal society in Kitchener, Ontario, founded by the General Church of the New Jerusalem (Swedenborgian) in 1963. There are similar communities in Philadelphia, Washington, Chicago, and London, England.

The church purchased several farms, formed a corporation to hold and sell the land, hired a landscape architect to lay out an imaginative community with winding roads and then built a church building, a school (grades K-8), and a community center. Starting in 1963, there are now 35 families living in Caryndale. Since the founding of the community only two families have left the community, quickly replaced by new members who were part of the Swedenborgian fellowship. Every Friday night the adults gather for dinner followed by a doctrinal class.

The total effect of Caryndale, located within the city limits of Kitchener, is a synchronized pattern of religious, educational, social, and cultural activities. In an urban area with members who are business and professional on the "outside" they have created a semicommunal society of impressive proportions. The price for this close-knit life is the separation from non-Swedenborgian people in Kitchener except through work or civic life. But, communalism has always sacrificed outside relationships for the intimacy of the insiders. It does this in order to enjoy the delights of fellowship, and, defensively, to minimize the erosion from hostile forces.

Another example of a semicommunal development is the York Center Community Cooperative founded by returning CPS men of the Church of the Brethren and teachers from Bethany Theological Seminary. Located 24 miles west of the Loop in Chicago, the community has 30 years of experience, proving that the precarious life of the hippie communes can be overcome in the hands of people of greater maturity and deeper commitments. Seventy-five families are living at York Center. In addition to yearning for closer fellowship, the York Center community was launched to break the color line in the Chicago suburbs and to permit people of limited capital to build homes on a half acre of land instead of the tiny lots now the hallmark of suburbia. When the community was started it was in an unincorporated area, hence, the co-op provided water, recreation, library, and fire protection. When hostility to racial minorities was demonstrated by a fiery cross visitation from the Ku Klux Klan, the co-op developed its own nonviolent police patrol—nonviolent since most of the men had been COs in the second World War.

Unlike Caryndale, York Center used the Rochdale economics of the co-op movement for the formal structures of the community. That is, a family joined by purchasing a membership in the co-op. This membership gave the possessors one vote in the business meetings of the community, a parcel of land, and the right to build a house with the limitations of a quit-claim deed which specified that the house could not be sold to anyone but a co-op member, a bylaw obviously aimed at avoiding members not in sympathy with the community.

Among the requirements in the early days were participation in a labor bank whereby each family was required to donate a certain number of hours of labor to the neighbor's building program and an equal amount to needs of the community.

As the years rolled on York Center lessened the Brethren inputs and greatly increased the emphasis on co-ops as the basic ideological foundation of the community. The York Center church was available nearby but not mandatory as in Caryndale.

York Center is highly diverse racially. It is a place where dissenters feel at home. It has provided a wholly new community of insight in the placid conformity of suburbia. It is a pattern which could be emulated many other places: private home ownership qualified by many features of mutual aid and cooperation among neighbors of common commitment; a community breaking the color line in the suburbs; and freedom to obtain employment on the outside.

It is a great disservice to the Russian commonwealth to assume that semicommunal life is desirable only for people fleeing from persecuting societies which require a new covenant with autocratic governments. Extricate Christian people from the sticky and precarious privilegiums and the question still remains: Can Christian people live with less than common ownership and more than private ownership? York Center, Caryndale, and many others suggest that the answer is "yes" in almost any part of North America. And especially as urbanism sweeps more and more people into urban and suburban areas.

While the insider-outsider issue remains as the central problem of all intentional communities, it compensates for this by a solid home base for witness and service to the outside world. If there are acts of nonconformity on the outside, the inside support system assures the nonconformist of support even though it cannot immunize him to sanctions, mild or brutal, from a culture which makes the deviant the target of punishment.

C. *Migration within and without North America.*

Surely one of the oldest strategies for people seeking an alternative to present socioeconomic problems is to move on to another place. In the case of the Old Colony people it is a quest for release from the encroachments of post-industrial societies; thus the migrations to Mexico and to the remote areas of Alberta and British Columbia that provide temporary isolation before the "world" moves up to the community.

Adventurism can also lead people to leave complicated modern societies for frontier living in Alaska, Australia, Guatemala, or New Zealand. Or, it can lead to the remote areas of Canada, either provincial or territorial. A tougher encounter with natural forces, the equalitarianism of the frontier, the return to greater handcraft—all these propel the migrant who may not have a strongly religious base.

Canada has also received many draft dodgers and deserters most of whom are staying permanently. These include a number of Mennonites whose major motif is freedom rather than economic change.

Be it political oppression, economic depression, anxieties that create restlessness, or despair over the urban rat race, there is always migration. While not like the classic eras when Europeans came to North America by the millions, migration is still a real option as one can see particularly well in Canada, where recent immigrants are to be found in large numbers in the affluent provinces. Most of these immigrants are only too eager to channel their reawakened economic motivation into the "rat race"—if they come into heavily populated urban-industrial communities. But, the migrants to frontier communities may peel off some of the overorganized dimensions of modern life for that pioneer lifestyle which has tested the characters of people for centuries.

It is good to have the option of migration to refocus and relocate the economic and social problem. One cannot migrate out of history except by death. But, one can leave Chortitza for Steinbach, and Steinbach for Winnipeg, and Winnipeg for Fort Vermilion.

D. *The small town: supplementing farming with small industry while providing a shelter from urban pathologies.*

In an earlier section we have commented on the agricultural-small business orientation of the small town, of which Archbold, Ohio, has been a symbol, with its furniture and farm machinery factories, meat-packing plant, and livestock auction. Absorbing the surplus of farm labor, few Archbold young people need to migrate to cities for employment.

The vigorous economies of the outstanding small towns of the United States and Canada are more than defensive citadels stemming migrational tides to the cities. Positively they have elicited the creative entrepreneural energies of gifted, highly motivated people. Occasionally, as in Hesston, Kansas, this creativity is so perfectly timed and so brilliantly executed that a company begins to knock on the doors of the mainstream of the economic order. An example of this is the Hesston farm implement company which has become an international operation, owning a Lear jet for its executives, holding board meetings in attractive places (recently in Brussels, Belgium), and claiming sales in the millions.

The Archbold and Hesston examples may suggest that it is only in small towns that the Mennonite flair for business can function. If this is true in the States, it is not true in Canada, where the Zehr Supermarkets of Kitchener, the Reimer Trucking Company of Winnipeg, and the Block real estate business in Vancouver are huge operations in a totally urban milieu, *i.e.,* areas of 200,000 to 1,000,000 population. Indeed Leo Driedger has pointed out that Canadian Mennonites in 1974 became a predominantly urban people whereas the United States brethren are still predominantly rural. This difference must not obscure the decline of farming everywhere, due to powerful forces of change in the North American economy.

If there are, however, continuing Archbold and Hesston options in the rural nonfarm communities, then the movement would be to "town" (rural nonfarm) from the farm, instead of to the huge urban centers. But quite apart from the movement to small towns and to large cities, the question before us is the "small town mix" as a model for economic life under Christian norms.

The small town can provide economic opportunity while avoiding separation from family and friends. Dynamic examples like Hesston and Archbold require growth in knowledge, skill, and insight into the products and markets of the local companies. The income levels can be quite good, even though scaled below big companies in big cities. The thriving small town also needs professionals such as teachers, doctors, dentists, and lawyers. The retention of the new economic and professional leadership augurs well for the local churches.

On the other side of the ledger, the possible illusion that these small-market companies are representative of the larger economic system of the corporations may create an ideological bias. Further, the small town has a natural predilection for conservative politics. There is tight social control over lifestyles. There is the balcony attitude whereby the great events of the day always take place "out there" but not "here" in the village. Even a dedicated local congregation may be no match for the subtle corporate pressures which the total village milieu place on all who dwell within it. There is the puzzle why the leading businessmen who prefer small towns spend so much time in the big cities selling, buying, and conferring. There is growing stratification between the major businessman and the remainder of the community.

In any case, the Canadian dynamics are primarily in the direction of the cities. It remains to be seen in the States if the burgeoning effect of higher education, electronic communications, Voluntary Service, the Goshen SST, and the austerity of the youth subculture can be contained within the boundaries of small town culture, dynamic or static. There is in megalopolis areas a nostalgic return to small towns by a small minority of victims of urban hysteria and paranoia. On the other hand, a sound prediction is a lessening hold of the small town option, despite the nostalgia and defeatism of some city dwellers. There are only a few dynamic small towns. Many are dying a slow death under the hammer blows of urbanism.

E. *Ethnic villagers or metropolitan remnant?*

After much research, Leo Driedger's question is before us (1975). The "ethnic villages" in the Canadian cities, principally in the West and overwhelmingly Russländer, are coping with a tough environment far better than rural life determinists and urban pessimists had ever expected.

The people in rural culture read and see the atrocities of city life and jump to the conclusion that cities are jungles beyond redemption. The facts are that cities are really constellations of small towns and neighborhoods which can be held together by territorial control, institutional completeness, social distance, and cultural identity, the latter consisting of language-use, endogamy, choice of friends, participation in church, parochial schools, and voluntary organizations. This neatly etched identity—the ethnic village—is something which can be measured in cross-cultural research.

After his painstaking research Driedger is quite blunt in his evaluation of what might be hailed as a great achievement, after the secularization warnings of a generation or two ago. Driedger speaks with direct effect when he says: "The basic shortcoming of the ethnic villager model is that it perpetuates ingroup solidarity to the extent that it creates social distance between the ingroup and others. The Christian gospel makes it clear that such a model is inadequate, if not heretical. The Christian community must serve as springboard to interaction, not separation" (1975:237). The dynamic of the gospel calls for a "metropolitan remnant."

Perhaps the issue between the ethnic village and metropolitan remnant bypasses the economic question. The remarkable thrust of the Winnipeg Mennonites into the economic life of the community may have been possible under the rubrics of either strategy. Given a city whose old British charter group was under heavy competition from vigorous newcomers mainly from Eastern Europe, the economic options for the Mennonites were as real as for anyone else. The construction industry, for example, was particularly available for enterprising Mennonites along with trucking and small manufacturing establishments like the DeFehr company. In addition, the professionals did quite well and the musicians were so numerous that a Master's thesis studied them as a subculture in the city. Everywhere there were opportunities for bright, disciplined, and increasingly educated people.

The foregoing picture of economically and socially successful people is an inadequate model for city dwellers under the dynamics of the biblical prophetic faith. A metropolitan remnant, faithful to the biblical calling, will seek to initiate a new way of life which will challenge the very foundations of its culture. J. S. Woodsworth, the Methodist minister and outstanding pacifist, quickly discovered in Winnipeg many years ago that his quest for new forms of church organization, new empathy with immigrants, and the rejection of war brought censure and conflict. In the House of Commons he was the only member of that body to vote against a declaration of war in 1939. Although respected as a man of integrity and sensitive conscience, he was a lonely, almost broken man after this experience as the voice crying in the wilderness. The synthesis of the Protestant economic ethic with ethnic enclaves in family, church, and community is not controversial, especially in Canada with its vertical mosaic. The witness of a messianic community is another matter.

It is obvious, however, that the ethnic villages in the Canadian cities are an advance on the melancholy failure of United States Mennonites in the big cities, starting approximately fifty to seventy years ago. All the branches of the church, for example, started rescue missions in Chicago which collapsed, one by one, after the second World War. With limited budgets, inadequate staffs, traditional programs, and a simple evangelical theology, the missions crumbled under the shifting, changing neighborhood developments. The Woodlawn Mennonite Church, with many more advantages from location adjacent to Mennonite Biblical Seminary, also collapsed after the seminary moved to Elkhart and the explosive neighborhood developments were too difficult to handle with the personnel available at that time.

There are several developments which hold promise for the future of urban Mennonites. The success of the Canadian ethnic villages takes away the automatic pessimism toward the city as a place of residence. The Voluntary Service units in such places as Atlanta, Cincinnati, and Hamilton are giving dozens of young people an early insight into the valid ways the church can be present in the city. The MCC service models have replaced the rescue missions. The presence of hundreds of professional and business people in the cities provides much more resiliency than the earlier migrants from the hinterlands.

With the rejection of the determinism of assimilation and with the encouragement of the foregoing developments, the challenge of a metropolitan remnant is top priority for the church of the 70s. Unlike the ethnic villagers whose mood is essentially defensive, the mood of the remnant must be bold and forward-looking. To those with other callings and vocations, there are the alternatives of migration, small towns and farms, communal and semicommunal patterns.

Conclusion

Anabaptist *Gelassenheit* and confrontation are gone, replaced by entrepreneural activities which are the back-up economic pattern for the vast institutional life of the church. The Hutterite model of total communality, in its various versions, is very much alive. The semicommunal models of Caryndale and York Center are attractive, workable, and underutilized. It was tragic that a semicommunal pattern could not survive in 19th-century Manitoba, but it is a warning that North American culture moves toward commercial farming and businesses rather than a solidarity economic pattern.

The church-state of Paraguay is neither desirable nor possible in North America, even as one admires the resiliency of these brethren and sisters in a primitive environment. In a different manner the Russian commonwealth is also not desirable or possible here. But, it will provide material for much reflection in the years ahead as this dazzling display of institutions and buildings comes to us like chapters of a book which are turned on a winter night.

It will help to set aside the rhetoric of the Anabaptist situation of the sixteenth century to describe fairly and accurately what economic and social institutions we do, *in fact,* have and what goals and models we *ought* to have. Looking over our shoulders will be the enormous array of church institutions and programs whose need for money is almost insatiable. Looking over the shoulders of the institutions are the heralds of the kingdom of God.

Expanding the
Vision of the Kingdom

Expanding the Vision of the Kingdom

The final set of essays deals with the larger relevance of the vision that informs the lifework of Guy Hershberger. Although Hershberger's main energies have been directed to and through Mennonite concerns and institutions, he has never lost sight of the wider realms to which his study of history and society had sensitized him.

Paul Peachey treats three aspects of ecumenical awareness: the pattern of relations among the Historic Peace Churches, the efforts at witness to and dialogue with representatives of global Christendom, and the theological meaning of ecumenical encounter. He presses Mennonites to reexamine their fundamental self-understanding with respect to the relation of sectarians to church-type Christianity.

In his effort to project the present interest in free church theology and practice into the future, Dale Brown wisely avoids oracular pronouncements, but he does suggest that the Anabaptist view of the church has particular relevance to the concerns of contemporary humankind. The need for roots, the desire for fellowship, the threat of uncontrolled power and self-destruction—to all of these the uncompromising stance of the free church claims to provide an answer.

To bring the volume to a fitting close, we present a recent example of Guy Hershberger's prophetic voice. His 1971 address is a thorough exposition, framed in relation to contemporary events and ideas, of the "colony of heaven" theme found in his earlier writings. Its style and method substantiate Robert Kreider's image of the scholar with Bible in one hand and newspaper in the other. Its content summarizes the message of this book: that the faithful community under the cross is the bearer of the kingdom of God.

15

The Peace Churches as Ecumenical Witness

Paul Peachey

I

Late in 1951 several representatives of the "continuation committee" of Historic Peace Church service agencies in Europe, an informal group active since 1947, called on W. A. Visser 't Hooft, the executive officer of the newly formed World Council of Churches(WCC) in Geneva. Their mission was to deliver a peace appeal to the WCC in the form of a pamphlet entitled "War Is Contrary to the Will of God." The pamphlet contained four theological statements, one from each of the three peace churches, and the fourth from the International Fellowship of Reconciliation (IFOR). The title, however, had been lifted from the report of the founding session of the WCC in Amsterdam in 1948, specifically the section of the report which dealt with international conflict.

This appeal to the new ecumenical body had been generated by the continuation committee. During the early postwar years representatives of the relief and service agencies of the peace churches in Europe maintained a continuing conversation about their work and concerns. This particular undertaking, however, was the fruit of the indefatigable conviction and faith of M. R. Zigler, then the senior representative of Brethren Service Commission in Europe. The Brethren had joined the WCC at the outset, and Zigler took the headquarters of their European service work to Geneva. It was Zigler's conviction that given the awful record of the churches' complicities in the wars among Western nations, this was the first question that would have to be faced if the churches were to be brought together. Ecumenical churchmen, on the other hand, appeared more preoccupied with the "scandal" that Christ's people are divided at the Lord's table. Zigler, with his gift for robust aphorisms, felt it to be more urgent that they first decide to "stop shooting each other." The wounds of World War II at the time, of course, were still fresh.

Paul Peachey is associate professor of sociology at Catholic University of America, Washington, D.C. He has worked with Mennonite Central Committee in Europe and East Asia, has directed the Church Peace Mission, and has published several books and articles on peace issues, religion, and sociology.

As a result of Zigler's prodding, Visser 't Hooft had invited the peace churches to submit a theological argument for the repudiation of war that WCC theologians might consider. He now met with their representatives to receive their document. But on discovering that they had not one, but four, messages, he declined their offering. If the several peace groups cannot agree on why they think war is wrong, and thereupon make a common declaration, he replied, how did they expect him to cope with the forty-odd bodies then comprising the WCC? In effect he told them that the peace churches would have to deal with the ecumenical question among themselves if they wished their witness to be heard ecumenically. Under this compulsion they eventually returned, more than a year later, with a single statement to which the WCC eventually responded.[1] Visser 't Hooft's ecumenical challenge, however, was not taken up, and it is to that challenge that the present paper is addressed.

The term "Historic Peace Churches," or more simply "peace churches," gradually found its way into church jargon after its first use in a conference of Brethren, Friends, and Mennonites held at Newton, Kansas, in 1935 (Bender, 1959).[2] The concept, however, was not a bolt from the blue. Since World War I, when conscientious-objector problems had arisen, and following which Mennonite and Brethren youths had served in Friends' Service Units in Europe, representatives of the three groups had been in frequent contact. Several conferences in the 1920s and 1930s had preceded the 1935 Newton gathering. Representatives of the three groups had already called on other religious bodies and on occupants of the White House in Washington to press the claims of peace. Thus it can be said that the coming together of the peace churches in a community of witness is a result of external challenge, from both church and state. The development of this community meant both *intension* and *extension,* a reflection on their own *identity* and on their common *mission.*

This twentieth-century crystallization of a peace church identity and witness was possible, however, because a commonality of historical experience already existed. Though each of the three movements had arisen independently, both the contexts of origin—established churches of Western Europe—and their inspiration were strongly similar. Both the Friends and the Brethren, who originated later, were soon in touch with Mennonites. These contacts, however, afford interesting illustrations of the fate of religious movements, for the most important early contacts appear to have been those involved in "sheep-stealing" [3] (Bender, 1959: Mallott, 1959). It appears that with the Mennonite movement in its second and then its third century, the early ardor had waned and some members no doubt were ready for greener pastures!

Between the two older bodies, the Mennonites and the Friends, Bender distinguishes three periods of interaction. The first, to which we have just referred, extended from 1655 to 1750, when Quaker missioners traveled on the continent (Fox's conversion occurred in 1643). The second was the colonial era during which Penn's New World colony (Pennsylvania) offered a haven to Mennonite immigrants. The third is the modern era dating from World War I. In fact, all three groups were in contact with one another, in varying ways, during the second and the third eras.

It is not our task here, of course, to trace the history of these common experiences. It is rather to recall the fact that the unity which the peace church label signifies, though the product of the twentieth century, has important historical roots. But what does this coming together in recent decades signify? Is it a mere happenstance? Is it something imposed by external events? Do the three groups merely share common memories, or does the peace church concept refer rather to a living and growing reality, a coming destiny rather than a fading memory? How do these groups see themselves? How are they viewed by other Christian groups? It is these questions which must engage us here.

II

In 1960, Esther B. Rhoads, then leader of the Friends Mission in Japan, retired after forty years of service there. Having originally gone to Japan as a one-year volunteer, she found instead her life vocation. Following a farewell service held on her behalf in the Friends meetinghouse in Tokyo, she commented on some of her experiences in private conversation. One persistent problem over the years had been the quality of spiritual nurture provided by the meeting for worship. She found that the Friends' "open meeting" presupposes a Christendom context, that is, a culture long influenced by, or suffused with, Christian concepts and influences. But in a meeting composed of new members, coming from a world as yet unfamiliar with the biblical tradition, how can members contribute substantively in spontaneous utterance? Esther Rhoads, of course, did not mean by this that England, where the Friends originated, for example, can be considered a

Christian society. Yet in fact she put her finger on the heart of the peace identity question. Do they exist only as reaction to a "great church," as parasite perhaps, or are they fulsome, and thus autonomous, bodies of Christ's people in their own right?[4]

Odd as this question may seem at first blush, it remains, ever since peace church beginnings, the most urgent question that they face. But a single or direct answer may not be possible. One can begin, perhaps, by asking what the founding fathers thought they were doing. That in itself would be a large undertaking of historical inquiry. Only a few comments will be possible here. Taking the oldest of the three groups, historians regard the Anabaptist movement as an effort to rebuild rather than to repair the existing churches, and thus as a "third way" alongside the Catholic church and its Protestant revision (Littell, 1958; Klaassen, 1973). At the same time, however, John Yoder has shown convincingly that during the early decades of that sixteenth-century movement, its spokesman continuously and repeatedly pressed the established churches for Bible-based discussions of the issues between them that both might come more fully into truth (Yoder, 1962). Seen from this perspective, Anabaptists apparently took the unity of Christ's people seriously and viewed themselves as fully rooted in the church universal. Despite this fact, however, separatism entered the very warp and woof of Mennonite identity. Hence the question: was this separatism implicit in their quest and thus inevitable? Was it rather the outcome of a movement thwarted, of a reconstruction aborted? On these questions critics and apologists, no doubt, will continue to disagree.

But what of subsequent developments? In contrast to the Catholic or people's church *(Volkskirche)* backdrop against which all three groups emerged, they were all by definition nonhierarchical and nonsacramental, the Friends more consistently so than the other two. All three viewed the modalities of worship and life as accidental rather than substantive in character. Worship was viewed not as a formal ritual reminiscent of ceremonies at royal courts, but as a common and deliberative search for the mind of Christ, specific to the situation. All three consciously rejected the doctrine of apostolic succession, as well as the belief that ritual acts in themselves afford objective guarantees of divine grace. Yet through the years each group has assimilated its own forms into its self-definition in a manner that may differ only outwardly from the Catholic sacramentalism that they reject. Though not codified in the canonical sense, and hence certainly more malleable and subject to revision "from below," their traditional structures are no more self-liquidating than are those of the established churches against which they arose. They have become "churches" like any of the other many scores of religious bodies that claim the designation "church." Their claims may be more modest than the claims of the larger bodies. But given the logic of their charter, their behavior as universal and self-sufficient bodies appears the more presumptuous. One recalls the parable of the son who claimed he would do his father's bidding but in fact did not go.

III

Leaving for the moment the question of peace church self-definitions, let us ask, How are they viewed ecumenically, from the outside? One day in 1949, Guy F. Hershberger drove to a Dominican monastery not far from Cologne, Germany, to call on an elderly monk, now deceased, named Franziskus Stratmann. Hershberger was seeking out pacifist Christians in Europe, and Stratmann was one of his discoveries. Stratmann was devoutly religious in the traditional Roman Catholic sense, and had written several books on Catholic saints. Nonetheless, he was informed by the deep conviction that the church must rise eventually to free herself from the curse of militarism, and he considered it his rather solitary vocation to work toward that distant goal. Shortly after Hershberger's visit, Stratmann's book on the church and war appeared (it must have been in press at the time), first in Germany and then also in England (Stratmann, 1950: 1956).

In keeping with his traditional outlook—this was well before Vatican II—"church" to Stratmann meant the church of Rome. The book is richly and broadly informative, yet he takes only a few quick glances at "the declarations of other Christians regarding the problem of war." These "other circles" were the leading bodies, such as Lutherans and Anglicans, in the WCC. But Stratmann's ecumenicity did not extend to the peace churches. Did the good monk not know his own Rhineland history well enough, one might ask, to know about Anabaptist pacifism? Were his cloister walls so high that he had not heard of Quaker service activities in the twentieth century? Hardly. In fact, he does refer briefly and appreciatively to Quakers in a discussion of conscientious objection in Anglo-Saxon lands. But by inference one must conclude that he would not have looked to peace church sources for normative or even didactic materials. Protestants might at least be recognized; they are separated brethren with whom future reunion is conceivable. But peace churches, if the inference is not mistaken, apparently belong in the Donatist bin where all schismatics without ecclesiastical status were filed from the fourth century onward.[5]

Meanwhile, of course, enormous changes have occurred. True, the ecumenical movement has not advanced as rapidly or as far as its advocates have hoped. Yet both the movement and the council (WCC) have grown, and while the church of Rome has not yet joined, it has taken steps which may some day lead to that result (Congar, 1972; Leeming, 1967). The ancient conception, which the established Protestant bodies shared with the Catholics, that the "sects" are heretical or schismatic or both, was in effect bypassed rather than resolved in the establishment of the World Council of Churches. Independent religious bodies who confess Jesus Christ as Lord and Savior, said the founding document, qualify for membership. While most Mennonites and some Friends stayed out of the Council, all three groups were numbered among the original membership. Later the New Delhi WCC Assembly (1961) added the disclaimer that membership in the WCC does not commit the body which joins to accept as valid the church order of any other member bodies. Thus the question as to whether the peace churches are "churches" or "sects" has not yet received an answer from ecumenical circles.

On the Roman Catholic side, however, important modifications have apparently occurred. A widely used and frequently republished German language Catholic church polity handbook, for example, introduces the concept *Freikirche* (free church) between the terms *Kirche* and *Volkskirche,* on the one hand, and *Sekte* on the other. The sect remains, as before, under censure. It is separatistic, individualistic, and self-centered in its inspiration, and rejects the church's true responsibility for the well-being of mankind. Heresy goes a step beyond sectarianism, since additionally it propagates false teachings (Algermissen, 1957).

The true church, as Algermissen sees her, is characterized basically by a "religious universalism which extends as far as the redemptive work of Christ," that is, to all mankind. This makes the church the great "educator" *(Erzieher)* of the human race. Between the true *Kirche,* which accepts this mandate, and the *Sekte* which does not, lies the *Freikirche* (free church). The free churches are those bodies which retain an inclusive character (by baptizing infants, thus including entire populations), but who separate from the state. "Free" thus refers to independence from the political "arm." But second, appealing directly to the late Fritz Blanke's classic little statement on the *Freikirche* (Blanke, 1955), Algermissen admits one further variant. The church is "free" in a further sense when membership is put on a voluntary basis. Examples of this second type, says Algermissen, are the Baptists and the Mennonites.

An article published in the United States in the *New Catholic Encyclopedia* moves in a similar direction, though the context leads to rather different terms. It must be remembered that in the United States all churches are in fact, though not in creed, "free churches," free in the above double sense. In any case, the writer of this article, Whalen, notes that a variety of church polities can be ranked as on a continuum. The critical threshold falls for him between the "cult" (characterized by both separatism and appeals to extra-biblical doctrines or authority) and "sect," a group rejecting the church's universal mission. Whalen's two examples of the "sect" so conceived are the Brethren and the Mennonites. Thus as for Algermissen the "free church" comes between the church in the full sense and the sect, so for Whalen the sect falls between the true church and "cult." Significantly, both locate peace churches in that middle category. Further, both recognize that one form may evolve into another, depending on circumstances and developmental stages (Whalen, 1967).

The import of these statements needs more treatment than is possible here. But though the process differs, perhaps there is a kindred trend in the WCC and the Roman Catholic developments. In both contexts attitudes toward the peace churches are undergoing redefinition. It would be naive, presumably, to conclude that other differences have disappeared. Yet Whalen's readiness to view the disagreement as summed up by the question of peace church withdrawal from social responsibility can be seen as a serious basis for genuine ecumenical engagement.

The Catholic doctrine of inclusiveness, of course, was shaped by the many centuries during which the church outwardly embraced entire peoples. But the "great churches," Catholic and Protestant, long ago had to cede that monopoly. As organizations, they exert ever diminishing influence on political and cultural life, and at least formally are under lessened political control. Perhaps because their own *Sitz im Leben,* their place in the scheme of things, approaches increasingly that of the peace churches, they are more ready to distinguish the latter from "cults" and "heretics."[6] No doubt, however, the peace churches have lost both their radical thrust and their contagious power. No longer do they endanger the status quo! Underlying their loss of dynamism may also slumber the uncertainty which is the subject of the present sketch: are the peace churches an elliptical focus of witness within the whole church, or separate embodiments of Christ's people universal? It is to this issue that we now at last turn.

IV

We shall take the former position here, that the break of the peace churches with the wider Christian community is a provisional one, not unlike an unresolved quarrel in some other context. The ecumenical conversation must be pursued, therefore, with a sense of both urgency and expectation.[7] The consequences of this assumption are drastic, both for peace church self-conceptions and for the ways in which they view the ecumenical movement and its goal. In the few remaining pages we can only hope to signal the direction serious inquiries will need to take. These two perspectives we shall treat in reverse order.

We can begin with the simple observation that the World Council of Churches, along with its member bodies, seeks the unity of divided Christendom. The founders of the Council were for the most part the high clergy of national churches and subsequently of the great denominations as well. At the time when the Council was formed, most of these bodies felt unable to accept the full validity of one another's sacraments. In the hope that this "scandal" could eventually be overcome, the upper clergy of the Church of England entered into conversation with their peers in the Church of Sweden, the Orthodox Church of Greece, and the like. At that stage, conversation with the little "free churches" or "sects" within their own geographic boundaries appeared to be another matter.

But is that truly the ecumenical problem? Surely, on the one hand, it is a violation of the unity of Christ's body when national boundaries become ecclesiastical boundaries as well, the more so when these are sanctioned by wars. On the other hand, it is inevitable that in England Christians speak English, in Sweden, Swedish, and in Greece, Greek. Not only is this permissible. The embeddedness of Christians in particular histories inheres in the Incarnation itself. Thus there are bound to be many "churches," many modalities of worship, life, witness, and service. Moreover in this age of global interdependence and mobilities, these modalities increasingly impinge on one another. The life of the worshiping community is thereby both enriched and complicated, since it must always "try the spirits" which come into its midst

(1 John 4:1). But the problem is not these diversities as such, but rather the human organizations erected upon them, and then endowed by both adherents and incumbents with sacred qualities which are by definition transcendental.[8] Merging these entities could never create the legitimacy and authenticity which they lack. Combining them, far from effecting a transformation, would only compound the confusion.

There is simply no way whereby one can integrate these ecclesiastical organizations, whether national or denominational, into the biblical conception of the faith community. There is no churchly reality or substance other than the grace whereby men and women become new creatures in Christ. Since the modern conciliar movement may yet be the instrument through which this will become evident, it certainly is not to be rejected out of hand. Indeed one may hope that much can come from the confrontations of the various churches with one another in the Council. But insofar as it is the hope thereby eventually to unite or even to coordinate the churches, in the terms of the perspectives here advanced, the WCC is a symptom of the problem, not its solution. The extent to which this awareness has already dawned within the movement is beyond the competency of this writer or this essay to ascertain.

Admittedly this argument is radical, and in terms of available alternatives or "models," hardly practical. But the answer lies in the Lord's future, not in some idyllic past. After all, problems concerning church polity arose already in New Testament times, and increased subsequently. Thus, though the biblical sources are normative, the early centuries dare not be romanticized. Yet the incubus of history must be recognized for what it is. Though fatal developments set in long before the age of Constantine, it is the integration of "Christianity" into the imperial order from the fourth century onward that underlies much of our difficulty even today. For a millennium and a half the Christian "religion" was a department of state, a means of social control, a societal cement. Sadly, most ecclesiastical liturgies and polities, including those of the peace churches, derive from the idioms of the Constantinian millennium.

Western Christian history appears thus as an ominous replication of the prostitution of the covenant of Abraham by the Hebrew monarchy. Despite the fact that on this point Jesus and the gospel could not have been more clear, the members of the new covenant have been no more ready than the members of the old to walk upright in the world, with only the rule of God between themselves and the primordial chaos. What had transpired in Solomon's Jerusalem was repeated

endlessly in the palaces and cathedrals in Europe. Meanwhile men and
women of faith, in the former as in the latter instance, bore the anguish
of the institutional powers which they could not revoke. Terrifying
though the naked rule of God may be, its challenge has never disappeared.

V

Finally, if the peace churches exist as ecumenical witness rather
than as "churches," what are the consequences of this definition for
their own life? As it turns out, this question cannot be answered "in
general." Rather, the reply will vary with the identity and position of
the respondent. As a problem, this question is most likely to be discussed by peace church elites, that is, by professional leaders. It goes
without saying that a peace church "clergy," in the terms here advanced, is a self-contradictory concept. Nonetheless, they exist, and
conceivably such elites may wish to look at alternatives.

First, they may undertake a reinterpretation and a redirection of
the respective ideologies (the term here is not pejorative) of these
groups. To some extent, historians and other scholars have done this in
the modern investigations of the origins of peace church movements.
By the very nature of the case, however, such efforts tend to lead to legitimation for modern developments rather than for basic redevelop-
ment. A radical reengagement with the beginnings and the basic logic
of these movements can have both *positive* and *negative import*—positive in that some of the creative service and witness expressions in the
modern era appear as consistent expressions of their genius and negative in that certain institutional and denominational tendencies will be
called into question.

Another option for peace church elites may be to accept, and to
expand on, the challenge which W. A. Visser 't Hooft flung down a
quarter of a century ago; that is, they could initiate merger talks among
Brethren, Friends, and Mennonites. Perhaps the WCC official was
right! Perhaps their *peace* witness would then become credible! Such
steps would be consistent with one feature of the ecumenical movement, namely the expectation that within the looser framework of the
conciliar movement, communions with common roots or similar
polities might forge ahead to effect mergers. Such steps can prepare the
way for wider union at some future time. Though in this case as with
reference to WCC generally, the present critique calls into question the
merger cure for the brokenness of Christian unity, it is an option which

may be worthy of consideration by those with less radical views.

A third possibility is that the peace church denominations might seek rather to dissolve themselves directly into larger currents or bodies in the ecumenical movement. Forty years ago a pioneer investigation of the missionary and philanthropic awakening among American Mennonites interpreted this institutional development as in fact a phase in the completion of the sect cycle. Social theories at the time suggested that sects are eventually reabsorbed by the parent bodies (Kaufman, 1931). Currently, of the three peace churches, it is the Brethren who have entered most deeply into the ecumenical movement, both in the United States and in the global dimension. The episode with which we began the present essay, namely the presence and the action of the Brethren with the WCC in Geneva, indicates that such relations can be productive. Indeed, if the present "schism" is in fact regarded as provisional, reassimilation in some form is the outcome to be expected, indeed sought. But since the basic issues raised by the peace church phenomenon have not been resolved, reabsorption appears premature.

A variation of this "assimilative model" can be called the "evangelical temptation," that is, merger into what has been called the "third force" of Christendom. Though this option appears unappealing to peace church majorities, parts of all three constituencies continue to be attracted by it. In some respects, in fact, affinity with the third force is greater than with the great churches. It is appealing where the great churches are weakest, namely in the emphasis on personal salvation. Yet the evangelical impulse all too often accepts a reductionism which cuts the life nerve of the peace church. For example, the executive of a "faith" mission declared before a gathering of missionaries in Tokyo some years ago, "Because the church has failed, God now saves only individuals!" These words were uttered, ironically enough, by a brother ready to contend at the drop of a hat for the plenary inspiration of the Bible, or against the unfaithfulness of the great churches, Catholic and Protestant. Somehow it did not occur to him that he was undertaking single-handedly a rather substantial revision of his plenarily inspired text. Yet even so, one can sympathize with those who choose the evangelical solution. In the end, however, the third force affinity is largely deceptive since in most evangelical modes the issues raised in the peace church witness all but evaporate.

The foregoing alternatives which peace church elites might consider, however, scarcely touch the issues which appear basic in the present critique. Given the tension between the basic peace church model and religious professionalism, moreover, certain questions are unlikely to be asked by professionals. Might the laity, then, be expected to ask the more difficult questions? Hardly, since few have the inclination or perhaps even the capacity to do so. To some extent, though hardly entirely so, this may be due to the practical bifurcation between laity and clergy (as religious professionals) that has transformed the structure of peace church life.

In the end, perhaps it must be admitted that it may be difficult to find anyone who will ask the right questions. Critics of the argument advanced in this paper may conclude that this may be its refutation; the proposed question may thus be shown to be unreal or wrong. But the question can nonetheless be stated and left with the reader. In other contexts it may receive fuller treatment. We shall state what appears to be the basic question by way of the visible-invisible church debate which in the sixteenth century played its part in defining the schism between the Protestant Reformation and the peace church. Not surprisingly, the line in that debate between theological truth and error lay not on the divide between those two camps but ran diagonally across them. Luther rightly insisted that the church, being rooted in grace, is perceptible only in faith. Peace church protagonists rightly insisted that the church is manifest in the visible acts of visible people. To ban the reality to the unseen and thus unverifiable world, while retaining a state-controlled social organization called church, could have only disastrous consequences for church and state alike. But to organize a "Believers' "Church, *i.e.,* to effect a social organization with a life of its own, not necessarily rooted in the dynamic of grace, leads in the end to a replication of the Roman Catholic confusion. Christ's community is diffuse within the society or "the world." It is not a separate nation or a social subsystem or group within the society or world. To invoke sociological inevitability at this point is a cop-out. Of course, social regularities operate when human beings interact. But it is the idioms of grace and of faith that define the church. To witness to that reality is the only identity which the "peace churches" possess.

16

The Free Church of the Future

Dale W. Brown

The Winter 1972 issue of *Brethren Life and Thought* was devoted to prophecies, hopes, models, and dreams for the Church of the Brethren by the year AD 2000. When I had finished sampling the special revelations of the rich variety of the contributors, I was convinced I had not really learned much of what the Church of the Brethren might look like at the end of our century. Rather, I had discovered a lot about the faith and dreams of my sisters and brothers. In times of rapid change, we are all destined to engage in futurology, attempting to speak about the future. Our temptation to believe that we can reduce this to an exact science or to feel we can attain any degree of certitude as to what we might engineer should be tempered by observing how far the respected prophecies of the futurologists of a decade ago are from the foreknowledge of current experts. When we read about the revolution in cybernetics and the resultant replacement of human labor by computerized technology, we were worrying about the utilization of leisure time on the part of the masses. We were promised a utopia in which a small percentage of humanity could meet the basic needs of all. Now futurologists are concerned about how long our planet can sustain life at all, given present demographical and ecological projections.

As our Anabaptist heritage has helped us to give priority to the *Way* over the most brilliant wisdom of ethicists, so should we give priority to the promises about God's future over the most sophisticated analyses of the futurologists. This does not mean that we cannot profit from the best studies of the human situation. It does mean that efforts, such as this one, should reflect on the meaning and mission of one stream of God's people, in this case the free church, in light of God's purposes. The growing identification of the author with the Anabaptist Vision and what he feels it has to offer will come forth more than any clairvoyant reading of the broader free church movement in the im-

Dale Brown, professor of Christian theology at Bethany Theological Seminary, Oak Brook, Illinois, is an active leader in the Church of the Brethren. He has published numerous articles and several books, including Brethren and Pacifism and the Christian Revolutionary.

mediate or distant future. In attempting to assess our current situation, however, it is inevitable that prophetic guesses will emerge.

Currently, free church theology seems to be approaching the status of a theological fad. In a New Year's issue of *The Christian Century*, John Howard Yoder made the top twenty list of "Who's Alive in '75?" Rationalizing the selection, the editors, likely represented by Martin Marty, "expect his influence to increase as more and more people seek biblical angles of vision on intractable world problems." As one for whom John Howard Yoder and other Mennonites had provided creative leadership many years ago, the present ascent to the top evokes mixed feelings of satisfaction and typical Anabaptist suspicion about ourselves when we gain this much acceptance by Protestantism's liberal voice.

In this selection the editors suggested that they might be reaching out to the growing numbers of evangelicals "with a social conscience." Most twentieth-century conservatives equated radical social witness with theological liberalism. Evangelical radicals, often referred to as a new breed of young conservatives, have been gratified to learn about a historical movement which was both biblically rooted and politically revolutionary. This growing alliance between the evangelical left and Anabaptists, as seen in such groups as the editors and readers of *Sojourners* (formerly *The Post American*), vindicates the stance of Guy Hershberger who was convinced that contemporary Mennonites belong neither in the Fundamentalist or liberal camp. Mennonites at their best should have repudiated the Fundamentalist translation of the corporate biblical faith into egocentric Protestant individualism, just as they rejected the human-centered, naively optimistic faith of liberalism. They should have offered a synthesis between the conservative concern for a genuine and moral personal lifestyle and the valid liberal expressions of kingdom theology.

We live in a time in which the evangelical renaissance will elicit a new dialogue with mainline churches. In such a milieu, a faithful free church model is strategically located, ecclesiologically and theologically, to offer a prophetic word to both camps as well as provide a third option which might serve for some as a bridge of reconciliation. In this we need to extend and revive Hershberger's dream. The continual recovery and articulation of the Anabaptist Vision is necessary to save us from an easy acculturation into either camp in the increasing polarization of our church life.

A similar role might be seen in reference to continuing expressions of the older Catholic-Protestant schism. Following the work of social historians like Troeltsch and Sweet, insiders such as Robert Friedmann (1973) and Walter Klaassen (1973) have insisted that the free church tradition is neither Catholic nor Protestant. Friedmann proposed that Anabaptism is neither a revised version of Catholic theology of sanctification nor Protestantism taken all of the way, but a new approach to the Word of God, one which he names "existential Christianity." He appropriated this term to refer to the stance in which faith and life, human and divine relationships, are inseparable. This led to Friedmann's tripartite analyses, such as his judgment that Catholic grace is interpreted as substance, Protestant grace as favor, and Anabaptist grace as creative love.

As it may be both necessary and helpful to thus differentiate the free church tradition from Catholicism and Protestantism, so it may be important to emphasize that in other respects the free church view is *both* Catholic and Protestant. Through its focus on the concrete life in an organized brotherhood, the free church vision shares the ecclesio-centric theology of Catholicism, the difference being that the locus of authority becomes the decisions of the disciplined brotherhood rather than the hierarchical structures of the established church. In accord with the Protestant principle of desacralizing of all human creeds, institutions, and efforts as subject to the judgment of God, the free church has been Protestant in its insistence on ever being open to new light as it breaks forth from the Word coming in the midst of community. In an era following a dramatic breakthrough in Catholic-Protestant relationships, the free church vision can offer new possibilities for consensus.

A proper focus on a peculiar calling, combined with affirmations of affinity with other streams of Christianity, should offer the basis for the free church ecumenical posture of the future. The free church has been forced to particular congregational identities because of the failure of the mainline churches to be free from subservience to the state and tribal culture. It is necessary to affirm this counterculture stance as an integral part of biblical expectations to be not conformed to this world. At the same time, the free churches originally sought dialogue and disputations with other Christians, in order to witness and be open to new possibilities of discipleship. They sought to become a corrective witness to what they regarded as the fallen state of the church. Again, we live in a time when faithfulness means nonconformity to the world, including the world of the mainline churches. At the same time it means that we will be open to every possibility for dialogue with the many winds of doctrine and styles of witness of Christian life. Isolated existence, protected by walls of separation, means that the witness God has entrusted can never be shared. On the other hand, complete acculturation into the society around us inevitably leads to the loss of anything to share.

We have seen how our post-Constantinian situation has created a climate to which free church theology can persuasively speak. This accounts for its current status as one of the fads. Let us hope that a fad may connote positive phenomena used by God as well as the more negative connotation of jumping on every bandwagon that comes along. Nevertheless, at a deeper level the Anabaptist position seeks to provide a witness even when what God wants us to represent is no longer a fad. With the demise of the popular peace movement, the healthy survival of jingoistic nationalism, the national refusal to change basic priorities, the advent of popular and personal religion, and the spectacle of counterculture dropouts buying into new configurations of Constantinianism, there are growing signs that a faithful minority people will still be needed. In our unjust, militaristic, and pagan society, we must still pray for the continuing recovery and incarnation of the Anabaptist Vision.

An ecumenical stance in its broadest sense is not limited to associations with other Christians. Ecumenicity involves the quality of our relationships with the entire world. Though we are called to be as "pilgrims," "exiles," "aliens," and "strangers" in this world, we are nevertheless called to be *in* the world. As pilgrims we are to go into all of the world inviting others to become citizens of a kingdom, which though not of the world, is in the process of establishing colonies in the midst of the world. For this reason Christian compassion requires that we be aware of the heartbeats, the yearnings, the true needs of others in our mediating the call to seek first the kingdom.

Presently, we do sense a real longing for rootage. The current fascination with antiques, the colonial nomenclature of suburban subdivisions, and the genealogical fad—all these may be symptomatic of a deeper yearning for foundations in a changing uncertain environment. When many are finding it difficult to identify with the American mainstream and current American values, we have experienced the attempt to find identity again in the heritage of many religious and ethnic traditions. Sociologists have been led to a new interest in the "unmeltable ethnics," whether Jewish, Nisei, Chicano, or black. We need to recognize that some of what we are experiencing in the free church revival is part of a larger sociological reality. The obvious danger in all of this is that we can so easily enshrine our heritage in the past so as to keep it from coming alive in the present. Many donors to the centers of historiography, which have been responsible for the recovery of the Anabaptist Vision, would be most uncomfortable with contemporary incarnations of their ancestral heroes in the faith.

Nevertheless, we do need to recognize the *kairos* situation for the Anabaptist Vision. One part of its radicalness is its desire to discern the roots or the heart of the faith. This focus on the faith and life of the early Christian community has been variously referred to as restitutionism, primitivism, restorationism, and apostolicity. The vision at its best offers historical paradigms, both in the early and sixteenth centuries, for styles of Christian community. Instead of an emphasis which focuses primarily on propositional statements which serve as foundations for faith or an apostolicity which offers the security of an infallible institution, here is a biblicism which holds up models of community relationships and faith for our appropriation.

But we need to keep this focus in proper balance. Elsewhere, I have referred to such an idealization of the early church as the pre-Constantinian myth; we are not dealing with one model, but many, and we must grant that the early church was not above reproach. One has only to examine Paul's correspondence with one church at Corinth to recognize that the early church was not morally pure, doctrinally sound, or organizationally stable. Even though it might be argued that it is the shape and style of life in struggling, believing, disciplining, and loving that is to be imitated, rather than any models of moral purity, there are still many historical problems with this myth. We might parenthetically add that the same is true of other meaningful myths, for example, the myth of apostolic succession. The advantage of focusing on the early community, however, instead of propositional truth or hierarchical continuity, is that the paradigm is historical and visible. At the same time, it cannot be defined legalistically and precisely without violating its dynamic nature.

Likewise, it should be pointed out that any such primitivism inevitably has to be combined with eschatology. The looking backward becomes an integral part of our looking forward. We attempt to find out who we were at our best as Christians in order to have a vision of who we should become. The vision of restitutionism did not lead the sixteenth-century Anabaptist merely to repeat the past, but to a positive movement forward in the history of the church, to a new creation which was something other than that found in the first centuries.

The power that such a restorationist vision has for providing anchorage in a messed-up world is intimately related to the widespread hunger for models of community. We have been attempting to live in the first era of human history lacking the benefits of a larger family. Even in the earlier decades of our century, most people on our planet were a part of a tribal entity, a farm community, an ethnic city neighborhood, a family church, or an atmosphere surrounded by relatives. It has been only in recent decades, with the scattering of the extended family due to the subservience of our destinies to the technological society, that the nuclear family has emerged as the small unit obligated to meet practically all of our existential and emotional needs. Previously, if parents did not relate as they should, there were grandparents, aunts and uncles, or others to provide the necessary resources for identity. I have listened to families, scattered in suburbia, who reminisce nostalgically for the old neighborhood where there was abundant intermingling in wrangling, playing, discussion, observing, or just sitting with others. Because the nuclear family has not been able to bear all of the needs carried by the extended family of the past, there exists the contemporary deep hunger for community.

In his community vision and efforts at mutual aid, Guy Hershberger was behind the times with his fellow Mennonites who were attempting to escape the narrow legalism and provincialism of their rural communities. But as is so often the case, in seeming to be behind the times, he was, in reality, ahead of the times. For many of the children of those who escaped the oppression of ossified communities have discovered that most American organizational socializing is superficial. Caught in the network of giant institutions, there is a new hunger for warm intimate relationships. Likewise most of the experimentation in communal and group living of the sixties has failed due to the dearth of moral and religious underpinnings. In the context of this crisis in familial structures and the resultant yearnings, the vision of the free church has a lot to offer.

A theologian from the Reformed tradition, Emil Brunner, has perhaps expressed more definitively than anyone the free church understanding of the nature of the body of Christ. He wrote that in the New Testament "the *Ekklesia* is never conceived of as an institution; but exclusively as a fellowship of persons, as the common life based in fellowship with Jesus Christ as a fellowship of the Spirit and a fellowship of Christ" (1962:21). He adds that a people "has" institutions, but never in the biblical sense do they understand themselves as an institution. Such a view of the priority of the visible fellowship builds on the fundamental theology that one cannot come to God except with one's brother or sister. Our relationship with God is integrally related to our relationships with others. The church, then, is nothing other than persons in fellowship, in fellowship with God and in fellowship with each other. People do not go to church; people are the church. One submits to discipline not because one is joining together with others to maintain perfection, but because, knowing one is a sinner, he or she acknowledges that God's help is mediated through a sister or brother. One participates in discipling others because one cares deeply. Such caring and sharing should extend to all of life, including even the offer of money and material goods for the common good. Baptism comes in response to the mediation of God's message and grace through the community and involves the making of a covenant with God and others for ministry and mission. Instead of choosing sides in the debate concerning the presence of Christ in the bread, the Anabaptist focus has been that the real presence of Christ is to be found in the body of Christ, the people who break bread together. This gift of fellowship and unity in the Spirit becomes a foretaste of the kingdom of God.

It does seem sad to observe folk who have been nurtured in this tradition, copying the Sunday school busing fad and other commercial Madison Avenue techniques, in order to be "evangelistic." In reality, a re-creation of the heart of the tradition, through caring and sharing fellowships combined with hospitality for the stranger and deep concern for the oppressed, would offer tremendous evangelistic potentialities in our type of world. Free church circles have spawned models of community such as Reba Place in Evanston, Illinois. As in the case of other communities, Reba Place illustrates something more than a sharing of material possessions, as good as this is. Appropriating the extended household model from the Church of the Redeemer in Houston, there is a genuine sharing of lives as more established families become the basis for admitting teenagers, single persons, and family units without one parent. Though not without many problems, in my judgment this sharing of all of life in creating new family units under Christ constitutes one of the beautiful evangelistic witnesses in our contemporary life.

In addition to answering the yearnings for rootage and for family-like communities, the free church model of voluntaristic committed fellowships is right for our pluralistic situation. As the free church challenged the synthesis known historically as *corpus christianum,* so there are growing signs that we live in a post-Constantinian, or in our context, post-American era. With Constantine the empire became holy. The church was regarded as the empire at prayer. Membership in the church and state coincided numerically. The early free church fathers were truly revolutionary in proposing voluntary membership, religious freedom, and the separation of church and state. We have lived through a period in which the American or Western empire has been identified by many with Christendom. The missionary advance of the churches was abetted by the worldwide influence of colonial domination, followed by the economic imperialism of giant corporations. Now it seems obvious that we are entering a time in which there must be major readjustments in the grossly unequal control of the world's resources by the affluent nations. In order to adjust psychologically to a lower standard of living, in order to take our place modestly as one nation in a family of nations there is needed the free church vision concerning the priority of loyalty to the kingdom over national allegiances.

Way back in 1927 in the first issue of *Mennonite Quarterly Review,* Guy Hershberger contributed the lead article on "False Patriotism," which is strikingly contemporary as I write in the atmosphere of the American Bicentennial. He wrote: "Merely because I love America is no indication that I must believe—and boast the belief—that the American people are 'more sincerely religious, better educated, of serener minds, and of purer morals' than the people of any other nation"(1927a:10). Such prophetic witness against American civil religion emerges logically from the free church tradition, especially in that wing which combines the principle of separation with the biblical command to love enemies. Disciples in this tradition have been often accused of an antistate bias. The truth of the matter is that Anabaptist theology has not espoused either anarchism or a hatred of the state. Rather, one's call to love all people and to place the claims of Christ's way of love above all other allegiances so challenges jingoistic attitudes as to evoke the wrath of those with narrow nationalistic identities. One becomes "counterculture" because one affirms a love for other cultures and the kingdom style for all cultures. This often results in alienation from the highly self-centered, materialistic, militaristic culture of one's own environment. There may not be a receptivity for it, but there is and will be a tremendous need for this aspect of the Anabaptist witness in a milieu which has shown few signs of real repentance from greedy consumerism or idolatrous devotion to making weapons of death. In our post-Constantinian situation, the might of the First and Second worlds should not be replaced by Third World peoples attempting to become first world powers, as much as by the vision of the coming kingdom of peace, righteousness, and justice.

The Anabaptist Vision can offer the church of the future models of witness whereby the polarity between personal evangelism and social responsibility is eliminated. The visible fellowship of believers becomes the primary witness in itself, the manifestation of the new aeon in the midst of the old, the tasting of the firstfruits of what God intends for the entire world. During the Vietnam War, governmental leaders easily dismissed pleas from leading churchmen because they knew that the prophetic utterances from ecclesiastical bureaucracies did not match the sentiments of the grass roots of the constituents. The Anabaptist view asserts that any authentic witness to brotherhood and justice in our world must be made in the context of some manifested firstfruits of the same. Through believer's baptism, individuals must come to a personal commitment to our Lord and His Way, but this involves a commitment to a fellowship which corporately witnesses to the world by being a witness, as well as proclaiming a witness to the coming kingdom.

The free church tradition offers faithfulness and simple obedience as the primary evangelistic and social strategy. Rather than a preoccupation with the virtues of either smallness or bigness or of success or failure, the focus is on faithful obedience. God might use such faithfulness for a cleansing of His church so as to leave only a remnant. Or He might use it for a great increase in the number of disciples. Rather than posing, "What would happen if our country would disarm?" we ask, "What does faithfulness to Christ mean for our situation?" In my own pilgrimage I became disillusioned with a political pacifism, one which promised that pacifism was to be the wave of the future and constituted a viable strategy for a peaceful world. When Reinhold Niebuhr and others forced me to a more realistic analysis, I had either to relinquish pacifism as a neat strategy or adopt the Anabaptist stance that peace was still the way, even though it might lead to a cross.

Having adjusted my priorities from "what will work" to "how best to be faithful" I have now come to feel that this less practical way from the viewpoint of the world's wisdom might point to an even greater realism. Rather than assuming that it is easy to calculate the consequences of ethical decisions in our complicated world, it is probably more realistic to recognize the impossibility of ever knowing the total context of our actions and thereby being able to predict the results of our actions. Dietrich Bonhoeffer, for example, reasoned that it was best to kill one man, Hitler, in order to thereby shorten the war and save the lives of many. Now, we are aware as he could not have been, of the rejection of all such schemes by the Allied leaders and their decision to refuse to negotiate with any new regime because of their stance of demanding unconditional surrender. We can never know for certain, but it appears that Bonhoeffer likely would have been more successful in saving lives in adhering to his more absolute allegiance to the way of the Sermon on the Mount as espoused in his *Cost of Discipleship.*

This assumption—that the foolishness of God's way is wiser than the wisdom of our social schemes—should be instructive in terms of how we relate to the powers and principalities. The question is frequently raised as to the nature of our Christian responsibility in the redemption of the institutions of our society. Rather than asking the question whether we should be in or outside the structures, we should pose how we might best be faithful. Sometimes faithfulness will lead to participation in structures, serving as leaven in the dough. This may be possible because of the greater openness of some institutions which have been more permeated by the Spirit of Christ. In other times and places, however, Christians have had so to struggle against the powers and principalities that faithfulness has required them to shake the dust off their feet and turn away. In the future faithfulness may produce the fruit of transforming power. But it may lead to the cross of confrontation with a system of death.

Anabaptists have been labeled as separatists and isolationists, imbibing a perfectionist ethic so as to pass by irresponsibly on the other side of the road. Though perhaps true of many subsequent varieties, such a caricature is unfair to the early Anabaptists who were found preaching in cities with evangelistic zeal, confronting leaders of church and state, and singing and witnessing to those gathered even when facing death. Their refusal to hold those public offices intimately related to the yielding of the sword did not keep them, even in some early instances, from holding offices serving the public good. They were nonresistant when it came to sticking up for their own rights. But this did not mean a total refusal to stand up against evil.

Guy Hershberger was right in emphasizing a thoroughgoing biblical nonresistance. He was probably overreacting to the faulty theology of liberalism, however, in his failure to work at how biblical nonresistance might be combined with a more aggressive witness to overcoming evil with good. Such a model might be found in the very first Anabaptist congregation in their protest procession against the town council. Outraged and desiring to witness, men, women, and children wearing willow twigs cried out: "Woe! Woe! Woe to Zurich!" In this case the "No" to injustice and intolerance was an integral part of saying "Yes" to the gospel.

Positively, the style of witness placed a strong accent on the importance of service. caring for one another, mutual aid in free church circles, logically led to compassion for others. There are records of early instances of aid extended by Dutch Mennonites to stranded Reformed refugees, victims of Huguenot persecutions, and expelled Schwenkfelders as they emigrated to America. All prophecies about our immediate future suggest that if we straighten out our own priorities, the ministry of almsgiving, of the cup of cold water, of humanitarian service may need to be very much with us. If this is true, we will need to become even more aware of the vulnerabilities of the service posture. Instead of getting to the source of the infection, it is argued, the church constantly applies Band-Aids. Sometimes such service makes life just tolerable enough for persons to endure the rotten systems which enslave. We often have adopted this role in order paternalistically to manipulate others into conforming to our middle-class values or our particular verbalization of the faith. We all are aware how it is not enough just to help; rather, we should be helping others help themselves. Though such criticisms are valid, the service motif is deeply rooted in Scripture, as in the parables of the last judgment and the Good Samaritan. Christian compassion becomes concrete through acts of service. I have observed that persons who become concerned about the sources of infection are usually those who have sympathetically put on a lot of Band-Aids.

John Howard Yoder in *The Politics of Jesus* (1972b) poses two assumptions which are entirely different from mainstream American religion. The first is the assertion, surprisingly documented by a wealth of biblical allusions, that the gospel is political. The teachings and life of Jesus speak to issues of justice and peace. In this Yoder corrects some revivalist, Pietist, and Fundamentalist tendencies to mistranslate biblical plural pronouns as singular, as well as the liberal judgment that Jesus either did not have a social ethic, or if He did, it is not relevant to our situation. The second major difference is in reference to the strategy for relating to politics. The common propensity of all of us is to know how the affairs of the world should be run. Therefore it is assumed that if somehow Christians could gain control, things would work out well. Yoder, however, advocates another way, one which he labels as "revolutionary subordination." Such a stance is truly revolutionary in that it stems from newfound freedom in Christ and identifies with the aspirations of the poor for justice. Such a stance is subordination as it features the style of patience, love, persuasion, suffering, teaching, and preaching rather than coercion and violence, as the way to the kingdom goal of justice and peace. After centuries of the way of death, the world of tomorrow needs the mind-blowing affirmation of the power of meekness, the ultimate triumph of the way of suffering love because of God's demonstration and promises of how resurrection follows the cross, victory arises out of suffering, and the death of the old foreshadows the hope in the coming of the new.

The apocalyptic world of the future may need more than anything else the free church interpretation of the future itself. Early Anabaptist theology did not stop with a backward look at the pristine primitive church. Rather, our fathers and mothers in the faith believed and experienced the biblical call for the death of the old and the birth of a new creation, which was seen not only as salvation for the individual but as the restoration of right relationships in all of life. Menno Simons wrote of two opposing princes and kingdoms. We live in a period of two overlapping aeons, one pointing backward to life lived apart from Christ, the other pointing forward to the fullness of the kingdom of God. This dualism between the kingdoms of this world and the kingdom of our Lord is something other than a dualism which regards the material creation as evil, in contrast to the nonmaterial which is spiritual. Nor is this a dualism which separates sharply this life from the next one to come in heaven or in the millennium. Rather, here is a dualism of the present and the coming, the now and not yet, in which "flesh" is life lived apart from God and "spirit" is life lived in proper relationship with God and others.

The social manifestation of the old aeon is often named "world," a New Testament word for the fallen creation. It is in this context that Jesus indicates that His kingdom is not of this world. Though not entirely limited to it, the new aeon is manifested visibly in the body of Christ. Christians can begin to participate presently in the coming kingdom. The way of the Sermon on the Mount dare not be pushed entirely into the future, to be obeyed only after Jesus returns. Rather, there exists a fervent expectation that the future kingdom will break into the present as an explosive force. Because of the promise that the kingdoms of this world will become the kingdom of our Christ, we can adopt the messianic license to begin now to play heaven on this dirty earth.

If the futurologists become even more pessimistic about the human prospect, there may be an even greater attraction to premillennial and dispensationalist interpreters. With them the Anabaptists can share a realistic analysis of the world, along with the faith that the kingdom will come through God's doings rather than ours. We may vary in the degree to which we engage in a greater literalization and schematization of the apocalyptic signs. The Anabaptist Vision, however, stands over against that of the premillennialists whenever the latter attempt to remove the Christian way entirely from the present to the future. Also rejected is the common tendency to picture the nature of our Lord differently,for example as a militant warrior, in His second coming than in the first. The Anabaptist Vision would behold a continuity between the style of the Suffering Servant who died on the cross and the Lamb's War of the Book of Revelation.

In brief, the faith of the free church shares with millennialists a common pessimism about human engineering of the world and an optimism about God's future. But it affirms more about the Spirit's power to work God's future in the present. The power of the pull of God's future is that it can begin to break into the present. It may well be the peculiar calling of the free church tradition to keep alive this optimism about God's activity, by incarnating and pointing to signs of the kingdom coming. This would continue the legacy of the saints of the free church tradition who witnessed most powerfully to the activity of God when things seemed to be at their worst.

I have often appropriated the word "vision" in sharing what is needed in the present and the future. This has been necessary because of my conviction that the Anabaptist Vision is not to be identified with most churches which historically come out of the free church tradition. In spite of our strong identification with our tradition and those people who have come out of it, we are painfully aware of the widespread lack of concretions of the free church vision at its best. Often, our life is in serious conflict with the vision which I have projected for the future. This leads me to suggest that the free church of the future may emerge where it is least expected. Today, there are signs that some so-called free churches are weary of hearing about the Anabaptist Vision, while it is coming alive in other circles and places. At the same time many folk in the free church tradition continue to acculturate to the mainstream, there are others who are discovering with joy the Anabaptist Vision.

At one of the Thanksgiving gatherings of evangelicals sharing social concerns, a brother from South America reported that in his part of the world there were only two options for the Christian. One was Marxist. By this he meant the choice of joining with those who were organizing to overthrow oppressive regimes by force in seeking justice for the people. The other was Anabaptist. By this I gathered he was referring to a faithful, suffering, counterculture movement pointing to the coming kingdom of peace, righteousness, and justice. Intensely interested, I drew him aside after the session. I queried as to what Anabaptist he had met or what literature he had been reading. What was his personal connection? He answered "none" and added: "It is simply the way it is in the situation in which we find ourselves today."

His choice may be a paradigm for more and more of our situations in the future. Whether this be the case or not, I do believe that the future of the free church may be found in lives like our brother from South America more than in many contemporary expressions which carry the label "free church." Though my own sociological identity is strong, my faith is not ultimately bound with the promise of the future success of the Church of the Brethren or the Mennonite cluster of denominations. But I do believe zealously that the vision of the disciple church for which God called out these people will survive in concrete witnessing communities of faith until the day when the kingdoms of this world truly become the kingdom of our Lord.

17

Our Citizenship Is in Heaven

Guy F. Hershberger

In the month of July the American people are accustomed to think and to speak in a special way of citizenship, of its meaning, its privileges and its obligations. This is so because it was on July 4, 1776, that the United States declared its independence from Great Britain so that henceforth its people thought of themselves no longer as British, but as American citizens.

Now there is a sense in which Christians may be American citizens, or British or Canadian citizens. Or citizens of Mexico or Japan or India or Israel or Jordan, or Ghana or Tanzania, or Costa Rica or Russia or China, or some other such earthly commonwealth. In this sense even the Apostle Paul referred to himself on one occasion as a Roman citizen and as a citizen of Tarsus. But Paul's mentioning of this kind of citizenship is incidental only, and its importance to him is ultimately insignificant, transitory, and ephemeral.

It is in passages like Philippians 3:20 that Paul speaks of the citizenship in which he really believed, when he says: "Our citizenship is in heaven." The Revised Standard Version says, "Our commonwealth is in heaven," which is to say that the country in which we have our citizenship is heaven. Practically every modern translation of the New Testament, in one way or another, says it this way: "Our citizenship is in heaven." The Greek word is *Politeuma,* from whose root we derive the English word "politics," and which in classical usage referred to government, or a constitution, or state. So this is our text this morning: "Our citizenship is in heaven" (Philippians 3:20).

The Apostle Peter uses similar language when he speaks to Christians as "a holy nation" whose citizenship is in heaven while living as strangers and pilgrims on the earth (1 Peter 2:9-11). Paul again calls the Ephesian Christians "fellow citizens with the saints and members of the household of God, built upon the foundation of the apostles and prophets, Christ Jesus himself being the chief cornerstone, in whom the

---

A sermon delivered at College Mennonite Church, Goshen, Indiana, July 18, 1971; edited and annotated in 1976.

whole structure is joined together and grows into a holy temple in the Lord; in whom you also are built into it for a dwelling place of God in the Spirit . . . that through the church the manifold wisdom of God might now be made known to the principalities and powers in the heavenly places" (Ephesians 2:19-22, 3:10, RSV).

In numerous places in the New Testament, as in this, Paul brings together in one package his teaching on the creative and redemptive work of Christ, and the lordship of Christ over the church, and over the principalities and powers in the heavenly places, and their earthly representatives, the rulers of states. Notice how he says it in Colossians 1:13-20: "He has delivered us from the dominion of darkness and transferred us to the kingdom of his beloved Son. . . . In him all things were created, in heaven and on earth, visible and invisible, whether thrones or dominions or principalities or authorities. . . . He is before all things and in him all things hold together. He is the head of the body, the church; he is the beginning, the first-born from the dead, that in everything he might be pre-eminent. For in him all the fulness of God was pleased to dwell, and through him to reconcile to himself all things, whether on earth or in heaven, making peace by the blood of his cross" (RSV).

Here we have a picture of Christ, first in creation, and then in the redemption of the fallen world. The redemptive process begins with Israel, the prophets, and the faithful remnant. Then Christ the Suffering Servant, the Redeemer himself, at the midpoint of redemption history, living, dying, and rising again, triumphant over death, hell, and the grave. Then the ascension to the highest heaven where He sits at the right hand of the Father, as Lord of all, both of the church and of the principalities and the powers and their agents. But the end is not yet. The great and final event is yet to come. Oscar Cullmann, writing with the closing events of World War II fresh in his mind, refers to the resurrection event as D-Day, with V-Day yet to come (1950:84, 141). Today the church, and we whose citizenship is in heaven, live in the end time between D-Day and V-Day as laborers together with our Lord for bringing all things to their final victorious, triumphant consummation.

Cullmann describes relationships in the present situation with the aid of two concentric circles with Christ at the center (1950: 188). Within the inner circle is the church, the body of Christ. Its members are the citizens of heaven. Between the inner and outer circles are the invisible, angelic heavenly powers and principalities, and their visible earthly representatives, the rulers of states. The Greek word for principalities or authorities, both visible and invisible as used in Colossians 1 is *exousiai* which is the same word used in Romans 13 where Paul speaks of the Roman government, which serves as part of God's program for the maintenance of social order.

Now Christ who is at the center of all this is Lord of all—Lord of the church (His body), and Lord of the invisible powers and the visible earthly rulers, emperors, kings, and presidents. The difference is that the church knows its Lord and labors together with Him for the redemption of the world, whereas the principalities and powers, neither the invisible heavenly nor the visible earthly powers, know their Lord. They are actually the enemies of their Lord. They think they are rulers in their own right, and indeed at times they become a terrible beast as one stage of the Roman Empire is described in Revelation 13. Even beastly rulers, however, cannot win, for the sovereign Lord holds them in check. And many rulers are under the control of Christ's lordship to such a degree that they are enabled to maintain a rule which is just and humane, even helping to advance the cause of Christ and His church. This is the good state of Romans 13. Or that of 1 Timothy 2:1-2 where Paul says: "I urge that supplications, prayers, intercessions, and thanksgivings be made for . . . kings and all who are in high positions, that we may lead a quiet and peaceable life, godly and respectful in every way" (RSV). Indeed the powers frequently become unconscious instruments of the redemptive process itself. When the Emperor Augustus (Luke 2:1) caused a census to be made bringing Joseph and Mary to Bethlehem where Christ was born, he was an instrument in the redemptive process, although without being conscious of the fact. Even more so was Pilate when God granted him power to bring the Christ-event "to its very climax, to the decision on the cross" (Cullmann, 1950: 190). When Jesus was questioned by Pilate, Jesus answered him, "You would have no power over me unless it had been given you from above" (John 19:11, RSV).

But now let us give our attention to the heavenly citizen as he walks, a stranger and a pilgrim, on the earth. Precisely what is his role first with respect to the church of which body he is a member, and then with respect to the visible kings, princes, and presidents, those agents of the invisible principalities and powers in the heavenly places?

Perhaps no one has given us a better answer to this question than the anonymous writer of the *Epistle to Diognetus,* written in the second century AD, a letter which is obviously a commentary on Philippians 3:20: "Our citizenship is in heaven." The epistle reads as follows:

Christians cannot be distinguished from the rest of the human race by country or language or customs. They do not live in cities of their own; they do not use a peculiar form of speech; they do not follow an eccentric manner of life. . . . Yet, although they live in Greek and barbarian cities alike, as each man's lot has been cast, and follow the customs of the country in clothing and food and other matters of daily living, at the same time they give proof of the remarkable and admittedly extraordinary constitution of their own commonwealth. They live in their own countries, but only as aliens. . . . It is true that they are "in the flesh," but they do not live "according to the flesh." They busy themselves on earth, but their *citizenship is in heaven.* They obey the established laws, but in their own lives they go far beyond what the laws require. . . . They are reviled, and yet they bless; when they are affronted, they still pay due respect. . . .

To put it simply: What the soul is in the body, that Christians are in the world. . . . The soul dwells in the body, but does not belong to the body, and Christians dwell in the world, but do not belong to the world. . . . The soul loves the flesh that hates it . . . ; in the same way, Christians love those who hate them. The soul is shut up in the body, and yet itself holds the body together; while Christians are restrained in the world as in a prison, and yet themselves hold the world together. (Richardson, 1953: 216-218; emphasis added).

Now let us note a few specific things which the heavenly citizen does to hold the world together—this alien world in which he dwells as a stranger and a pilgrim.

1. *First, he is obedient to the Great Commission as given by our Lord in Matthew 28:18-20.* Take a good hard look at these words. Weigh each one carefully and you will see in them everything of which we have been speaking and much more besides. *All authority in heaven and earth has been given to me.* Here is the lordship of Christ over the church, over the angelic powers, and over their visible agents the rulers of states and heads of governments. *Go therefore and make disciples of all nations.* This means preaching the good news of salvation from sin, and of reconciliation with God through the atoning work of Christ. In the case of the Jews this meant bringing them to understand that justification comes not by works of the law but by faith in Christ.[1] In the case of the Athenian philosophers on Mars' Hill it meant Paul's declaration that God is a person, not an impersonal world spirit; that He is a personal, intelligent creator, not a cosmic force identical with the creation; that He is Lord of His creation, of all in heaven and in earth; that salvation is not a process of self-purification with absorption in an impersonal

cosmic soul as its goal; but that God is a righteous God calling all men to repentance from sin; that repentance is followed with faithful discipleship, hearing and obeying the voice of Christ who has come to teach His people Himself; and that the same Christ will walk with His faithful disciples to the end of the age, even to that great day when all shall stand before the Lord of glory and every knee shall bow and tongue confess that Jesus Christ is Lord to the glory of God the Father.

2. *In the second place the heavenly citizen in his sojourn on the earth proclaims the lordship of Christ directly to principalities and powers themselves.* The Apostle Paul proclaimed his faith in Jesus Christ and the hope of the resurrection, before Roman officials; he witnessed prophetically concerning righteousness and temperance and judgment which is to come (Acts 24:25). In our service this morning we confessed in unison again the Apostles' Creed in which we reiterated that our Lord Christ had suffered under Pontius Pilate. Speaking historically, the mention of Pontius Pilate in the creed owes its origin to the fact that the earliest formulas of faith were spoken in persecution, before pagan courts, where Christians testified to the fact that Pilate himself was an instrument used of God in the redemptive process which brought Christ to the cross.

Menno Simons gave witness to rulers of his time, both of repentance and righteousness and judgment and justice, admonishing them to "take heed wisely, rightly to execute your responsible and dangerous office according to the will of God" (1956:197).

Christians in our day must also witness to the powers that be. The invitation to faith, including its full meaning in true discipleship, must be extended to all men, including government officials. On the other hand, ever mindful that God abandons neither the state nor its rulers, even in their rebellion against Him, the Christian must, when the response is something less than Christian faith, hold forth the claims of Christ's lordship, even upon the sub-Christian and the pagan state.

This witness may be carried on by word of mouth, through oral or written conversation with officials of state, whether national or local; by means of the printed page; through works of mercy, such as feeding the hungry or clothing the naked; by a ministry of reconciliation in areas of tension, whether these be racial or social tensions in our own land, or colonial, nationalistic, or political tensions abroad; or by other means consistent with New Testament teaching and practice.

3. *In the third place the heavenly citizen does not belong within the power structure of the principalities and authorities.* "What the soul is in

the body, that Christians are in the world," says the *Epistle to Diognetus.* "The soul dwells in the body, but does not belong to the body. Christians dwell in the world, but do not belong to the world." Since the writer of the epistle did not claim to be a psychologist, it would be fruitless to quibble about the psychological precision of his analogy. But the meaning of the analogy is clear enough. Neither does his statement give a detailed blueprint for the Cristian's political relationships, participations, and abstentions. But here again the principle is clear. Christians "busy themselves on earth, but their citizenship is in heaven. They obey the established laws, but in their own lives they go far beyond what the laws require. . . . They are reviled, and yet they bless; when they are affronted, they still pay due respect."

That Christians by their verbal testimony and their performance must and do make their impact on the performance of the state is clear enough. The persistent witness and patient suffering of the Anabaptist fathers eventually led to freedom of religion within the nations of the Western world. The firm position on Christian race relations taken by the churches in the early 1960s convinced even segregationist congressmen and senators of the need for civil rights legislation. There is no doubt that civilian voluntary service programs sponsored by various private agencies, including the significant Mennonite Central Committee Pax program, were among the precedents followed by the United States government when it established the Peace Corps. And the MCC Peace Section and the National Interreligious Service Board for Conscientious Objectors, from their offices in Washington, maintaining a constant watch on proceedings on Capitol Hill, are good examples of citizens of heaven, witnessing to principalities and powers concerning that which is required of them under the lordship of Christ.

Every good thing, however, is accompanied by its own peculiar temptations. Close proximity to the seat of political power with some knowledge of its workings sometimes brings the temptation to operate within the power structure itself. If a heavenly citizen has an obligation to testify of righteousness to men in power, would it not be even better to wield the power himself, for then it would surely be used aright? Indeed this was the great temptation of Jesus Himself—the temptation of power, prestige, and possession—which Karen Horney tells us is at the heart of the neurotic personality of our time (Horney, 1937). But in the case of Jesus the significant fact is that He successfully resisted the temptation. It was His calling to be the Suffering Servant in whose steps the Christian is summoned to follow.

This is not to say, of course, that it is impossible for a pacifist elected to Congress to maintain an antiwar position in the face of the Pentagon and the military-industrial complex whose influence is so dominant in our time. But it is to state my conviction that to do so is very difficult, and that in the great majority of cases the love of power for its own sake seems eventually to become so dominant as to vitiate its use for righteous purposes.

My own personal acquaintance with many of our peace-loving Friends, the Quakers, together with long study of their history, has convinced me that the Quaker influence for peace has been greatest when and where they remained outside the political power structure, and weakest when and where they became involved on the inside. George Fox, the preacher-founder, remained outside the political structure, suffering persecution, imprisonments, and beatings as he literally turned the other cheek. He saw "the origin of war in the lusts of men and in their disobedience and treason toward Jesus Christ" (Jones, 1972:54), and in an encounter with Oliver Cromwell the military dictator of the commonwealth he fearlessly declared that he was a "son of God who is sent to stand a witness against all violence and against all the works of darkness, and to turn people from the darkness to the light, and to bring them from the occasion of . . . war" (Fox, 1952:197).

It was William Penn who took a different course, hoping to operate the government of colonial Pennsylvania on the basis of Matthew 5 and Romans 12. This was to be, in his own words, a government like that before the fall of Adam when man, God's deputy, ruled the world and "there was no need of coercive or compulsive means."[2] Within a few short years, however, the peaceful Quakers in the Assembly were asked by the Crown for military appropriations at a time when the Assembly itself was engaged in a bitter struggle with the Executive Council as to whether the latter should continue to exercise the power of initiative in legislation or whether this power should be transferred to the Assembly. When the request for military funds came, the Assembly first offered religious objections to the request, but seeing their opportunity they compromised their peace principles and passed the military appropriation bill with a rider attached giving the coveted power of initiative to the Assembly. Illustrations such as this could be cited by the score to show how step by step the Quakers in the government of Colonial Pennsylvania sold their peace principles for added bits of power until after seventy-five years the so-called Holy Experiment came to its end.[3]

Happily, however, while Quakers inside the government were selling their faith in exchange for political power, Friends like John Woolman on the outside continued to walk the way of the Suffering Servant that true Quakerism might not perish from the earth, even as some Quakers today continue their mission as true witnesses to the way of peace while one of their number is a member of Congress, serving on the House Armed Services Committee where as late as 1967 he was the author of proposed legislation designed to induct conscientious objectors into the armed forces.[4] Within the body of Christ it ought not be necessary for members outside the power structure to spend their time undoing the harm done by members within that structure.

4. *In the fourth place, they whose citizenship is in heaven, carry on their witness in the spirit of the Suffering Servant.* The heavenly citizen is a nonconformist in the sense that he does not conform to the evil ways of an evil society. Indeed he is opposed to the evil and cries out against it. But if he is *only* a nonconformist, if he is unable in the spirit of the Suffering Servant to proclaim and to exemplify the *better* way, he is likely to end up merely fighting evil with more evil. Citizens of heaven "are reviled, and yet they bless," says the *Epistle to Diognetus.* "When they are affronted, they still pay due respect."

At the University of Notre Dame a few weeks ago the graduating class heard a most significant address by the commencement speaker, Kenneth Keniston, a psychologist of the Yale Medical School, who chose as his subject: "Agony Stalks the Campus: the Lost Ecstasy of Youth." The address was an analysis of what Keniston believes to be the cause for the silence, the "eerie tranquility," of the American university campus during the past academic year, as compared with the tumult of the 1960s. The catalyst which precipitated the new quietism, Keniston believes, was two events, two deaths: (1) "the murder of an innocent onlooker by Hell's Angels at the rock festival at Altamont"; and (2) "the killing of an innocent graduate student in the terrorist bombing of the mathematics building at the University of Wisconsin" (1971:1).

Two major causes for the student protests of the 1960s were the Vietnam War and the oppression of blacks and other minorities in our own country. Thus it was violence against which the students were protesting—violence on the part of the American nation against the innocent Vietnamese and violence on the part of American society against its own minorities. The assumption of the student protest movement and of the counterculture generally was that violence is something to be associated with the establishment. Not until Altamont and Madison were students awakened to the fact that "the potential for violence lies not only within the rest of American society, but within the student movement itself."

It is true enough that the violence "out there" was far greater than that within the counterculture, but what brought the agony on the campus was the sudden realization that "the counterculture itself became infected by the very violence it nominally opposed. The shouted obscenity calculated to offend the policeman was all along a form of violence. . . . During the earlier era it was possible for student activists to blind themselves to their own rage, to see themselves as happy exceptions to that morbid fascination with violence which affects our nation as a whole. The violent rhetoric that came to provoke the student movement could be passed off as mere talk. But when that rhetoric culminated in murder, then the members of the student movement had to face for the first time their own complicity with the very violence against which they struggled."

Confronted with this new realization, says Keniston, "the same students who last year were working toward major changes in national priority . . . have this year fallen silent. . . . They have turned inward— to meditation . . . to communes in the mountains." While Keniston believes that this new introspectiveness and self-examination testifies "to the ultimate sanity and decency of most student activists," he also warns against the danger that the present agony of disillusion may lead to despair, causing the student movement to "continue to fragment, splinter, go underground, be suppressed, and eventually disappear" without bringing to fruition its great potential for good. In order that this may not happen he appeals for a turn from a movement of mere opposition to one of affirmation, a movement formed by "an alliance not merely of the young, the privileged and the educated, but of those who are not young or privileged, or educated, and of that vast majority of Americans who refuse to ally themselves with either camp" (Keniston, 1971:1-3).

We should be grateful indeed that the student violence of which Keniston speaks was not characteristic of Mennonite campuses. But there is in this, nevertheless, a lesson for all Mennonites, students and others alike. The great lesson for Mennonites from this analysis, it seems to me, should be a realization of the need for a renewed and deepened commitment to the way of the Suffering Servant, the way of love and nonresistance in our relations with our fellowmen, with the state, and even our enemies. Violence cannot be overcome by violence, nor even by nonviolence which has a violent spirit pent up within itself. Nothing less than outgoing, suffering love will do. Citizens of heaven "are reviled," says the *Epistle to Diognetus,* "and yet they bless; when they are affronted, they still pay due respect.... The soul loves the flesh that hates it . . .; in the same way, Christians love those who hate them."

5. *In the fifth place, they whose citizenship is in heaven keep the Christian mission—evangelism and service—in proper balance.* Moffatt's translation of Philippians 3:20 reads this way: "We are a colony of heaven." Just as the incarnate Son of God literally came down to earth and lived the heavenly life on the earth at the same time that His preaching was pointing the way to heaven—so must His disciples comprise a heavenly society here in this world. They must preach the way to heaven and at the same time feed the hungry, heal the sick, and witness for peace and against war, and all Christians, whatever their race or color or station in life, must learn to live together as brethren or else it is not a colony of heaven. "Men will come from east and west, and from north and south," said Jesus, "and sit at table in the kingdom of God." And if this is to be our experience when we get to heaven we citizens of heaven must get a little practice in this kind of thing while we are here on the earth.

The colony of heaven on the earth has two integral parts, the heavenly and the earthly, which must not be separated. Many Christians, however, have difficulty here. Some are so overwhelmed by the experience of peace and inner joy which comes with personal salvation that they are content to shelter themselves safely within the rifted rock where the storms of life do not molest and where they need not hear the call of the needy, the sick, and the oppressed. Salvation, yes. But, service to a needy world, no. "That is humanitarian social service. I am interested in spiritual things." "In the rifted rock I'll hide me, till the storms of life are past, all secure in this blest refuge, heeding not the fiercest blast." Some others, even some who are nominal Christians, keenly aware of the world's economic and social needs, its suffering and injustice, become wholly involved with this problem and often render an important humanitarian service, but without regard to the inner spiritual needs of those whom they are serving in a material way. They feel no call to lead men to a personal experience with Jesus Christ. They would establish a heaven on earth without the resources of heaven—without leading men to know the Savior of men—the One who is Lord of heaven and earth, at whose feet every knee shall bow.

But the New Testament way is to feed the hungry and to clothe the naked, even as the MCC motto itself says, "In the Name of Christ." When the authorities in Jerusalem were annoyed because Peter and John had healed a crippled man, and because they were teaching the people and proclaiming in Jesus the resurrection from the dead, they arrested them and brought them to trial. "And when they had set them in the midst, they inquired, 'By what power or by what name did you do this?' Then Peter, filled with the Holy Spirit, said to them, 'Rulers of the people and elders, if we are being examined today concerning a good deed done to a cripple, by what means this man has been healed, be it known to you all . . . that by the name of Jesus Christ of Nazareth, whom you crucified, whom God raised from the dead, by him this man is standing before you well. . . . And there is salvation in no one else, for there is no other name under heaven given among men by which we must be saved' " (Acts 4:7-12, RSV).

It was this same gospel of redemption through Christ and holy living and service in His name which was preached by Menno Simons when he said: "These regenerated people . . . know war no more. . . . They comfort the afflicted; assist the needy; clothe the naked; feed the hungry. . . . Therefore we preach . . . by day and by night, in houses and in fields . . . hither and yon . . . with possessions and blood, with life and death" (1956:94f.)

This is keeping the message of personal salvation and service to one's fellowmen in the name of Christ together, even as Jesus and the apostles themselves kept them together.

6. *In the sixth place they whose citizenship is in heaven maintain a keen sense of destiny. Theirs is a living hope.* If the risen Christ is Lord of the universe, there is more to this life than problems and conflict and tension. "I consider," says Paul, "that the sufferings of this present time are not worth comparing with the glory that is to be revealed to us" (Romans 8:18, RSV). Indeed, the glory which is to be is revealed even now. Not the least feature of this hope is the inner sense of satisfaction experienced by the Christian as he presses toward the ultimate goal, conscious that he is making his contribution to the realization of the kingdom now. He who possesses this hope has within himself the only motive power for true progress in this age.

Christian ethics and the hope for the future belong together. In Paul's first epistle to the Corinthians there are two classic chapters, the thirteenth on Christian love, and the fifteenth on the resurrection and the future life. There is good reason for the close proximity of these two themes, for the love portrayed in the former chapter is inconceivable in this age except through the power of the risen Christ. The Christian ethic is a divine ethic, not man-made. He whose life and hope are in the eternal world will have a prophetic message for this age. He who is comfortably adjusted to the present age has no prophetic message regarding the future. Christian ethics and Christian eschatology belong together. When the Greco-Roman world charged the early Christians with social irresponsibility as they sought first the kingdom of God and its righteousness, Origen the church father replied that "men of God are assuredly the salt of the earth: they preserve the order of the world; and society is held together as long as the salt is uncorrupted."[5] Chrysostom said that when Christians pray, "Thy will be done in earth, as it is in heaven," and act upon their own prayer, they are laboring to "make the earth a heaven" (quoted in Petry, 1956: 103). And Walter Rauschenbusch, whose own eschatology was based on human development, found it necessary to admit that the principles of the Sermon on the Mount have had a tragic fate when accepted only as social ideals to be realized by a social order which is anthropocentric and this-worldly in its orientation. "Only those church bodies which have been in opposition to organized society," he says, "and have looked for a better city with its foundations in heaven, have taken the Sermon on the Mount seriously" (1918:134).

The Christian realizes that he is caught up in the stream of redemptive history; that this stream has been made effective for his personal redemption in Christ. Once this has occurred he becomes a colaborer with God, an ambassador for Christ, God through him making his appeal to men that they may be reconciled to God and thus also enter the stream of redemptive history as it moves forward to flood tide.

It is from this redemptive stream that Christian ethics flows. Since it is a holy stream of which the Christian is a part, his ethics are of the same holy substance as the stream itself. The question is no longer, What should or can I do in the light of my present situation? The question is rather, What does the holy stream of redemptive history require of the present situation? As Oscar Cullmann says, this sets the moral law of the Decalogue "in the light of the imminent kingdom of God, that is, sets it in the situation in which one must be radically obedient to the divine will at every moment" (1950:226).

Merely to refrain from destroying the body of one's fellowman no longer satisfies the requirements of the sixth commandment. What is now required is the way of love and the cross, following the steps of the Suffering Servant who for our sake emptied Himself in complete self-giving service. The way of the cross is eschatologically oriented. He who follows in this way finds himself so absorbed in the discharge of his ultimate responsibility to the kingdom of God that he cannot be too much disturbed by ideas of responsibility for a social order based on lesser foundations. "The abiding characteristic of true Christian social thought," says Ray Petry, "is that it is not coordinated with the present society as the true center of reference. Because of this, alone, kingdom-destined men can give the present its true, socializing impact. . . . To be truly productive, the present social order must respond to, and be broken into, by the future and eternal one" (1956:67-68).

Therefore, Christian friends, having been reconciled to God through Christ who has given unto us the ministry of reconciliation, let us have this mind among ourselves which we have in Christ Jesus, following His steps in the way of the cross, blameless and innocent, children of God without blemish in the midst of a crooked and perverse generation, among whom we shine as lights in the world. Let us run with perseverance the race that is set before us, looking unto Jesus the pioneer and perfecter of our faith, who has disarmed principalities and powers, and triumphed over them, and will in His own time bring all things to their consummation and make all things new, whence He shall reign forever and ever. I am the Alpha and the Omega, says the Lord God, who is and who was and who is to come, the Almighty. Amen.

A Bibliography of the Writings of
Guy F. Hershberger, 1922-1976

Compiled by Elizabeth Hershberger Bauman

The following listing of Guy F. Hershberger's writings is organized chronologically, so that the scholar may see the historical development of Hershberger's thought over a fifty-year span of time. The manuscript materials are to be found either in the Mennonite Historical Library or in the Archives of the Mennonite Church, both located on the campus of Goshen College, Goshen, Indiana 46526; the individual entries are so noted.

Abbreviations used throughout the bibliography include: AMC for Archives of the Mennonite Church, *AAAPSS* for *The Annals of the American Academy of Political and Social Science*, CL for *Christian Living*, CH for *Church History*, GH for *Gospel Herald*, MComm for *Mennonite Community*, *ME* for *Mennonite Encyclopedia*, MHL for Mennonite Historical Library, *MQR* for *Mennonite Quarterly Review*, *MVHR* for *Mississippi Valley Historical Review*, YCC for *Youth's Christian Companion*.

1922

a. "The Pharisees." Paper written 1922 for course at Hesston College. Handwritten. Goshen, Ind. AMC. Hist. Mss. 1-171 Box 14.

1923

a. "The Call of the Church for Trained Men." *Hesston College Journal* 10 (Commencement 1923): 49-50.

b. "The Seer of the Ages." *Hesston College Journal* 10 (Aug.-Sept. 1923): 1-4.

1924

a. "The Influence of Pagan Thought and Religion, Especially Greek, on Historical Christianity." Paper written Dec. 5, 1924, for course at University of Iowa. Typewritten. Goshen, Ind. AMC. Hist. Mss. 1-171 Box 13.

1925

a. "The Evangelical Movement in England." Seminar report made Jan. 22, 1925, for course at University of Iowa. Typewritten. Goshen, Ind. AMC. Hist. Mss. 1-171 Box 13.

b. "An Inquiry into the Origins of the Anabaptist Movement." Unpublished Master's thesis, University of Iowa, 1925.

1927

a. "False Patriotism." *MQR* 1 (Jan. 1927): 9-27; (Apr. 1927): 29-45.

1928
a. "Endowment Gifts an Expression of Confidence in the Church." *Christian Monitor* 20 (1928): 338-39.
b. "The Mennonite Attitude and the Modern Peace Movement as Illustrated by the St. Louis Meeting of the World Alliance for International Friendship through the Churches." *MQR* 2 (1928): 111-18.
c. [Review.] Morrison, Charles Clayton. *The Outlawry of War: A Constructive Policy for World Peace.* Chicago: Willett, Clark and Colby, 1927. In *MQR* 2 (1928): 159-75.

1929
a. "After Eleven Years." *Goshen College Record* 31 (Nov. 1929): 1-2.

1930
a. "Foreign Claims in Regard to Repudiated American State Debts." Paper written for course at University of Chicago, 1930. Typewritten. Goshen College Library.
b. [Review.] Smith, C. Henry. *The Coming of the Russian Mennonites. An Episode in the Settling of the Last Frontier, 1879-1884.* Berne, Ind.: Mennonite Book Concern, 1927. In *MQR* 4 (1930): 72-77.
c. [Review.] Wedel, P. P. *Kurze Geschichte der aus Wolhynien, Russland nach Kansas ausgewanderten Schweizer-Mennoniten.* Moundridge, Kan.: Privately printed, 1929. In *MQR* 4 (1930): 72-77.

1931
a. [Review.] Curti, Merle E. *The American Peace Crusade, 1815-1860.* Durham: Duke University Press, 1919. In *MQR* 5 (1931): 68-72.
b. [Review.] Meyer, Ernest L. *"Hey! Yellowbacks!" The War Diary of a Conscientious Objector.* New York: John Day Co., 1930. In *MQR* 5 (1931): 72-77.

1933
a. "Religion in Politics and Social Reform." Typewritten. 1933. Goshen, Ind. AMC. Hist. Mss. 1-171 Box 12.

1935
a. "Do We Know Where We Stand on the War Question?" *YCC* 16 (1935): 792.
b. "Is Alternative Service Desirable and Possible?" *MQR* 9 (1935): 20-36.
c. "The Mennonite Conference on Peace and War." *Goshen College Record* 36 (Mar. 1935): 1.
d. "Quaker Pacifism and the Provincial Government of Pennsylvania, 1682-1756." Unpublished PhD dissertation, University of Iowa, 1935.

1936
a. "Can the American Revolution Be Justified?" *YCC* 17 (1936): 320.
b. "The Conversion of Menno Simons." *YCC* 17 (1936): 177-78.
c. "Is Modern Religious Liberalism a Force for Peace?" *Goshen College Record* 37 (Jan. 1936): 1-3; also in *GH* 28 (1936): 994.

d. "John M. Brenneman's Pamphlet on War." *YCC* 17 (1936): 216.

e. "Later Life of Menno Simons." *YCC* 17 (1936): 187.

f. *Nonresistance and the State: The Pennsylvania Quaker Experiment in Politics, 1682-1756.* Scottdale, Pa.: Mennonite Publishing House, 1936.

g. "Peace Movements That Have Failed in Time of Need." *YCC* 17 (1936): 248.

h. "The Pennsylvania Quaker Experiment in Politics, 1682-1756." *MQR* 10 (1936): 187-221.

i. "Some Mennonite Experiences During the Civil War." *YCC* 17 (1936): 296.

j. "Some Religious Pacifists of the Nineteenth Century." *MQR* 10 (1936): 73-86.

k. "Was the War of 1812 Justified?" *YCC* 17 (1936): 351.

l. "What Did Jesus and the Apostles Say about War, Peace, and the State?" *YCC* 17 (1936): 8.

m. "What Did the Early American Mennonites Do about War?" *YCC* 17 (1936): 136.

n. "What Did the Early Christians Think about War and State?" *YCC* 17 (1936): 40.

o. "What Did the Early Mennonites Say about War and Peace?" *YCC* 17 (1936): 112.

p. "What Did the Mennonites Do in the American Revolution?" *YCC* 17 (1936): 176.

q. "What Shall We Think of the War with Mexico?" *YCC* 17 (1936): 392.

r. "Why Have Many Christians Forgotten the Bible Teachings on Peace?" *YCC* 17 (1936): 80.

1937

a. "How the American Churches Made Themselves Believe That the World War Was a Holy War." *YCC* 18 (1937): 528.

b. "The Origin of the Peace Problems Committee." *YCC* 18 (1937): 664.

c. "The Program and Work of the Peace Problems Committee." *YCC* 18 (1937): 704.

d. "Quaker Experiment in Politics." *Religious Digest* 18 (Mar. 1937): 79-83. Condensed from *MQR* 10 (1936): 187-221.

e. [Review.] Niebuhr, H. Richard; Pauck, Wilhelm; and Miller, Francis P. *The Church Against the World.* New York: Willett, Clark and Co., 1935. In *MQR* 11 (1937): 228-31.

f. "War Is a Maker of Hatred and Lies." *YCC* 18 (1937): 560.

g. "Was the Civil War Necessary to Free the Slaves?" *YCC* 18 (1937): 424.

h. "What Did the Church Do to Help Our Young People During the World War?" *YCC* 18 (1937): 632.

i. "What Is the Meaning of the War in China?" *YCC* 18 (1937): 764a.

j. "What Meanest Thou, O Sleeper?" *Goshen College Record* (May 1937): 1.

k. "What Shall a Christian Youth Do in Time of War?" *YCC* 18 (1937): 600.

l. "Why Did the United States Enter the World War?" *YCC* 18 (1937): 496.

m. "Why Did the United States Have a War with Spain?" *YCC* 18 (1937): 464.

n. "Why Is the Mennonite Church Doing Relief Work in Spain?" *YCC* 18 (1937): 808.

1938
a. "A Call to Peace from the Cotswold Bruderhof." *YCC* 19 (1938): 414c.
b. "Christians Must Exercise Good Will Toward All People." *YCC* 19 (1938): 143-44.
c. "Memorials of Peace and Memorials of War." *YCC* 19 (1938): 216.
d. "The Mennonite General Conference States Its Position on Peace and War." *YCC* 19 (1938): 87.
e. "Military Training in Schools and Colleges." *YCC* 19 (1938): 111-12.
f. "On Being True to the Faith of the Fathers." *YCC* 19 (1938):296.
g. "Quaker Pacifism and the Provincial Government of Pennsylvania, 1682-1756." *University of Iowa Studies in the Social Sciences. Abstracts in History III* 10 (Feb. 15, 1938): 7-18.
h. "Render unto God the Things That Are God's." *YCC* 19 (1938): 47.
i. "We Cannot Support War, Directly or Indirectly." *YCC* 19 (1938): 256.
j. "Why Do the Nations Spend Money for That Which Is Not Bread?" *YCC* 19 (1938): 5.

1939
a. "Military Conscription and the Conscientious Objector." *YCC* 20 (1939): 809-10.
b. "Noncombatant Military and Noncombatant Civilian Service." *YCC* 20 (1939): 832.
c. "Nonresistance and Industrial Conflict." *MQR* 13 (1939): 135-54.
d. "One War Leads to Another." *YCC* 20 (1939): 800.
e. "Pacifism and the State in Colonial Pennsylvania." *CH* 8 (Mar. 1939): 54-74.
f. "Reflections on Armistice Day." *YCC* 20 (1939): 776.
g. [Review.] Hull, William I. *The Rise of Quakerism in Amsterdam, 1655-1665.* Swarthmore: The College, 1938. In *CH* 8 (1939): 380-82.

1940
a. *Can Christians Fight? Essays on Peace and War.* Scottdale, Pa.: Mennonite Publishing House, 1940.
b. "French Conscientious Objectors: Henri Roser." *YCC* 21 (1940): 328.
c. "French Conscientious Objectors: Philippe and Pierre Vernier." *YCC* 21 (1940): 344.
d. "The Friendly Association (1756-64)." *Dictionary of American History* 2 (1940): 348.
e. "A Letter to the President Suggesting Alternative Service for Mennonite Youth in Case of War." *YCC* 21 (1940): 192.
f. "Maintaining the Mennonite Rural Community." *MQR* 14 (1940): 214-23.
g. "Mennonites and Conscription in the World War." Prepared for use by Peace Problems Committee in view of approaching conscription (Burke-Wadsworth Bill). Typewritten. 1940. Goshen, Ind. MHL.
h. "The Methodist Church and the Conscientious Objector." *YCC* 21 (1940);296.
i. "Nonresistance in Time of War." *YCC* 21 (1940): 8.
j. "Objectors to War in England." *YCC* 21 (1940): 312.
k. "The Pemberton Papers in the Historical Society of Pennsylvania." Typewritten. 1940.

l. "The Pennsylvania Quaker Experiment in Politics." *Dictionary of American History* 4 (1940): 385.
m. "A Plan of Action: Suggestions for Mennonite Young Men of Draft Age in Case of War." *YCC* 21 (1940): 178-179.
n. "Questions for Nonresistant Christians." *GH* 33 (1940): 323, 338, 371, 386, 418, 435, 450, 466, 514, 530, 546, 562, 642, 658, 675, 738, 754. A series of seventeen articles.

1941

a. [Review.] Brinton, Howard H. *Quaker Education in Theory and Practice.* Pendle Hill Pamphlet, no. 9. Wallingford, Pa.: Pendle Hill Publications, 1940. In *MVHR* 28 (1941): 136-37.
b. [Review.] Eddy, Sherwood. *The Kingdom of God and the American Dream: The Religious and Secular Ideals of American History.* New York: Harper and Row Publishers, 1941. In *MVHR* 28 (1941): 313-14.
c. [Review.] Fries, Adelaide L., ed. *Records of the Moravians in North Carolina.* Vol. 6, 1793-1808. Raleigh: North Carolina Historical Commission, 1943. In *Pennsylvania Magazine of History and Biography* 67 (1941): 414-15.
d. [Review.] Gingerich, Melvin. *The Mennonites in Iowa.* Iowa City: State Historical Society of Iowa, 1939. In *MQR* 15 (1941): 142-43.
e. [Review.] Melcher, Marguerite Fellows. *The Shaker Adventure.* Princeton: Princeton University Press, 1941. In *MVHR* 28 (1941): 314.
f. [Review.] Wenger, John C. *History of the Mennonites of the Franconia Conference. Telford, Pa.: Franconia Mennonite Historical Society, 1937.* In *MQR* 15 (1941): 141-42.

1942

a. *Christian Relationships to State and Community.* Mennonites and Their Heritage, edited by Harold S. Bender, no. 5. Akron, Pa.: Mennonite Central Committee, 1942.
b. "The Economic Life of the Mennonite Community." *GH* 34 (1942): 452.
c. [Review.] Kirby, Ethyn W. *George Keith, 1638-1716.* New York: Appleton-Century, 1942. In *MVHR* 29 (1942): 253.
d. "Suggestions for Improving the Small Christian Community." In *Proceedings of the First Conference on Mennonite Cultural Problems, pp. 48-59. North Newton, Kan.:* The Bethel College Press, 1942. Held at Winona Lake, Ind., Aug. 7-8, 1942.

1943

a. "Biblical Nonresistance and Modern Pacifism." *MQR* 17 (1943): 115-35.
b. "Peace and War in the New Testament." *MQR* 17 (1943): 59-72; also in *La Voz Menonita. Revista Evangelica Mensual* 12 (1943): 416-25.
c. "Peace and War in the Old Testament." *MQR* 17 (1943): 5-22; also in *La Voz Menonita. Revista Evangelica Mensual* 12 (1943): 371-82.
d. [Review.] Blake, Israel G. *The Holmans of Veraestan.* Oxford, Ohio: Mississippi Valley Press, 1943. In *MVHR* 30 (1943): 295-96.
e. [Review.] Boettner, Loraine. *The Christian Attitude Toward War.* Grand

Rapids: Wm. B. Eerdmans Publishing Co., 1940. In *MQR* 17 (1943): 53-55.
f. "Why I Am a Nonresistant Christian." Typewritten. Address given frequently *ca.* 1943ff. Goshen, Ind. AMC. Hist. Mss. 1-171 Box 11.

1944
a. "Mennonites in the Civil War." *MQR* 18 (1944): 131-44.
b. "Questions on Mennonite Community Life." *GH* 36 (1944): 1075, 1091, 1107; 37 (1944): 4, 36, 52, 68, 229, 293, 309, 325, 340, 372, 397, 557, 572, 597, 620, 636, 653. A series of twenty articles.
c. *War, Peace, and Nonresistance.* Scottdale, Pa.: Herald Press, 1944. 2d. rev. ed., 1953; 3d rev. ed., 1969.

1945
a. "Appreciating the Mennonite Way of Life." *GH* 38 (1945): 444.
b. "Conference on Mennonite Community Life." *MQR* 19 (1945): 75-78.
c. "How Will Mennonite Mutual Aid Assist the Person Who Needs Help?" *GH* 38 (1945): 508.
d. "How Will Mennonite Mutual Aid Obtain Its Working Capital?" *GH* 38 (1945): 492.
e. "The Mennonite Community: A Syllabus." A course in the Farm and Community School, CPS Camp No. 138, Unit 2, Malcolm, Neb., 1945. Mimeographed. Goshen, Ind. MHL.
f. "Mennonite Mutual Aid Is Now Organized." *GH* 38 (1945): 477.
g. "Mennonites and Materialism." *GH* 37 (1945): 828-29.
h. "Mutual Aid for Sharing of Losses in Case of Calamity, Sickness or Death." Typewritten. *Ca.* 1945-47. Goshen, Ind. AMC. Hist. Mss. 1-171 Box 40.
i. [Review.] Brinton, Howard H., ed. *Byways in Quaker History: A Collection of Historical Essays by Colleagues and Friends of William I. Hull.* Wallingford, Pa.: Pendle Hill Publications, 1944. In *CH* 14 (1945): 134-35.
j. [Review.] Cummings, Hubertis. *Richard Peters, Provincial Secretary and Cleric, 1704-1776.* Philadelphia: University of Pennsylvania Press, 1944. In *CH* 14 (1945): 77.

1946
a. "A Baptist Minister on Nonresistance." *GH* 39 (1946): 639.
b. "Biblical Nonresistance and Modern Pacifism." *GH* 39 (1946): 461.
c. "The Church of the Brethren and War." *GH* 39 (1946): 638.
d. "Conscientious Objectors in Prison." *GH* 39 (1946): 460.
e. "CPS Guinea Pig Projects Commended." *GH* 39 (1946): 639.
f. "The New Leviathan." *GH* 39 (1946): 459.
g. "A New Postwar Peace Movement." *GH* 39 (1946): 639.
h. "Says Truman Pardons Pendergast Vote-Stealers, But Not CO's." *GH* 39 (1946): 640.
i. "The Supreme Court and Conscientious Objectors." *GH* 39 (1946): 460-61.

1947
a. "Appreciating the Mennonite Community." *MComm* 1 (Jan. 1947): 6.

b. "A Christian Community at Work." *MComm* 1 (Sept. 1947): 16.
c. "John Horsch, a Proponent of Biblical Nonresistance." *MQR* 21 (1947): 156-59.

1948

a. "The Significance of the Mennonite World Conference." *MComm* 2 (Sept. 1948): 24.
b. "Wider Horizons for the Community." *MComm* 2 (Jan. 1948): 13.

1949

a. "Die sozialen Folgerungen der Wehrlosigkeit." Typewritten. 1949. Goshen, Ind. AMC. Hist. Mss. 1-171 Box 12.

1950

a. "Christian Nonresistance: Its Foundation and Its Outreach." In *Proceedings of the Fourth Mennonite World Conference,* pp. 244-52. Akron, Pa.: Mennonite Central Committee, 1950. Held at Goshen, Ind. and North Newton, Kan., Aug. 3-10, 1948.
b. "Christian Nonresistance: Its Foundation and Its Outreach." *MQR* 24 (1950): 156-62.
c. "Das Verhältnis zwischen dem materiellen und geistlichen Leben der amerikanischen Mennoniten." Typewritten. *Ca.* 1950. Goshen, Ind. AMC. Hist. Mss. 1-171 Box 12.
d. "Die Stellung der Mennoniten zur Politik." Typewritten. 1950. Goshen, Ind. AMC. Hist. Mss. 1-171 Box 11.
e. "The Disciple of Christ and the State." In *Report of the MCC Peace Section Study Conference,* pp. 53-58. Held at Winona Lake, Ind., Nov. 9-12, 1950.
f. "Men Wanted." *GH* 43 (1950): 1065.
g. "Report on My Term of Service for the Peace Section of the Mennonite Central Committee, June 10, 1949 to August 21, 1950." Mimeographed. Goshen, Ind. MHL.
h. "Types of Modern Pacifism." Paper read at Indiana Academy of the Social Sciences, 1950. Typewritten. Goshen, Ind. AMC. Hist. Mss. 1-171 Box 11.

1951

a. "Christian Nonresistance: Its Foundation and Its Outreach." *GH* 44 (1951): 1002.
b. *The Mennonite Church in the Second World War.* Scottdale, Pa.: Mennonite Publishing House, 1951.
c. "Mennnonite Life in the Swiss Jura of Today." *MComm* 5 (Mar. 1951): 17.
d. "Mennonite Principles: A Re-examination." *MComm* 5 (Dec. 1951): 17.
e. "Re-examining Mennonite Practices in the Application of Christian Principles to Everyday Living." In *Report of the Study Conference on Christian Community Relations,* pp. 18-25. Sponsored by Committee on Industrial Relations of Mennonite Church, Goshen, Ind. Held at Laurelville Mennonite Camp, July 24-27, 1951.

f. [Review.] Fretz, J. Winfield, *Christian Mutual Aid: A Handbook of Brotherhood Economics*, Akron, Pa.: Mennonite Central Committee, 1947. In *MQR* 25 (1951): 225-26.
g. [Review.] Hartzler, J. S. *Mennonites in the World War, or Nonresistance Under Test.* Scottdale, Pa.: Mennonite Publishing House, 1921. In *MQR* 25 (1951): 229-30.
h. "The Saving Remnant." Address first given Jan. 1951, Goshen College, Goshen, Ind. Typewritten. Goshen, Ind. AMC. Hist. Mss. 1-171 Box 11.

1952
a. "Church and State: The Mennonite View." Paper read at the annual meeting of the National Association of Evangelicals, Social Action section, 1952. Mimeographed. Goshen, Ind. MHL.
b. *Conscientious Objectors in Europe.* Washington, D.C.: National Service Board for Religious Objectors, 1952. Excerpt from "Report on My Term of Service for the Peace Section of the Mennonite Central Committee, June 10, 1949 to August 21, 1950."
c. "Islands of Sanity." *GH* 45 (1952): 293-94.
d. [Review.] Drake, Thomas E. *Quakers and Slavery in America.* New Haven: Yale University Press, 1950. In *MQR* 26 (1952): 92-94.

1953
a. "Das Evangelium und unsere heutigen sozialen Probleme." In *Die Gemeinde Christi und ihr Auftrag: Vorträge und Verhandlungen der Fünften Mennonitischen Weltkonferenz,* pp. 218-35. Karlsruhe, Germany: Heinrich Schneider, 1953. Held at St. Chrischona near Basel, Switzerland, Aug. 10-15, 1952.
b. [Review.] Fosdick, Raymond B. *Within Our Power: Perspective for a Time of Peril.* New York: Longmans, Green and Co., 1952. In *AAAPSS* 287 (1953): 217-18.
c. [Review.] Sibley, Mulford Q., and Jacob, Philip E. *Conscription and Conscience: The American State and the Conscientious Objector, 1940-1947.* Ithaca: Cornell University Press, 1952. In *MQR* 27 (1953): 351-55.

1954
a. "Relations with Labor Organizations." *CL* 1 (Dec. 1954): 36.

1955
a. "The Agricultural Community in the Service of Christ." *CL* 2 (June 1955): 26.
b. "Alert to the Question of Labor Union Relations." *CL* 2 (Jan. 1955): 26.
c. "Anabaptism and Brotherhood Economics." *CL* 2 (Aug. 1955): 26; (Sept. 1955): 26.
d. "Archbold." *ME* 1 (1955): 146.
e. "Christian Labor Relations." Mimeographed. 1955. Goshen, Ind. Goshen College Good Library.
f. "Committee on Economic and Social Relations." *ME* 1 (1955): 650-51.

g. "Conscientious Objector." *ME* 1 (1955): 692-99.
h. "Continued Study on Labor Union Relations." *CL* 2 (Feb. 1955): 26.
i. "Labor Union Relations: The Basis of Understanding." *CL* 2 (Mar. 1955): 26.
j. "Love and Justice in Economic Relations." *CL* 2 (Oct. 1955): 26.
k. "Rural Life in a Changing World." *CL* 2 (May 1955): 26.
l. "Social Science Textbooks in Mennonite Colleges." In *Proceedings of the Tenth Conference on Mennonite Educational and Cultural Problems,* pp. 9-22. Held at Mennonite Biblical Seminary, Chicago, Ill., June 16-17, 1955.
m. "When Capitalism Goes Astray." *CL* 2 (Nov. 1955): 26.

1956
a. "The Christian Attitude Toward Labor Unions." *CL* 3 (Aug. 1956): 26.
b. "The Christian's Accommodation to the Organized Industrial Order." *CL* 3 (Dec. 1956): 22.
c. "Fulton County." *ME* 2 (1956): 417-18.
d. "Henry Nunn Sets an Example." *CL* 3 (Nov. 1956): 23.
e. "Hershberger." *ME* 2 (1956): 714-15.
f. "Litigation in Mennonite History." In *Peace Problems Committee Papers Prepared and Discussion Summaries, Conference on Nonresistance and Political Responsibility,* pp. 32-34. Held at Laurelville Church Center, Sept. 21-22, 1956.
g. "The Modern Social Gospel and the Way of the Cross." *MQR* 30 (1956): 83-103.
h. "The Nonresistant Christian Betwixt Management and the Union." *CL* 3 (Sept. 1956): 26.
i. "Promoting Christian Employer-Employee Relations." *CL* 3 (Oct. 1956): 22.

1957
a. "The Disciple of Christ and the State." Paper read at Conference on Christian Responsibility and the State, Nov. 15-16, 1957, Chicago, Ill. Mimeographed.
b. "Introduction." *The Recovery of the Anabaptist Vision.* Edited by Guy F. Hershberger. Scottdale, Pa.: Herald Press, 1957.
c. "Labor Unions." *ME* 3 (1957): 266-67.
d. "Litigation." *ME* 3 (1957): 375-77.
e. "The Mennonite Community." *ME* 3 (1957): 619.
f. "Mennonite Community Association." *ME* 3 (1957): 619.
g. "Mennonite Mutual Aid Organizations." *CL* 4 (Apr. 1957): 22.
h. "Mennonite Relief and Service Committee." *ME* 3 (1957): 635-36.
i. "Mennonite Relief Commission for War Sufferers." *ME* 3 (1957): 636-37.
j. "Nonresistance." *ME* 3 (1957): 897-906.
k. "Nonviolence." *ME* 3 (1957): 908.
l. *The Recovery of the Anabaptist Vision; a Sixtieth Anniversary Tribute to Harold S. Bender.* Edited by Guy F. Hershberger. Scottdale, Pa.: Herald Press, 1957.
m. [Review.] Peterson, H. C., and Fite, Gilbert C. *Opponents of War, 1917-*

1918. Madison: University of Wisconsin Press, 1957. In *AAAPSS* 313 (1957): 154-55; also in *MQR* 31 (1957): 302-303.

n.[Review.] Williamson, Geoffrey. *Inside Buchmanism: An Independent Inquiry into the Oxford Group Movement and Moral Re-armament*. New York: Philosophical Library, 1954. In *AAAPSS* 313 (1957): 180-81.

1958

a. "The Christian Redemptive Approach to the World in the History of Christendom." Paper read at Theological Workshop, Aug. 1958, Goshen College, Goshen, Ind. Duplicated. Goshen, Ind. AMC. Hist. Mss. 1-171 Box 10.

b. [Review.] Davidson, Robert L. D. *War Comes to Quaker Pennsylvania, 1682-1756*. New York: Columbia University Press, Temple University Publications, 1957. In *Bulletin of Friends Historical Association* 47 (1958): 113-15; also in *William and Mary Quarterly* 15 (1958): 532-34.

c. [Review.] Reimer, Gustav E., and Gaeddert, G. R. *Exiled by the Czar: Cornelius Jansen and the Great Mennonite Migration, 1874*. Newton, Kan.: Mennonite Publication Office, 1956. In *MQR* 32 (1958): 163-65.

d. *The Way of the Cross in Human Relations*. Scottdale, Pa.: Herald Press, 1958. An expansion of the Conrad Grebel lectures delivered in 1954.

1959

a. "August 6: A Day of Intercession." *GH* 52 (1959): 663.

b. "The Cross in Personal Relations." *CL* 6 (July 1959): 27.

c. "A Newly Discovered Pennsylvania Mennonite Petition of 1755." *MQR* 33 (1959): 143-55.

d. "Pacifism." *ME* 4 (1959): 104-105.

e. "Race Relations." *ME* 4 (1959): 241.

f. "Relief Work." *ME* 4 (1959): 284-91.

g. "Social Behavior and a Clear Conscience." Address given *ca.*1959 at Goshen College, Goshen, Ind. Typewritten. Goshen, Ind. AMC. Hist. Mss. 1-171 Box 12.

h. "Usury." *ME* 4 (1959): 791-92. Coauthor, Melvin Gingerich.

1960

a. "Christian Ethics in the Rural Economy." *Town and Country Church* , no. 154 (Nov. 1960), pp. 7-12.

b. "The Christian Witness, Catholicism, and a Presidential Year." *GH* 53 (1960): 841 and 861.

c. "The Christian Witness to the State." *GH* 53 (1960): 647, 713, 826, 913, 1001. A series of five articles.

d. "Martin L. King: Professor's View." *The Elkhart Truth* 65 (Mar. 17, 1960): 15.

e. "Nonresistance, the Mennonite Church, and the Race Question," *GH* 53 (1960): 577. f. "Questions of Social Concern for Christians." *GH* 53 (1960): 252, 276, 292, 316, 340, 364, 396, 420, 444, 492, 508, 532, 556, 580, 600, 620, 660, 684. A series of eighteen articles.

f. "Questions of Social Concern for Christians." *GH* 53 (1960): 252, 276, 292,

316, 340, 364, 396, 420, 444, 492, 508, 532, 556, 580, 600, 620, 660, 684.
A series of eighteen articles.
g. "Why I Am an Anabaptist-Mennonite." *GH* 53 (1960): 949.

1961
a. "The Main Point: Doing What Is Right." *CL* 8 (Apr. 1961): 11.
b. "Mennonites and Government: A Historical Perspective." IN *Our National Government and the Christian Witness: Seminar Report, pp. 11-16.* Sponsored by Mennonite Central Committee Peace Section, Akron, Pa., Held at Washington, D.C., Apr. 27-29, 1961.
c. [Review.] Bainton, Roland H. *Christian Attitudes Toward War and Peace: A Historical Survey and Critical Re-evaluation.* Nashville: Abingdon Press, 1960. In *MQR* 35 (1961): 322-24.
d. "The Tragedy of the Empty House." *GH* 54 (1961): 733-35.

1962
a. "Civil Defense: Guest Editorial." *GH* 55 (1962): 995-96.
b. "A Mennonite Analysis of the Montgomery Bus Boycott." Intercollegiate Mennonite Peace Fellowship, 1962. Mimeographed. Goshen, Ind. MHL.
c. *Military Conscription and the Conscientious Objector: A World-Wide Survey.* Akron, Pa.: Mennonite Central Committee Peace Section, 1962.
d. "Military Conscription and the Conscientious Objector: A World-Wide Survey, with Special Reference to Mennonites." Paper presented at the Seventh Mennonite World Conference, Kitchener, Ont., Aug. 7, 1962. Mimeographed. Goshen, Ind. MHL.
e. [Review.] Ramsey, Paul. *War and the Christian Conscience: How Shall Modern War Be Conducted Justly?* Durham: Duke University Press, 1961. In *AAAPSS* 344 (1962): 144-45.
f. [Review.] Sappington, Roger E. *Brethren Social Policy, 1908-1958.* Elgin, Ill.: Brethren Press, 1961. In *MVHR* 49 (1962): 357.
g. [Review.] Schaff, Philip. *America: A Sketch of Its Political, Social, and Religious Character.* Edited by Perry Miller. Cambridge: Harvard University Press, Belknap Press, 1961. In *AAAPSS* 339 (1962): 196.
h. "World Wide Report on Military Draft and CO's." In *The Lordship of Christ: Proceedings of the Seventh Mennonite World Conference,* edited by C. J. Dyck, pp. 544-48. Scottdale, Pa.: Mennonite Publishing House, 1962. Held at Kitchener, Ont., Aug. 1-7, 1962.
This is the conclusion of a research paper, the body of which was published separately as a pamphlet, *Military Conscription and the Conscientious Objector: A World-Wide Survey, 1962.* The original unabridged paper, "Military Conscription and the Conscientious Objector: A World-Wide Survey, with Special Reference to Mennonites," is mimeographed, 1962.

1963
a. "The Christian Witness to the State: Guest Editorial." *GH* 56 (1963): 363.
b. "The Committee on Economic and Social Relations Is Important Too." *GH*

56 (1963): 384.

c. "The Contribution of J. E. Hartzler to Goshen College." Paper read to the Goshen College faculty, 1963. Typewritten.

d. *Das Täufertum, Erbe und Verpflichtung.* Edited by Guy F. Hershberger. Stuttgart: Evangelisches Verlagswerk, 1963. German translation of *The Recovery of the Anabaptist Vision.*

e. *"Einführung." Das Täufertum: Erbe und Verpflichtung.* Edited by Guy F. Hershberger. Stuttgart: Evangelisches Verlagswerk, 1963.

f. "How Important Is the Peace Problems Committee?" *GH* 56 (1963): 346-47.

g. "Mennonites and the Current Race Issue: Observations, Reflections, and Recommendations Following a Visitation to Southern Mennonite Churches, July-Aug. 1963, with a Review of Historical Background." Mimeographed. Goshen, Ind. MHL.

1964

a. "A Christian Witness on Race Relations Now." *GH* 57 (1964): 425.

b. "Concerning the Reliability of Statements of Carl McIntire." *GH* 57 (1964): 602.

c. "Definition and Scope of Christian Mutual Aid." In *Proceedings of All-Mennonite Conference on Christian Mutual Aid*, pp. C1-C14. Held at Smithville, Ohio, June 4-6, 1964.

d. "Harold S. Bender and His Time." *Harold S. Bender: Educator, Historian, Churchman.* Edited by Guy F. Hershberger. Scottdale, Pa.: Herald Press, 1964.

e. "Harold S. Bender and His Time." *MQR* 38 (1964): 83-112.

f. *Harold S. Bender, Educator, Historian, Churchman.* Edited by Guy F. Hershberger. Scottdale, Pa.: Herald Press, 1964.

g. "Lessons from Anabaptist History for the Church Today." *MCC News Service*, Apr. 7, 1964. Abridged edition of a paper presented at the Mennonite Conference on Race Relations, Atlanta, Ga., Feb. 24-25, 1964.

h. "Lessons from Anabaptist History for the Church Today." Paper presented at the Mennonite Conference on Race Relations, Atlanta, Ga., Feb. 24-25, 1964. Mimeographed. Goshen, Ind. MHL.

i. "Moral Issues in the Election of 1964." *GH* 57 (1964): 826.

j. [Review.] Ramsey, Paul. *War and the Christian Conscience: How Shall Modern War Be Conducted Justly?* Durham: Duke University Press, 1961. In *MQR* 38 (1964): 73-74.

k. "A Senator Speaks to the Churches." *GH* 57 (1964): 666.

l. "A Study of Church-State Relations." *GH* 57 (1964): 889-90.

1965

a. "Capital Punishment." *GH* 58 (1965): 339.

b. "From Words to Deeds in Race Relations." *GH* 58 (1965): 121.

c. "The Mennonite Peace Witness Beyond North America." *GH* 58 (1965): 427.

d. "Mennonites and the Negro Revolution." In *Proceedings of the Fifteenth Conference on Mennonite Educational and Cultural Problems*, pp. 112-22. North Newton, Kan.: The Mennonite Press. Held at Bluffton

College, Bluffton, Ohio, June 10-11, 1965.
e. "Proposed Statement on Capital Punishment." *GH* 58 (1965): 632-34.
f. "Washington Visitation on Vietnam." *GH* 58 (1965): 520.

1966

a. "The Committee on Peace and Social Concerns (of the Mennonite Church) and Its Predecessors." Mimeographed. 1966. Goshen, Ind. MHL. Summary review of the witness of the Mennonite Church, through the CPSC and its predecessors, to other Christians, to the state and to society, with respect to peace and the social implications of the Gospel, 1915-66.
b. "The Congregation and Its Need for a Diaconate in a Changing Era." Paper read at meeting of Mennonite Mutual Aid Association, Nov. 11, 1966, Chicago, Ill. Mimeographed. Goshen, Ind. AMC. Hist. Mss. 1-171 Box 10.
c. "Reflection on Capital Punishment Resolution." *GH* 59 (1966): 107-108.

1967

a. "Christian Attitudes Toward Nuclear Warfare." In *Program Guide,* edited by Arnold Roth, pp. 104-106. Scottdale, Pa.: Herald Press, 1967.
b. "Christians the Conscience of Society." *Goshen College Bulletin* 61 (Feb. 1967):3.
c. "Christians the Conscience of Society." *GH* 60 (1967): 934-36.
d. "A New King Who Did Not Know Joseph." Sermon delivered at College Mennonite Church, July 2, 1967, in Goshen, Ind. Duplicated. Goshen, Ind. AMC. Hist. Mss. 1-171 Box 14.
e. "Our Peace Witness in the Wake of May 18." *GH* 60 (1967): 803, 821, 847, 874, 889, 918, 944, 963, 983, 1018, 1039, 1063, 1090, 1114, 1134; 61 (1968): 7, 33. A series of seventeen articles.
f. "Questions Raised Concerning the Work of the Committee on Peace and Social Concerns (of the Mennonite Church) and Its Predecessors." Mimeographed. 1967. Goshen, Ind. MHL. Summary review of questions raised concerning the work of the CPSC and its predecessors, particularly concerning witness to other Christians, to the state, and to society, with respect to peace and the social implications of the Gospel, and concerning inter-Mennonite and inter-denominational cooperation in carrying on this work, 1925-66.
g. "What Color Is Christ?" In *Program Guide,* edited by Arnold Roth, p. 149. Scottdale, Pa.: Herald Press, 1967.

1968

a. "Conscience of Society." *GH* 61 (1968): 150-51.
b. "Current Antiwar Sentiment." *GH* 61 (1968): 86.
c. "The Current Upsurge of War Objection." *GH* 61 (1968): 57.
d. "How Protest." *GH* 61 (1968): 127.
e. "A Mennonite Office in Washington?" *GH* 61 (1968): 186.
f. "Pacifism." *Encyclopedia Americana* 21 (1968): 93-96.
g. "Protest Against Evil." *GH* 61 (1968): 104.

h. "War and the New Morality." *The Reformed Journal* 18 (Feb. 1968): 21-24.
i. "Will Conscription End?" *GH* 61 (1968): 203-204.
j. "You Are the Salt of the Earth." Sermon delivered at College Mennonite Church, Aug. 4, 1968, in Goshen, Ind. Duplicated. Goshen, Ind. AMC. Hist. Mss. 1-171 Box 14.

1969
a. "The Christian and the Draft." Address given at Campus Church, July 1969, at Goshen College, Goshen, Ind. Typewritten. Goshen, Ind. AMC. Hist. Mss. 1-171. Box 10.
b. [Review.] Durnbaugh, Donald F., ed. *The Brethren in Colonial Pennsylvania: A Source Book on the Transplantation and Development of the Church of the Brethren in the Eighteenth Century.* Elgin, Ill.: Brethren Press, 1967. In *CH* 38 (1969): 124-26.
c. [Review.] Toews, John B. *Lost Fatherland: The Story of the Mennonite Emigration from Soviet Russia, 1921-1927.* Scottdale, Pa.: Herald Press, 1967. In *CH* 38 (1969): 383.
d. "You Are the Salt of the Earth." *GH* 62 (1969): 6-9.

1970
a. "Historical Background to the Formation of the Mennonite Central Committee." *MQR* 44 (1970): 213-44.

1971
a. [Review.] Johnpoll, Bernard K. *Pacifist's Progress: Norman Thomas and the Decline of American Socialism.* Chicago: Quadrangle Books, 1970. In *AAAPSS* 397 (1971): 185-86.
b. [Review.] Libby, Frederick J. *To End War: The Story of the National Council for Prevention of War.* Nyack, N.Y.: Fellowship Publications, 1969. In *AAAPSS* 397 (1971): 184-85.
c. "Our Citizenship Is in Heaven." Sermon delivered at College Mennonite Church, July 18, 1971, in Goshen, Ind. Typewritten. Goshen, Ind. AMC. Hist. Mss. 1-171 Box 54.
d. [Review.] Pickvance, T. Joseph. *George Fox and the Purefeys: A Study of the Puritan Background in Fenny Drayton in the 16th and 17th Centuries.* London: Friends' Historical Society, 1970. In *MQR* 45 (1971): 389-90.

1972
a. [Review.] Chatfield, Charles. *For Peace and Justice: Pacifism in America, 1914-1941.* Knoxville: University of Tennessee Press, 1971. In *CH* 41 (1972): 418-19.

1973
a. "Conscientious Objector." *Encyclopaedia Britannica* 6 (1973): 366-68. Coauthor, John Moss.

1974
a. "The People of God, Then and Now," *GH* 67 (1974): 6-8.

b. [Review.] Yoder, John Howard. *The Politics of Jesus.* Grand Rapids: Wm. B. Eerdmans Publishing Co., 1972. In *MQR* 48 (1974): 534-37.
c. "The New Birth: A New Life, A New Social Order." Sermon delivered at Trinity Mennonite Church, June 2, 1974, in Glendale, Ariz. Typewritten. Goshen, Ind. AMC. Hist. Mss. 1-171 Box 54.
d. "Prophets, Priests, and Kings: Civil Religion, Then and Now." Sermon delivered at Trinity Mennonite Church, March 3, 1974, in Glendale, Ariz. Typewritten. Goshen, Ind. AMC. Hist. Mss. 1-171 Box 54.
e. "Robert Friedmann: In Remembrance." *MQR* (1974): 197-200.
f. "The Times of Sanford Calvin Yoder: The Mennonite Church and the First Fifty Years of Goshen College." In *An Evening to Honor Sanford Calvin Yoder,* pp. 7-40. Goshen, Ind.: Goshen College, 1974.

1975
a. "From 'God and His People' to 'God and Country.' " Typewritten. July 1975. Goshen, Ind. AMC. Hist. Mss. 1-171 Box 54.
b. "In Tribute to Melvin Gingerich." *Mennonite Historical Bulletin* (Oct. 1975): 2-4.
c. [Review.] Wellenreuther, Hermann. *Glaube und Politik in Pennsylvania 1681-1776: Die Wandlungen der Obrigkeitsdoktrin und des "Peace Testimony" der Quäker.* Köln und Wien: Böhlau Verlag, 1972. In *The American Historical Review* 80 (1975): 1380-81.

1976
a. [Review.] Estep, William R. *The Anabaptist Story.* Revised edition. Grand Rapids, Mich.: Wm. B. Eerdmans Publishing Company, 1975. In *The American Historical Review,* in press.
b. [Review.] Kauffman, J. Howard, and Harder, Leland. *Anabaptists Four Centuries Later: A Profile of Five Mennonite and Brethren in Christ Denominations.* Scottdale, Pa., and Kitchener, Ont.: Herald Press, 1975. In *The American Historical Review,* in press.
c. [Review.] Roberts, Arthur O. *The Association of Evangelical Friends: A story of Quaker renewal in the twentieth century.* Newberg, Ore.: The Barclay Press, 1975. In *CH,* in press.

NOTES

Chapter 1: Theron Schlabach, "A Mennonite Vision"

1. This essay rests on extensive research in Guy Hershberger's writings (see the Bibliography in this volume) and related documents and archival material, and on some interviews with key figures in the story. In order to avoid cumbersome apparatus, the text published here documents only direct quotations and some other major items. A mimeographed list of all sources consulted, keyed to the published essay, is available from the publisher.

2. How to label accurately the various Mennonite branches, and yet maintain smooth prose, is always troublesome for historians of Mennonitism. In this chapter the term "Mennonite Church" (capitalized) refers to that branch of Mennonites that has its press at Scottdale, Pennsylvania, and its major board offices at Elkhart, Indiana, that is, the branch sometimes labeled with the prefix "Old" or the parenthesis (MC). References to the general conference of that branch will use lower case letters, to distinguish from the General Conference Mennonite branch.

3. For further interpretation of the "Great Awakening" or "quickening" period, see *A New Rhythm for Mennonites* (Schlabach, 1975), a booklet which is actually the projected first chapter of my forthcoming book on the mission movement of the Mennonite Church.

4. These quotations are from Byers and Hartzler letters to Menno S. Steiner, found in the Steiner papers, Mennonite Church Archives (Goshen, Indiana).

5. For a succinct and direct dispensationalist reply to Hershberger's interpretation of the Old Testament, see J. Irvin Lehman, "A Criticism of the Article 'Peace and War in the Old Testament,' " *The Sword and Trumpet* 11 (July 1943), 28-31.

6. From the report of the Committee on Industrial Problems, published under the title "Mennonites and Industrial Organizations," *Gospel Herald* 30 (Feb. 10, 1938), 989-990.

Chapter 2: Leonard Gross, "History and Community"

1. For Hershberger's interpretation of this whole era, see his "The Times of Sanford Calvin Yoder: The Mennonite Church and the First Fifty Years of Goshen College" (1974d).

2. See Blanke (1961), Wenger (1970), and Yoder (1973), especially chapter two.

3. Hershberger's unpublished Master's thesis is entitled "An Inquiry into the Origins of the Anabaptist Movement" (1925b).

4. See also Hershberger's article "Is Modern Religious Liberalism a Force for Peace?" (1936c).

5. See 1958d, 127-151, for Hershberger's comprehensive treatment of this theme.

6. See Footnote 2.

7. Arnold Toynbee, whose mind-set and views to be sure reflect something of nineteenth-century liberalism, has an insightful word for the contribution of the brotherhood approach in his lifelong interest in helping to lift all of current civilization beyond a world of war and conflict: "Human history presents some striking illustrations of the eventual triumph, contrary to all apparent likelihood, of principles held by tiny minorities who have stood for these principles wholeheartedly and who have therefore been prepared to suffer for their principles to any extent. Time and again, martyrdom has proved more potent than the physical force that is wielded by governments." (1969: 210-211.)

Chapter 3: Robert S. Kreider, "Discerning the Times"

1. The preparation of this essay is based on wide reading in the writings of Guy

Hershberger. For this the bibliography in this volume may be consulted. In addition to the works cited, the files of the following periodicals were particularly helpful: *Christian Exponent, Gospel Herald, Goshen College Record,* and *Hesston College Journal.* The writings of Melvin Gingerich, Rodney J. Sawatsky ("The Influence of Fundamentalism on Mennonite Nonresistance, 1908-1944," msc, 1973, Goshen College Historical Library), and Sanford yoder yielded much information and many insights. In an effort to understand the themes and critical issues during the past eighty years the author was aided by interviews with a number of persons who have known this period of Mennonite history.

Chapter 4: Millard C. Lind, "Biblical Hermeneutics"

1. *War, Peace, and Nonresistance* included chapters on both Old and New Testaments. Another chapter distinguished between biblical nonresistance and other types of pacifism. *The Way of the Cross in Human Relations* begins with two chapters on biblical foundations, and utilizes Scripture references throughout.

2. In some respects a case can be made that the synagogue has been closer to the teaching of Jesus than has the mainline church. *The Anchor Bible* commentary series, edited by W. F. Albright and D. N. Freedman, is an example of the ecumenical character of contemporary biblical studies.

3. For discussion of Anabaptist hermeneutics, see Bender (1938), Kaufman (1951), Wenger (1938), Klassen (1966a and 1966b), and Yoder (1966).

4. See Riedemann (1970) for an example of the Anabaptist attitude toward government. Two of my former students, David Mann and Frederic A. Miller, have written papers on this subject.

5. See Zimmerli (1965); I have written a response to this book (Lind, 1966).

6. Quoted by Albrektson (1967). Albrektson's book is a criticism of this concept among Old Testament specialists. In my opinion his work does not demolish the point, but qualifies it.

7. I quote McKane at some length because he is not a pacifist nor an Anabaptist, and thus should not be suspect because of his presuppositions. McKane himself rejects the prophetic ethic in favor of the ethic of "responsibility" of ancient Near Eastern wisdom (pp. 129f.). But if McKane is correct in his contrast of these two ethics, it is then evident on which side this puts the ethics of Reinhold Niebuhr, e.g., *Moral Man and Immoral Society.* His ethic is contrary to that of the prophets and Jesus and is more in line with NE statecraft. This is the fundamental issue between the Bible and its environment; this is what Genesis 3 is about. See my unpublished paper, "The Anomaly of the Prophet."

8. For the importance of Isaiah 53 to the New Testament interpretation of Jesus, see Dodd (1965). Hooker (1959) may be successful in qualifying Dodd's thesis, but in my judgment does not demolish his argument.

9. For a statement of the differences between Bright and Noth, see Bright (1956).

10. Von Rad makes a sharp distinction between the confessional character of biblical faith and the way the events "really happened." "These two pictures of Israel's history lie before us—that of modern critical scholarship and that which the faith of Israel constructed—and for the present, we must reconcile ourself to both of them." He holds that modern critical scholarship is "rational and 'objective'; that is, with the aid of historical method and presupposing *the similarity of all historical occurrence,* it constructs a critical picture of the history as it really was in Israel" (italics mine). In a footnote he sympathetically quotes E. Troeltsch: "The means by which criticism is at all possible is the application of analogy. . . . But the omnicompetence of analogy implies that all historical events are identical in principle" (1962:107).

Chapter 5: C. Norman Kraus, "The Disciple Community"

1. See, for example, J. I. Lehman, *God and War* (1942), which argues against Hershberger.

2. Donald Dayton suggests that the Holiness churches were caught in somewhat the

same relation to Fundamentalism, and are now reassessing. See "The Holiness Churches: A Significant Ethical Tradition" in *The Christian Century,* XCII (1975), 192-201.

3. John Howard Yoder has argued that the normative Mennonitism of this period was modeled after the Reformed tradition (Yoder, 1970).

4. For a study of the concept of salvation suggested here, see chapter 4, "The Saving Community" in my book (Kraus, 1974).

5. At least three attempts have been made to enter the dialogue with a contribution of systematic nature: J. C. Wenger, *Introduction to Theology* (1954), Gordon Kaufman, *Systematic Theology* (1969), and Ed. G. Kaufman, *Basic Christian Convictions* (1972). Each of these has addressed a different audience, and had a different purpose in mind.

6. See Ephesians 2:14 ff. This is only one of the many ways in which Scripture speaks about salvation.

Chapter 8: Calvin Redekop, "Institutions and Gospel"
1. The first part of this paper relies heavily on materials discussed in *Institutionalism and Church Unity,* edited by Nils Ehrenstrom and Walter Muelder (1963). Another significant book is James Gustafson's *Treasure in Earthen Vessels* (1961).

2. In our analysis the relationships of institutions and power in the Christian movement will be treated in itself, but we cannot ignore the fact that the Christian tradition developed out of a Jewish tradition that conveyed to the Christian tradition a vast and powerful social institutional system. (See R .P. C. Hanson, "Institutions in the Early Church," in Ehrenstrom and Muelder, 1963.) In this essay, we refer to the Christian tradition or Christian church as the Christian movement, to emphasize the response of persons to a call, and to downplay the structural/institutional aspects, which receive special emphasis in the argument itself.

3. The emphases introduced here under "being" and "doing" are of course gross oversimplifications of a complex philosophical tradition. The concepts of ontology and teleology are only several that are related to the topic. But it is possible to speak of orientations in philosophical thinking which have emphasized the primacy of existence (existentialism) as over against goal-oriented action (process philosophy).

4. Max Weber defined power as "the probability that one actor within a social relationship will be in a position to carry out his will despite resistance, regardless of the basis on which this probability rests" (1947:152). Institutions have been generally defined in the text. But there are other dimensions that need delineation. "Institution" is normally defined as involving a value system, a set of norms which determine how the values are to be achieved, a set of symbols that express the values and norms, and facilities which provide the materials for goal achievement. "Organization" is a term used in conjunction with institutions, and refers to the specific structure, and the persons involved. Thus the Sunday school is an institutional complex, and the specific incarnation such as the First Baptist Church Sunday school is an example of an organization.

5. This statement reveals the paradoxical nature of the relationship between being and doing. The New Testament abounds with references to the new status which is achieved without any effort, yet constantly reiterates the need for Christians to strive for and achieve the new being. In theological language, it is the faith/works dilemma, and it would be fruitless to comment on this dilemma any further, more than to call attention to the centrality of this problem for the Christian movement.

6. This review of Parsons' work is necessarily oversimplified (if indeed it can be simplified or understood at all). I have combined his first and second dimension because they refer to the same dynamic from two different perspectives.

7. Another significant corollary which cannot be expanded here is the way institutional power begets more power—the power of position can often be used to arrogate more power. Thus for example an editor of a church paper not only exercises the power of publication of ideas, but of information, influence, and the like.

8. The Free Church revolt has been characterized in many ways, but its central dynamic seems to have been the rejection of the use of power in achieving the Christian gospel's objectives. Thus the terms "magisterial reformation" and Free Church have been used to distinguish the differences (see the essays by Bender, Littell, and Yoder in Hershberger, 1957l).

9. Treatment of the concepts of institutions and power is remarkably absent in the writing of modern Anabaptist/Mennonite scholars. *The Mennonite Encyclopedia* contains no reference to power or institutions. The *Mennonite Quarterly Review* in its indexes has no reference to power and has one reference to institutions which states: "Institutions, Charitable and philanthrop: See hospitals" (p. 17). Power, when it is discussed, is almost always found in the discussion of the relation of the church and state, and of course power in that context is eschewed. In one reference to power (1944c:49) Guy Hershberger states: "The Jews for the most part had a wrong idea of what the Messiah and his kingdom would be like. They were looking for a military leader who would overthrow the Roman conqueror and establish a political state of prestige and power. It seems that in His great temptation Jesus was actually tempted to follow this course. . . . But Jesus rejected the temptation and followed the way of love and suffering, for which purpose He had come into the world." In this context, the analysis of institutions and force forms the foundation for the relationship of the Christian community and the world. But one cannot conclude from this, as has normally been done, that therefore the Free Church has nothing to do with power and institutions. The "Reiseprediger" in the Mennonite church in Russia, the bishop in the Franconia conference, to list only a few instances, exercised a lot of power, usually in a salutary sense and for the empowerment of the laity, but nevertheless, they had and used power. It is interesting that everyone knew the leaders had power, but rarely was it ever discussed in open or scholarly ways.

Chapter 9: J. R. Burkholder, "Mennonite Ethics."

1. J. Lawrence Burkholder, in his instructive *Mennonite Encyclopedia* essay on ethics (1959:1079-1083), notes that no American Mennonite has written a book on ethics as a theological discipline, although the writings of Guy F. Hershberger in effect serve this function for the brotherhood. Since 1959, several works have appeared that qualify this statement. Gordon Kaufman's *The Context of Decision* (1961), although not developed explicitly from Anabaptist-Mennonite presuppositions, does represent a self-consciously Mennonite voice. John Howard Yoder, in a series of books (1964; 1971; 1972a; 1972b), deals with both the theological-biblical foundations and the socio-political implications of Christian nonresistance, even though none of these writings could properly be called a treatise on ethics.

Clarence Bauman's doctoral dissertation on *Gewaltlosigkeit* (1968) is a highly important study of the 16th-century formation of the nonresistant ethic. Walter Klaassen's review (1969:333) calls attention to Bauman's demonstration that nonviolence is central and integral to basic Christian affirmations concerning the cross, the resurrection, and the nature of the church.

The only book that, by its title, appears to speak to our theme, is a disappointment. Although Abraham P. Toews in *The Problem of Mennonite Ethics* claims to fill a gap in the literature by setting forth "in simple fashion the biblicistic belief of the Mennonites and their uncompromising nonconformity" (1963:x), the work falls far short of the goal. The range of the literature surveyed is impressive, but it has not been digested or systematized. The book is burdened with an indiscriminate mix of quotations (often incorrectly cited) scattered across centuries and lacking focus and organization.

2. Paul Peachey in a 1956 essay entitled "The Mennonite Ethical Dilemma" called attention to the "deep gulf" between the official ethic of the denomination and the compromises occasioned by participation in the economic ethos of the world. "The time has

come when we shall have to admit officially what some of us have concluded—that awful fact, *the necessity of compromise.* Or we shall have to accept a thoroughgoing restitution, which may cost us much of our wealth and even our church institutions." (Peachey, 1956b:1074.)

In precise terms, Peachey's dilemma is not well phrased, for it tends to confuse the theoretical and the practical questions in ethics. If a "thoroughgoing restitution" is possible, then the problem is a practical one of obedient response. But if compromise is indeed necessary, then the ethic itself is inadequate. For an ethic that in its basic formulation rejects compromise, but cannot be practiced in the real world without compromise, must be judged irrelevant. It may serve as a reminder of the inevitability of sin, as a Lutheran-Niebuhrian emphasis, but it is not very useful as a guide to Christian behavior.

3. This statement is quoted from a paper "The Role of the Mennonite Church in Civil Rights Concerns," presented by Hershberger at a conference on urban-racial concerns as reported in *Gospel Herald* 58 (Mar. 30, 1965), p. 279. Further study of Hershberger's response to the civil rights movement would demonstrate his recognition that Martin Luther King, Jr.'s philosophy represented a new approach to conflict situations that had not been anticipated in Hershberger's earlier critique of Gandhian nonviolence. Compare the viewpoint in *War, Peace, and Nonresistance* (1944c:219-229) with his encyclopedia essay on "Nonviolence" (1957k) and his analysis of the Montgomery bus boycott (1962b).

Chapter 12: John A. Lapp, "Civil Religion"

1. The article "Civil Religion in America" appeared originally in the Winter 1967 issue of *Daedalus* entitled "Religion in America." The Bellah article has been reprinted in the excellent compilation by Russell Richey and Donald G. Jones: *American Civil Religion* (1974). Bellah has further developed his thinking in *The Broken Covenant: American Civil Religion in Time of Trial* (1975).

2. For the Hebrew struggle with civil religion, see Mendenhall (1973).

Chapter 13: Emma LaRocque, "The Ethnic Church"

1. See "Forum" in *Festival Quarterly* 2 (No. 3, August-October, 1975), 10-11. Readers may also be interested in my brief essay, "The Cross-Cultural Youth Convention" in *Gospel Herald* 68: 561.

Chapter 15: Paul Peachey, "Ecumenical Witness"

1. This statement was eventually published, together with the reply on behalf of the WCC by Reinhold Niebuhr and Angus Dun and a further peace church statement (Zigler, 1958).

2. Speaking at a similar conference more than 25 years later, Kenneth Boulding, the noted Quaker economist, observed that the past five centuries had each produced a peace church. To the Mennonites (16th century), the Friends (17th), the Brethren (18th), he added the Seventh-Day Adventists (19th), and Jehovah's Witnesses (20th). The two last groups, however, were sufficiently different in origin and rationale to remain outside the Historic Peace Church fraternity. Boulding wished to dramatize the default of the "great churches" and in that sense his point is well taken.

3. The term refers to instances where a religious movement seeks adherents among members of other religious groups.

4. This writer, on an assignment in Japan under the Peace Section of the Mennonite Central Committee at the time of the above incident, experienced the same difficulty in slightly different form. That assignment was itself a product of the wider peace church ferment which is the subject of the present sketch. For most of the Japanese, however, the debates between Anabaptists and the "great churches" were remote and incomprehensible. But the Mennonite "peace worker," outside the Christendom context, found he had

only a few tools in his chest. It was easier, though not necessarily more effective, to argue church and state questions with Lutherans than to answer questions real to the Japanese!

5. Thomas Heath, formerly of the Dominican House of Studies in Washington D.C., currently director of the novitiate in St. Stephen's Priory, Dover, Mass., is preparing for publication a translated anthology of Stratmann's writings.

6. Marxist Radical Reformation historians believe that the greater tolerance which the "great churches" show toward the "sects" is the result of the defensive position into which they have been placed by modern secular forces (Zschäbitz, 1958).

7. This clearly appears to be the logic of Yoder's conclusion (Yoder, 1962).

8. Some scholars use the term *reification* (related to the word "real") to characterize the process whereby an idea or concept comes to be treated as an object or as concrete reality. A network of human interactions thus may be treated as though it possessed real being, as a spiritual or "metaphysical" entity. In the present instance the error is compounded by the fact that "church" (as in "Church of England" or "Mennonite Church") is not only reified, but is associated with the sacred or transcendental qualities thought to inhere in "church" viewed as the body of Christ.

Chapter 17: Guy F. Hershberger, "Our Citizenship"

1. John H. Yoder, in *The Politics of Jesus* (1972), chapter 11, building on the work of Krister Stendahl and Markus Barth, spells out in an impressive manner the social and ethical dimension of justification by grace through faith, a dimension long obscured by the distorted classical Protestant interpretation of the Pauline doctrine. Far from being seen as a mere forensic imputation of righteousness, justification is rather a new creation enabling men and women in Christ to see their fellow human beings as Christ sees them, thus breaking down the wall of separation between Jews and Gentiles and all other social barriers which are the source of untold unethical practices and injustices. "When anyone is united to Christ, there is a new world, the old order has gone, and a new order has already begun" (2 Cor. 5:17, NEB).

2. See the preface to the *Frame of Government for Pennsylvania,* in *Pennsylvania Colonial Records,* 1:29, and Historical Society of Pennsylvania, Dreer Collection, *Letters and Papers of William Penn,* 38.

3. Numerous accounts of this political struggle have been published. For example, Hershberger (1936h:1939e); E. B. Bronner, *William Penn's "Holy Experiment"* (Temple University Publications, 1962). The most recent significant analysis is Hermann Wellenreuther, *Glaube und Politik in Pennsylvania 1681-1776* (Böhlan Verlag, Cologne and Vienna, 1972).

4. Congressman William G. Bray of the sixth Indiana district, a Quaker, a member of the House Armed Services Committee, in 1967 inserted in the original House Bill for the extension of the draft (the current law would have expired on July 1, 1967) a provision that conscientious objectors should be inducted into the armed forces, with the possibility of their being furloughed for civilian service while remaining under military authority. E. Raymond Wilson of the Friends Committee for National Legislation with the help of other Friends, Mennonites, and others, led the protest against this proposal which resulted in the deletion of the Bray provision before the bill came to the floor of the House in May 1967.

5. From the apology "Contra Celsus," quoted in Roberts and Donaldson (1925: vol. 4,666)

GENERAL BIBLIOGRAPHY

All references to published materials are indicated by a parenthesis at an appropriate point in the text. The information in the parenthesis enables location of the source by author and date. The abbreviations used in this bibliography are *ME*, for *The Mennonite Encyclopedia* (Harold S. Bender and C. Henry Smith, eds.; Scottdale: Mennonite Publishing House, 1955-1959) and *MQR*, for *The Mennonite Quarterly Review*. References to Guy Hershberger's writings may be located in the preceding specialized bibliography.

Albrektson, Bertil. 1967. *History and the Gods.* Sweden: C.W.K. Gleerup.

Algermissen, Konrad, 1957. *Konfessionskunde.* Celle: Buchhandlung Josef Giesel (seventh edition).

Angus, Samuel. 1925. *The Mystery-Religions and Christianity.* London: J. Murray.

Auerbach, Erich. 1957. *Mimesis: The Representation of Reality in Western Literature.* New York: Doubleday Anchor.

Bainton, Roland. 1941. "The Left Wing of the Reformation." *Journal of Religion* 21:124-134.

Barclay, Harold. 1969. "The Protestant Ethic versus the Spirit of Capitalism?" *Review of Religious Research* 10:151-158.

Bauman, Clarence. 1968. *Gewaltlosigkeit im Täufertum: Eine Untersuchung zur theologischen Ethik des oberdeutschen Täufertums der Reformationszeit.* Leiden: E. J. Brill.

Bellah, Robert N. 1974. "Civil Religion in America." In *American Civil Religion.* Russell E. Richey and Donald G. Jones, eds. New York: Harper & Row.

_____. 1975. *The Broken Covenant: American Civil Religion in Time of Trial.* New York: Seabury.

Bender, H. S. 1927. "To the Youth of the Mennonite Church." *MQR* 1:ii.

_____. 1938. "The Theology of Conrad Grebel." *MQR* 12:27-54.

_____. 1944. "The Anabaptist Vision." Reprinted in *The Recovery of the Anabaptist Vision.* Guy F. Hershberger, ed. Scottdale: Herald Press, 1957.

_____. 1953. "Outside Influences on Mennonite Thought." *Mennonite Educational and Cultural Problems Proceedings, 1953.*

_____. 1955. "The Anabaptists and Religious Liberty in the Sixteenth Century." *MQR* 29:83-100.

_____. 1956. "The Pacifism of the Sixteenth Century Anabaptists." *MQR* 30:5-18.

_____. 1959. "Society of Friends." *ME* 4:561-565.

Bender, Ross T. 1971. *The People of God.* Scottdale: Herald Press.

Berger, Peter L. 1969. *The Sacred Canopy: Elements of a Sociological Theory of Religion.* New York: Doubleday.

Blanke, Fritz. 1955. *Kirche und Sekten.* Zürich: Zwingli-Verlag.

————. 1961. *Brothers in Christ.* Scottdale: Herald Press.

Bright, John, 1956. *Early Israel in Recent History Writing.* Chicago: A. R. Allenson.

Brunner, Emil. 1953. *The Misunderstanding of the Church.* Philadelphia: Westminster.

————. 1962. *The Christian Doctrine of the Church, Faith, and the Consummation: Dogmatics, Volume III.* Philadelphia: Westminster.

————. 1963. "The Significance of the Old Testament for Our Faith." In *The Old Testament And Christian Faith.* Bernhard Anderson, ed. New York: Harper & Row.

Burkhard, Samuel. 1918. Letter to J. F. Balzer. In J. F. Balzer Collection, Mennonite Library and Archives, Bethel College, North Newton, Kansas.

Burkholder, J. Lawrence. 1958. "The Problem of Social Responsibility from the Perspective of the Mennonite Church." Unpublished ThD dissertation. Princeton Theological Seminary.

————. 1959. "Ethics." *ME* 4: 1079-1083.

————. 1963. "The Peace Churches as Communities of Discernment." *Christian Century* 80:1072-1075.

————. 1965. "The Church a Discerning Community." *Gospel Herald* 58: 113, 116, 131-132.

Campbell, Will D. and Holloway, James Y. 1970. *Up to Our Steeples in Politics.* New York: Paulist Press.

Clark, Stephen B. 1972. *Building Christian Communities.* Notre Dame, Indiana: Ave Maria Press.

Clasen, Claus-Peter. 1972. *Anabaptism: A Social History, 1525-1618.* Ithaca: Cornell University Press.

Coffman, John S. 1924. "The Spirit of Progress." *Christian Exponent* 1:6-7, 24.

Congar, Y.M.J. 1962. "Oekumenische Bewegung." *Lexikon Für Theologie und Kirche,* Vol. VII. Freiburg: Herder Verlag.

Cullmann, Oscar. 1950. *Christ and Time.* Philadelphia: Westminster.

DeKoster, Lester. 1975. "Anabaptism at 450: A Challenge, A Warning." *Christianity Today* 20:11-16.

Dodd, C. H. 1965. *The Old Testament in the New.* Philadelphia: Fortress.

Dombois, Hans, 1963. "The Church as *Koinonia* and Institution." In *Institutionalism and Church Unity.* Nils Ehrenstrom and Walter Muelder, eds. New York: Association Press.

Driedger, Leo. 1975. "Canadian Mennonite Urbanism: Ethnic Villagers or Metropolitan Remnant?" *MQR* 49:226-241.

Dyck, Cornelius J. 1967. *An Introduction to Mennonite History.* Scottdale: Herald Press.

Ehrenstrom, Nils and Walter Muelder, eds. 1963. *Institutionalism and Church Unity.* New York: Association Press.

Ellul, Jacques. 1967. *The Political Illusion.* New York: Random House.

————. 1975. *The New Demons.* New York: Seabury.

Epp, Frank, 1974. *Mennonites in Canada.* Toronto: Macmillan of Canada.

Fox, George, 1952. *The Journal of George Fox* (John L. Nickalls Edition). Cambridge, England: Cambridge University Press.

Francis, E. K. 1955. *In Search of Utopia.* Glencoe, Illinois: Free Press.

Fretz, J. Winfield. 1939. "Mutual Aid Among Mennonites." *MQR* 13: 28-58, 187-209.

Friedmann, Robert. 1956. "Gelassenheit." *ME* 2:448-449.

———. 1967. "The Essence of the Anabaptist Faith: An Essay in Interpretation." *MQR* 41:5-24.

———. 1973. *The Theology of Anabaptism.* Scottdale: Herald Press.

Gingerich, Melvin. 1975. Interviews with Guy F. Hershberger, March 27 and April 3, 1975 at Glendale, Arizona. Transcript in Archives of the Mennonite Church, Goshen, Indiana.

Gish, Arthur G. 1970. *The New Life and Christian Radicalism.* Grand Rapids: Eerdmans.

———. 1973. *Beyond the Rat Race.* Scottdale: Herald Press.

Groff, Warren F. 1969. "A Believing People: Theological Interpretation." In *The Concept of the Believers' Church.* James Leo Garrett, Jr., ed. Scottdale: Herald Press.

Gustafson, James. 1961. *Treasure in Earthen Vessels.* New York: Harper.

Habegger, David. 1959. " 'Nonresistance and Responsibility'—A Critical Analysis." *Concern,* No. 7 33-40.

Hammond, Phillip E., and Benton Johnson. 1970. *American Mosaic: Social Patterns of Religion in the United States.* New York: Random House.

Handy, Robert T. 1971. *A Christian America: Protestant Hopes and Historical Realities.* New York: Oxford University Press.

Hanson, R. P. C. 1963. "Institutions in the Early Church." In *Institutionalism and Church Unity.* Nils Ehrenstrom and Walter G. Muelder, eds. New York: Association Press.

Harper, Michael. 1973. *A New Way of Living.* Plainfield, N.J.: Logos International.

Harrison, Paul M. 1959. *Authority and Power in the Free Church Tradition.* Princeton: Princeton University Press.

Hatch, Nathan O. 1974. "The Origins of Civil Millennialism in America: New England Clergymen, War with France and the Revolution." *William and Mary Quarterly* (Third Series) 31: 407-430.

Hatfield, Mark. 1976. *Between the Rock and a Hard Place.* Waco, Texas; Word.

Hauerwas, Stanley. 1974. *Vision and Virtue: Essays in Christian Ethical Reflection.* Notre Dame, Indiana: Fides Publishers.

Herberg, Will. 1974. "America's Civil Religion: What It Is and Whence It Comes." In *American Civil Religion.* Russell E. Richey and Donald G. Jones, eds. New York: Harper & Row.

Hess, J. Daniel. 1966. "Guy F. Hershberger: Tiller of Ideas." *Christian Living* 13:21-23, 37.

Hillerbrand, Hans J. 1958. "The Anabaptist View of the State." *MQR* 32:83-110.

Hooke, S. H. 1958. *Myth, Ritual and Kingship.* Oxford: Clarendon Press.

Hooker, Morna D. 1959. *Jesus and the Servant.* London: S.P.C.K.

Horney, Karen. 1937. *The Neurotic Personality of Our Time.* New York: W. W. Norton.

Hostetler, John A. 1974. *Hutterite Society.* Baltimore: Johns Hopkins University Press.

Howe, Mark DeWolfe. 1965. *The Garden and the Wilderness: Religion and Government in American Constitutional History.* Chicago: University of Chicago Press.

Hudson, Winthrop S. 1953. *The Great Tradition of the American Churches.* New York: Harper & Row.

———, ed. 1970. *Nationalism and Religion in America: Concepts of American Identity and Mission.* New York: Harper & Row.

Hutchinson, John A. and McDonald, Lee C. 1965. *Myth, Religion and Politics.* Nashville: Division of Higher Education of the Methodist Church.

Jackson, Dave and Neta. 1974. *Living Together in a World Falling Apart.* Carol Stream, Illinois: Creation House.

Jones, Ilion T. 1954. *A Historical Approach to Evangelical Worship.* New York: Abingdon Press.

Jones, T. Canby. 1972. *George Fox's Attitude Toward War.* Annapolis, Maryland: Academic Fellowship.

Juhnke, James C. 1970. "Mennonite Benevolence and Civic Identity: The Postwar Compromise." *Mennonite Life* 25:34-37.

———.1975. *A People of Two Kingdoms: The Political Acculturation of the Kansas Mennonites.* Newton, Kansas: Faith and Life Press.

Kauffman, Daniel. 1898. *Manual of Bible Doctrine.* Elkhart, Indiana: Mennonite Publishing Co.

——— . 1914. *Bible Doctrine.* Scottdale: Mennonite Publishing House.

——— . 1919. "Christianity's Greatest Foe." *Gospel Herald* 11:921.

——— . 1928. *Doctrines of the Bible.* Scottdale: Mennonite Publishing House.

Kauffman, J. Howard, and Leland Harder. 1975. *Anabaptists Four Centuries Later: A Profile of Five Mennonite and Brethren in Christ Denominations.* Scottdale: Herald Press.

Kaufman, Edmund G. 1931. *The Development of the Missionary and Philanthropic Interest Among the Mennonites of North America.* Berne, Indiana: Mennonite Book Concern.

———.1972. *Basic Christian Convictions.* N. Newton, Kansas: Bethel College.

Kaufman, Gordon D. 1951. "Some Theological Emphases of the Early Swiss Anabaptists." *MQR* 25:75-99.

——— . 1958. "Nonresistance and Responsibility." *Concern,* No. 6:5-29.

——— . 1961. *The Context of Decision: A Theological Analysis.* New York: Abingdon.

——— . 1969. *Systematic Theology: A Historicist Perspective.* New York: Scribner's.

Keniston, Kenneth. 1971. "Agony Stalks the Campus; the Lost Ecstasy of Youth." *Chicago Sunday Sun-Times,* June 27, Section 2, pp:1-3.

Klaassen, Walter. 1969. Review of *Gewaltlosigkeit im Täufertum* by Clarence Bauman. *MQR* 53:333-336.

——— . 1971. "The Nature of the Anabaptist Protest." *MQR* 45: 291-311.

——— . 1973. *Anabaptism: Neither Catholic nor Protestant.* Waterloo, Ontario: Conrad Press.

Klassen, Peter James. 1964. *The Economics of Anabaptism 1525-1560.* The Hague: Mouton and Co.

Klassen, William. 1966a. "Anabaptist Hermeneutics: The Letter and the

Spirit." *MQR* 40:83-96.

_____ . 1966b. "The Relation of the Old and the New Covenants in Pilgrim Marpeck's Theology." *MQR* 40:97-111.

Krahn, Cornelius. 1959. "Russia." *ME* 4:381-392.

Kraus, C. Norman. 1974. *The Community of the Spirit.* Grand Rapids:Eerdmans.

Leeming, B. 1967. "Ecumenical Movement." *New Catholic Encyclopedia.* Vol. V: 96-100. New York: McGraw-Hill.

Lehman, J. Irvin. 1942. *God and War.* Scottdale: Mennonite Publishing House.

Light, Donald and Suzanne Keller. 1975. *Sociology.* New York: Alfred Knopf.

Lind, Millard. 1966. "The Hermeneutics of the Old Testament." *MQR* 40:227-237.

Littell, Franklin H. 1957. *The Free Church.* Boston: Starr King Press.

_____ . 1958. *The Anabaptist View of the Church.* Boston: Starr King Press.

_____ . 1960. "The Work of the Holy Spirit in Group Decisions." *MQR* 34:75-96

_____ . 1961. *A Tribute to Menno Simons.* Scottdale: Herald Press.

_____ . 1964. *The Origins of Sectarian Protestantism.* New York: Macmillan Company.

Long, Edward LeRoy, Jr. 1967. *A Survey of Christian Ethics.* New York: Oxford University Press.

Mallott, Floyd E. 1959. "Church of the Brethren." *ME* 1:421-424.

McKane, William. 1965. *Prophets and Wise Men.* Naperville, Illinois: Alec R. Allenson, Inc.

McLoughlin, William. 1974. "Revivalism." In *The Rise of Adventism.* Edwin Gaustad, ed. New York: Harper & Row.

Mead, Sidney E. 1975. *The Nation with the Soul of a Church.* New York: Harper & Row.

Mendenhall, George E. 1973. *The Tenth Generation: The Origins of the Biblical Tradition.* Baltimore: Johns Hopkins University Press.

Menno Simons. 1956. *The Complete Writings of Menno Simons.* John C. Wenger, ed. Scottdale: Herald Press.

Meyer, Albert J. 1958. "A Second Look at Responsibility." *Concern,* No. 6:30-39.

Miller, John W. 1975. "The Mennonite Church in 2025?" *Gospel Herald* 68:573-575.

Moltmann, Jürgen, et al. 1974. *Religion and Political Society.* New York: Harper & Row.

Neill, Stephen. 1964. *The Interpretation of the New Testament: 1861-1961.* London: Oxford University Press.

North, Christopher R. 1956. *The Suffering Servant in Deutero-Isaiah.* London: Oxford University Press.

_____ . 1964. *The Second Isaiah.* Oxford: Clarendon Press.

Noth, Martin. 1958. *The History of Israel.* New York: Harper.

_____ . 1962. *Exodus: Old Testament Library.* Philadelphia: The Westminster Press.

Novak, Michael. 1974. *Choosing Our King: Powerful Symbols in Presidential Politics.* New York: Macmillan.

O'Connor, Elizabeth. 1964. *Call to Commitment.* New York: Harper & Row.

————. 1971. *Our Many Selves.* New York: Harper & Row.

Oetting, Walter. 1964. *The Church of the Catacombs.* Saint Louis: Concordia Publishing House.

Parsons, Talcott. 1951. *The Social System.* Glencoe, Illinois: The Free Press.

Peachey, Paul. 1954. *Die soziale Herkunft der Schweizer Täufer in der Reformationszeit: Eine religionssoziologische Untersuchung.* Karlsruhe: Verlag Schneider.

————. 1956a. "Anabaptism and Church Organization." *MQR* 30:213-228.

————. 1956b. "The Mennonite Ethical Dilemma." *Gospel Herald* 49:1073-1074.

————. 1962. "Our Social Ministry in the Gospel." *MQR* 36:227-235.

Petry, Ray. 1956. *Christian Eschatology and Social Thought.* New York: Abingdon.

Pritchard, James B. 1969. "The Sumerian King List." *Ancient Near Eastern Texts.* Princeton: Princeton University Press.

Quiring, Walter, and Helen Bartel. 1974. *In the Fullness of Time, 150 Years of Mennonite Sojourn in Russia.* Kitchener, Ontario: Aaron Klassen.

Ramsey, Paul, 1950. *Basic Christian Ethics.* New York: Scribner's.

Rauschenbusch, Walter. 1918. *A Theology for the Social Gospel.* New York: Macmillan.

Redekop, Calvin. 1970. *The Free Church and Seductive Culture.* Scottdale: Herald Press.

————. 1973. "Religion and Society: A State Within a Church." *MQR* 47:339-357.

————. 1974a. "A New Look at Sect Development." *Journal for the Scientific Study of Religion* 13:345-352.

————. 1974b. "Anabaptism and the Ethnic Ghost." Unpublished paper presented to the Tuesday Seminar, Goshen College, October 22, 1974.

Redekop, John H. 1968. *The American Far Right.* Grand Rapids: Eerdmans.

————. 1972. *Making Political Decisions: A Christian Perspective.* Scottdale: Herald Press.

Richardson, C. C., et al, eds. 1953. *Early Christian Fathers.* Philadelphia: Westminster.

Richardson, Herbert. 1974. "Civil Religion in Theological Perspective." In *American Civil Religion.* Russell E. Richey and Donald G. Jones, eds. New York: Harper & Row.

Richey, Russell E., and Donald G. Jones, eds. 1974. *American Civil Religion.* New York: Harper & Row.

Riedemann, Peter. 1970. *Confession of Faith.* New York: The Plough Publishing House.

Roberts, Alexander, and James Donaldson, eds. 1925. *The Ante-Nicene Fathers.* New York: Scribner's.

Sandeen, Ernest R. 1970. *The Roots of Fundamentalism.* Chicago: University of Chicago Press.

Sanders, Thomas G. 1964. *Protestant Concepts of Church and State.* New York: Holt, Rinehart and Winston.

Schaller, Lyle. 1975. *Hey, That's Our Church.* New York: Abingdon.

Schlabach, Theron F. 1975. *A New Rhythm for Mennonites: The Mennonite*

Church and the Missionary Movement, 1860-1890. Elkhart, Indiana: Mennonite Board of Missions.

Sider, Ronald J., ed. 1974. *The Chicago Declaration.* Carol Stream, Illinois: Creation Press.

Smucker, Don E. 1953. "The Theological Basis for Christian Pacifism." *MQR* 27:163-186.

Smylie, John. 1963. *The Christian Church and National Ethos.* Washington, D.C.: The Church Peace Mission.

Stratmann, Franziskus. 1950. *Krieg und Christentum Heute.* Trier: Paulinus Verlag.

————. 1956. *War and Christianity Today.* London: Blackfriars.

Tawney, R. H. 1926. *Religion and the Rise of Capitalism.* London: J. Murray.

Tillich, Paul. 1951. *Systematic Theology: Volume I.* Chicago: University of Chicago Press.

————. 1954. *Love, Power, and Justice.* New York: Oxford University Press.

Toews, Abraham P. 1963. *The Problem of Mennonite Ethics.* Grand Rapids: Eerdmans.

Tolles, Frederick Barnes. 1963. *Meeting House and Counting House.* New York: W. W. Norton and Co.

Toynbee, Arnold, 1969. *Experiences.* New York and London: Oxford University Press.

Tuchman, Barbara W. 1966. *The Proud Tower.* New York: Macmillan.

Turner, Victor W. 1974. "Metaphors of Anti-Structure in Religious Culture." In *Changing Perspectives in the Scientific Study of Religion.* Allan W. Eister, ed. New York: John Wiley and Sons.

Tuveson, Ernest Lee. 1968. *Redeemer Nation: The Idea of America's Millennial Role.* Chicago: University of Chicago Press.

von Rad, Gerhard. 1962. *Old Testament Theology I.* Edinburgh and London: Oliver and Boyd.

Wagner, Jonathan F. 1974. "Transferred Crisis: German Volkisch Thought Among Russian Immigrants to Western Canada." *Canadian Review of Studies in Nationalism* 1:202-217.

Warfield, Benjamin B. 1952. *Biblical and Theological Studies.* Philadelphia: The Presbyterian and Reformed Publishing Company.

Weber, Max. 1930. *The Protestant Ethic and the Spirit of Capitalism.* London: G. Allen and Unwin, Ltd.

————. 1947. *The Theory of Social and Economic Organization.* Glencoe, Illinois: The Free Press.

Wenger, J. C. 1938. "The Theology of Pilgrim Marpeck." *MQR* 12: 205-256.

————. 1950. *The Doctrines of the Mennonites.* Scottdale: Mennonite Publishing House.

————. 1954. *Introduction to Theology.* Scottdale: Herald Press.

————. 1970. *Conrad Grebel's Programmatic Letters of 1524.* Scottdale: Herald Press.

Whalen, W. J. 1967. "American Sects and Cults." *New Catholic Encyclopedia.* Vol. XIII:31-34. New York: McGraw-Hill.

White, Theodore H. 1975. *Breach of Faith: The Fall of Richard Nixon.* New York: Atheneum.

Williams, George Huntston. 1969. "A People in Community: Historical Background." In *The Concept of the Believers' Church*. James Leo Garrett, Jr., ed. Scottdale: Herald Press.

Williams, Robin M. 1951. *American Society: A Sociological Interpretation*. New York: Alfred A. Knopf.

Wills, Gary. 1972. *Bare Ruined Choirs: Doubt, Prophecy, and Radical Religion*. New York: Doubleday.

Yoder, John Howard. 1954. "The Anabaptist Dissent: The Logic of the Place of the Disciple in Society." *Concern*, No. 1:45-68.

──────. 1955. "Reinhold Niebuhr and Christian Pacifism." *MQR* 29: 101-117.

──────. 1962. *Täufertum und Reformation in der Schweiz*. Karlsruhe: Verlag H. Schneider.

──────. 1963. Review of *The Context of Decision*, by Gordon Kaufman. *MQR* 37: 133-138.

──────. 1964. *The Christian Witness to the State*. Newton, Kansas: Faith and Life Press.

──────. 1966. "The Hermeneutics of the Anabaptists." Unpublished paper.

──────. 1967. "Binding and Loosing." *Concern*, No. 14:2-32.

──────. 1969. "A People in the World: Theological Interpretation." In *The Concept of the Believers' Church*. James Leo Garrett, Jr., ed. Scottdale: Herald Press.

──────. 1970. "Anabaptist Vision and Mennonite Reality." In *Consultation on Anabaptist-Mennonite Theology*. A. J. Klassen, ed. Fresno, California: Council of Mennonite Seminaries.

──────. 1971. *Nevertheless: A Meditation on the Varieties and Shortcomings of Religious Pacifism*. Scottdale: Herald Press.

──────. 1972a. *The Original Revolution: Essays on Christian Pacifism*. Scottdale: Herald Press.

──────. 1972b. *The Politics of Jesus*. Grand Rapids: Eerdmans.

──────. 1973. *The Legacy of Michael Sattler*. Scottdale: Herald Press.

──────. 1974. "The Biblical Mandate." In *The Chicago Declaration*. Ronald J. Sider, ed. Carol Stream, Illinois: Creation House.

Yoder, Sanford Calvin. 1959. *The Days of My Years*. Scottdale: Herald Press.

Zigler, M. R. (Chm.). 1958. *The Christian and War. A Theological Discussion of Justice, Peace, and Love*. Amsterdam: Continuation Committee of the Historic Peace Churches in Europe.

Zimmerli, Walther. 1965. "Promise and Fulfillment." In *Essays on Old Testament Hermeneutics*. Klaus Westermann, ed. Richmond, Virginia: John Knox Press.

Zschäbitz, Gerhard, 1958. *Zur Mitteldeutschen Wiedertäuferbewegung nach dem Grossen Bauernkrieg*. Berlin: Rütten & Loening.

GENERAL INDEX

INDEX OF
BIBLICAL REFERENCES